□□□□□□□□□□□□□□□□□□□□□□□□□□□

FEELING FREE
TO BE LIKE CHRIST

□□□□□□□□□□□□□□□□□□□□□□□□□□□

MEN'S BIBLE STUDY
Personal / Group

LEVEL 1

□

*The hidden secrets to a victorious life
that you won't hear in Church*

□

Jackie Goldsmith

Feeling Free To Be Like Christ – Men's Bible Study – Personal / Group – Level 1

ISBN: 9781087210216

Second Edition – (Updated & Expanded)

Text copyright © 2019 by Jackie Goldsmith

CONTENTS

A solid foundation

In a world of ever-increasing challenges faced by men, there are certain secrets to living a victorious life. These secrets are available to any man who is ready and willing to know them and use them. They are hidden in the scriptures recorded in the Bible, and they offer true empowerment to every man. Knowledge of these hidden secrets is essential for any man who wants to be the true master of life's challenges and the true master of his own self. You have found this book, and this book has found you, because you are ready for this information.

If you are new to the scriptures recorded in the Bible, this book, *Feeling Free To Be Like Christ (Level 1)*, is a good place to begin. The information which is shared in it will give you a head-start on your journey toward greater self-knowledge and understanding. On the other hand, if you are familiar with the scriptures recorded in the Bible, this book is your opportunity to understand even more. Much of what you will see and hear in this book is not taught in Church. Many things, which may be puzzling you, will become crystal clear.

Also, if you have lost faith in God or never had much faith at all, or if you have been challenged by certain issues in your life which have negatively affected you, this book is your opportunity to have self-renewal, recover your good feelings and give yourself a fresh start. There is no judgment or condemnation in this Men's Bible Study. You are encouraged to give the information in this book a chance to serve you and assist you in your spiritual development and personal empowerment.

You may be wondering: *"Is there really a spiritual aspect to my life? And, if there is, why should I pay any attention to it?"* Every man is, at the same time, physical and non-physical. The physical human body is the 'house' within which the non-physical (i.e. spiritual) being lives.

There are many men who don't see themselves as being 'religious' in a traditional sense. Yet they have recognized that the spiritual aspect of their lives is significant; and they have decided to pay attention to it. They have recognized that their spiritual aspect will empower them to deal with life's challenges successfully and masterfully. Therefore, these men have questions as to how to consciously walk the spiritual path. On the other hand, there are many men who are already consciously on the spiritual path. These men are interested in finding their purpose in life. They want to know: *"What am I called to do in service to others?"* Even after finding their purpose, some men still feel as if they could be and do much more.

Perhaps you are curious about such things.

However, once you decide to pay attention to the spiritual aspect of your life, there may be certain issues regarding your understanding of yourself, of other persons, of life, of God and of the Bible which you may need to address first. These issues may be causing difficulties and setbacks in your daily life right now; and they can become major roadblocks on the spiritual path if they are left unresolved or misunderstood. So, before you begin the Lessons at Level 1 of this Men's Bible Study, please use the following questions to identify any such issues which apply to you:

☐ Have you ever wondered why there are so many religious groups which are teaching so many opposite interpretations of the Bible, and have you also wondered whether it is possible for you to know the truth?

☐ Do you feel that God is both good and evil, or that God is unfair, or that God is an absent stranger, or that perhaps there is no God?

☐ Do you feel as if there is a gap of separation between you and

God, and have you wondered how you can close that gap?

☐ Does God seem to be far away from you, and have you been trying in vain: to reach out to God; or to feel God's presence; or to feel a connection with God?

☐ Have you ever wondered whether there is an effective way to develop your faith, and to get your faith to produce results for you?

☐ Are you troubled by negative feelings such as frustration, guilt, shame, fear, self-criticism, self-condemnation, inadequacy or powerlessness, and have you ever wondered if there is an effective way for you to master these feelings?

☐ Do you habitually think and speak negatively about yourself?

☐ Do you feel that, no matter how hard you try, you are just not good enough; and have you been trying unsuccessfully to finally feel right about yourself?

☐ Do you feel that you are in some way a sinner?

☐ Do you feel that, if you were a better person, then you would be more worthy of God's love?

☐ Are you having trouble getting past your past?

☐ Are you living under the burden and threat of 'sin', and are you terrified that you might end up in 'hell'?

☐ Are you having difficulty breaking unwanted habits, and are there weaknesses in your character which you have been fighting but without success?

☐ Are you haunted by unpleasant memories?

☐ Do you feel that you have done things which are unforgiveable, or do you feel that you have made so many mistakes that your life can never be fixed?

☐ Do you feel as if you are not measuring up to the standard of who and what you 'should' be as a 'good Christian'?

☐ Have you been trying (and failing) to act like Christ?

☐ When you face challenges, do you sometimes find yourself wondering: "What would Jesus do?"

☐ Have you been trying in vain to reach that elusive goal of Christian perfection?

☐ Does your life feel like a battleground, and do you feel as if you are constantly under attack?

☐ Are you pretending to be someone whom you are not, just so you can fit in with your religious group?

☐ Do you have a desire to dig deeper into the secrets of the Bible?

☐ Do you have challenges in understanding the Bible, and do you feel that there is crucial information in the Bible that you may be missing?

☐ Have you ever wondered why some Bible verses contradict each other?

☐ Have you ever read the Bible and wondered why the God spoken of in the Old Testament seems so different in character than the Heavenly Father spoken of in the New Testament?

☐ Have you been searching for the secret ingredient of a victorious life?

☐ And, most importantly, have you ever asked yourself: "Who am I, and why am I here on Earth?"

If you have answered 'Yes' to any of these questions, the secrets which are shared in the 7 Lessons in this book will help you to overcome these challenges and to answer these questions, plus many more. As you go through this book, you will also become fully aware of a life-changing truth which Jesus Christ taught about you. This truth is available to you, now that you are willing to receive it.

As students of the Master-Teacher Jesus Christ, our goal is: *to be like Christ.* Everything else is secondary. All other things will fall into place when we are truly like Him.

If you are wondering whether it is possible to truly be like Christ, the answer is: Yes, it is possible. However, before we can be like Christ, it is necessary to fully understand the truth about who Christ is, and the truth about who we are. This truth is rarely, if ever, taught in Church; and this is one reason why some Christians struggle spiritually and mentally.

When you have completed Level 1 in this Men's Bible Study, you will realize that your real challenge is <u>not</u> negativity, or past mistakes, or a lack of faith, or an unwanted habit, or a weakness, or sin, or not feeling good enough. If you face any such challenge, it is just a shadow cast by the real obstacle in your spiritual path. The real obstacle is that there is information about your true identity which you are missing. You are much, much more than you may presently believe. Once you know the whole truth of your identity, the truth will set you free to be like Christ.

There are three Levels in this Men's Bible Study series. Level 1 is the Introductory Level, Level 2 is the Intermediate Level and Level 3 is the Advanced Level. Each book in the series contains 7 Lessons. These books may be used for personal reflection or for group discussion. The secrets shared in these books are easy to understand and easy to apply to your everyday life. Once you begin to apply these secrets, you will see positive results in your life in a very short time without having to experience frustration or struggle.

The scriptures recorded in the Bible all have an obvious, literal meaning, which any man who reads the Bible can understand. However, there are also higher meanings which are hidden in secret beneath the surface of the scriptures. More and more of these higher meanings will unfold to us as we go Lesson by Lesson and step by step through this Men's Bible Study.

This book, *Feeling Free To Be Like Christ (Level 1)*, offers you a solid foundation of truth upon which to build an ever-increasing understanding of how to live victoriously. It will give you access to a greater perception of the truth about yourself, about other persons, about life, about God and about the Bible. It is designed to help you to enhance and upgrade how you see yourself. The other books in this Men's Bible Study series will give you access to even higher levels of information once you have completed Level 1.

Now, here are some suggestions so you can get the most from this Men's Bible Study.

How to get the most from this
Men's Bible Study

As you go through each Lesson, let the information really sink in. Each time you go through a Lesson you will gain more understanding.

Be receptive to what you see and hear in this Bible Study, even though it may be new to you, or may be different from what you have previously understood. Keep an open mind; and be willing to see familiar scriptures from the Bible in a new light.

Go through each Lesson at your own pace. There is no pressure to go through an entire Lesson in a day. Each Lesson is divided into segments; so you can pause at the end of a segment if you choose to do so.

Give quality time to the Lesson, preferably at a fixed time each day if possible. If despite your best efforts your schedule does not allow for this, then each day at whatever time works for you, go through as much of the Lesson as time allows. You will find that it is best to not skip a day in using this book. As a child of God, your time is precious; and yes, you are a child of God, even if you have been told otherwise.

If you have any negative feelings or ideas associated with the word 'God', you can use the word 'Good' instead of 'God' as you go through this book. The true God is All Good. Good is all that the true God is; for the true God is Infinite Unconditional Love. (We will investigate this in more detail later on in this book.)

Be sure to use the Supporting Scriptures, the Affirmation and also the questions and answers given in the Review which follow each Lesson. When you do so, you will deepen the impression in your mind of everything which you have seen and heard in the Lesson. Also, be sure to make use of the self-empowerment Techniques which are shared throughout this book.

When you have completed Level 1, move on to the next book in the series which is titled *Feeling Free To Be Like Christ (Level 2);* and then move on to the final book titled *Feeling Free To Be Like Christ (Level 3)*. Doing so will give you the full benefit from the series. Each Lesson provides a foundation for the following Lesson; and each book provides a foundation for the following book. So be sure to go through the Lessons and the books in sequence, and don't skip over any of the Lessons.

Certain words and phrases in this book have been written in block capitals, some in bold print, and some in italics. Some words have also been underlined. This is done either to draw your attention to certain information or to impress certain truths upon your mind in such a way that you will easily remember them. It is not meant in any way to 'shout' at you.

You may recommend to other persons that they use this book and go along with us on this journey to greater self-knowledge and spiritual understanding. However, as you go through this book, keep your focus on you.

Remember that, sometimes, positive adjustments will happen rapidly. At other times, they may take more time. Be patient. The more open and receptive you are to the information in this Bible Study and the more you review the information, the more profound will be your transformation. If there is some issue or situation in your life which you really want to improve, there is a simple, practical and effective way to do so. You can use the Mind Renewal Technique which will be shared with you in Lesson 2 of this book.

Now let's begin Lesson 1.

(Before you start this Lesson, you are encouraged to first go through the preceding sections of this book if you haven't already done so; i.e. A solid foundation and How to get the most from this Men's Bible Study.)

Lesson 1: Who do you think you are?

WORD FOR TODAY: "Beloved friends, right now we are the sons of God..."   (1st John 3:2)

Truth is hidden in the Bible

There are many men who know the Bible, but they do not know the Truth. This statement may sound strange, but let's think about it for a moment. How can it be possible for a man to be well-versed in the scriptures which are recorded in the Bible, and yet not know the Truth which the Bible contains? It is possible because Truth is hidden in the Bible.

Truth is eternal and universal. Truth is dynamic and ever-unfolding. There are many levels of Truth which are recorded in the Bible; and each level is higher and wider than the one before. Truth is always unfolding, and there is always more Truth to be known. Therefore, when a man desires to know the Truth, he becomes willing to keep progressing from an understanding of truth to an understanding of higher Truth.

The Bible tells us that John, the beloved disciple of Jesus Christ, wrote these words: *"I have no greater joy than to hear that my children are following the truth" (3rd Epistle of John, verse 4).* The spiritual path is the path of Truth. When you follow Truth and keep progressing in the path of Truth, everything becomes clear. There is no more confusion and no more controversy. One of the most significant levels of understanding to which the path of Truth will take you is: *the Truth of who you really are.* This is a vital Truth for you to explore and understand. However, this Truth is not taught in school; and rarely, if ever, is it taught in Church.

Now you may be wondering: "Why is it so important for me to know the truth of who I really am?" We find the answer in the secrets shared by the Master-Teacher Jesus Christ in a well-known passage from the Bible. This passage is recorded in The Gospel of John, chapter 8, verses 31-36; and here's what it says:

"Jesus said to those Jews who believed on Him, 'If you follow My teaching, then you really are My disciples. And **you will know the truth, and the truth will make you free.'**

They answered Him: 'We are the descendants of Abraham. We have never been anybody's slaves! So how can you say that we will be set free?'

Jesus replied: 'I tell you this timeless truth: Anyone who lives a sinful life is a slave to sin. A slave has no permanent place in the family, but a son belongs to the family forever. So if the Son makes you free, you are truly free'." (Please read these verses a second time before moving on. Let them sink in.)

The Jews in Jesus' day had access to the scriptures which now make up the larger section of the Bible, and which are collectively known as 'The Old Testament'. (The scriptures which now make up the smaller section of the Bible, collectively known as 'The New Testament', were not yet written.) Knowledge of these scriptures was a major part of Jewish culture. Therefore, these Jews had been rigorously taught these scriptures from childhood, and could quote long passages from memory. Yet, we have just read that Jesus boldly told them that they still did not know the Truth.

▣ Therefore, the first lesson which we learn from our main text recorded in John 8:31-36 is: **It is possible for a man to be well-versed in scriptures and yet not know the Truth.** A man may have an extensive knowledge of scriptures, and may even have read the entire Bible from beginning to end several times, and yet may lack the knowledge of the Truth which the Bible contains. This is possible because Truth is hidden in the scriptures recorded in the Bible. Many men know the Bible but they do not know the Truth.

The importance of Mind Renewal

Our main text, which we have just read, conceals one of the most significant teachings of Jesus Christ. So let's analyze it and find the divine Truth hidden within it.

Let's look at the first part of the text. *"Jesus said to those Jews **who believed on Him**, 'If you follow My teaching, then you really are **My disciples**. And you will know the truth, and **the truth will make you free.**'*

*They answered Him: 'We are the descendants of Abraham. **We have never been anybody's slaves!** So how can you say that we will be set free?' "* (John 8:31-33)

The text tells us that these Jews, to whom Jesus Christ was speaking, were people "who believed on Him". However, even though they were sincere believers in Jesus Christ, they were not free. When Jesus Christ told these believers that they needed to be set free, they were very offended. Many modern-day believers in Jesus Christ would probably react in a similar way.

Traditionally, we have been told that, once we believe in Jesus Christ, we will automatically experience a wonderful, higher level of freedom which is available through Him. However, the text, which we have just read, tells us that this is not so at all. The text clearly tells us that Jesus was speaking to people "who believed on Him". He was speaking to sincere believers in Jesus Christ. Yet, these believers were still not truly free because they did not know the Truth. So, we have learned three lessons from this text so far:

▣ **It is possible for a man to study the Bible and to be well-versed in the scriptures and yet not know the Truth;**

▣ **It is possible for a man to be a sincere believer in Jesus Christ and yet not know the Truth; and**

▣ **It is possible for a man, who is a sincere believer in Jesus Christ, to be restricted and controlled by the same things which used to restrict and control him before he became a believer; because so long as a believer does not know the Truth, he is not free.**

Therefore, knowledge of the scriptures is not enough to set a man free. Being a sincere believer in Jesus Christ is not enough to set a man free. A man becomes free when he knows the Truth. "He whom the Son sets free is free indeed"; this is true. However, there is a certain level of Divine Truth which a man is required to understand before the Son can set him free. He is required to open his mind to this higher level of truth, so that he can be free to be like Christ. This is why Jesus told these believers: "...follow My teaching..."

Why were these believers offended when Jesus told them that they needed to be set free? They were offended because, while Jesus was speaking to them, they were imagining themselves being held in *Physical Captivity,* which is *restriction and control of the body.* So they argued with Jesus and said: "We have never been anybody's slaves!"

However, when Jesus told these believers that they were not free, He was not speaking of Physical Captivity. He was speaking of a type of captivity which is not easy to detect. Jesus was in fact telling them that, even though they were physically free, and even though they were diligent students of the scriptures, and even though they sincerely believed in Him, they were still not truly free because they were in a state of *Mental Captivity*; which is *restriction and control of the mind.* Mental Captivity was preventing them from recognizing, understanding and knowing the Truth. It was also preventing them from being truly free in their minds. And yet, these believers were completely unaware that they were in a state of Mental Captivity.

◙ Therefore, the fourth lesson we learn from the text in John 8:31-36 is: **It is possible for a man to be physically free but yet, at the same time, be restricted and controlled in his thinking, without ever being aware of it.** These mental restrictions create a state of Mental Captivity which will negatively affect every facet of his existence. Mental Captivity will prevent him from knowing the Truth and from being truly free.

We pride ourselves on our physical freedoms such as: freedom of movement, freedom of speech, freedom of assembly and freedom of expression, just to name a few. We will go to great lengths to preserve these physical freedoms, and will resist anyone or anything which seems to threaten these freedoms in any way. However, Jesus Christ is teaching us that, no matter how many physical freedoms we enjoy, *we are not truly free unless our mind is free.*

Now at this point you might be saying to yourself: *"But my mind is already free. No one can tell me what to think! I can direct my own thoughts in any way I choose. So why would I need to take any further steps in order to experience mental freedom?"*

Water, by its very nature, is free to flow in any direction. However, if a large volume of water is released onto land where deep and wide channels already exist, the water is going to take the path of least resistance. It is going to flow along the channels which are already prepared. Similarly, whether we know it or not, we have all been exposed to intensive mental conditioning while we were progressing from childhood to adulthood in the world system. Mental conditioning has trained us and programed us to think in certain negative ways and along certain negative lines. Therefore, over the years, this mental conditioning has cut deep and wide 'channels' in our minds, even though we may not be aware of it. We are free to think in any way we choose.

However, just like water, our thoughts will always tend to flow along those 'channels' which mental conditioning has already created in our minds.

So we never assume or take for granted that we are mentally free. When we value mental freedom enough to closely examine our own way of thinking, we can ensure that we are truly free. These Jewish believers assumed that they were completely and totally free; but they were not. They were physically free, but their minds were being held captive. And yet, they were completely unaware that they were in a state of Mental Captivity.

We all have grown up in a world system which has subtly conditioned us and *programed* us from childhood to think in certain negative ways. For example, it is no coincidence that all the audio and visual broadcasts in the electronic media are called *'programs'*. Whether they are cartoons, game shows, award shows, talk shows, movies, dramas, sitcoms, games, galas, music videos, interviews, discussions, debates, newscasts, documentaries, speeches, advertisements, etc., notice that they are all called *'programs'* and are generally referred to as *'programing'*. They are designed to influence us and to program us to obey 'World System Thinking'. So, here's a suggestion: From now on, whenever you watch and/or listen to these 'programs', protect your Mental Freedom by constantly asking yourself: "How is this 'program' trying to influence my thinking?"

What is the world system? The world system is the overarching framework which organizes, governs and controls civilization on Earth. It is made up of a network of many mini-systems such as: the political system, the financial system, the banking system, the legal system, the military system, the commercial system, the science and technology system, the communication system, the education system, the social system, the 'class and collar' system, the racial system, the sport and entertainment system, the drug and pharmaceutical system and the health system, just to name a few. As civilization has progressed, these mini-systems have become ever more integrated and sophisticated; and they impact the lives of nearly every person on Earth. The agenda of the world system is to maintain and increase its control of mankind and its domination of the Earth.

Over thousands of years, the world system has mastered the art of controlling the masses of people on Earth. The world system has figured out that if it tries to forcibly control us physically, we tend to resist; but if it controls us mentally without us knowing it, we will put up no resistance. Once mental control is achieved, it is very easy to control us physically, and to get us to act and react in ways which serve the world system's interests. Therefore, for thousands of years, physical slavery was the order of the day; but that lasted until the world system figured out that there is no need to put chains and shackles on people's feet if you have already chained and shackled their thinking. When the system physically chained and shackled one group of people, the rest of the people enjoyed some measure of freedom. However, by mentally chaining and shackling all people, freedom is just an illusion.

A physically free man can be easily manipulated and controlled without him knowing it. This is possible as long as he is not aware of how crucial Mental Freedom is. Also, a man who is a sincere believer in Jesus Christ, and who is very knowledgeable of the Bible, can be easily manipulated and controlled without him knowing it. This is possible so long as that sincere believer is not aware of the importance of Knowing the Truth. Therefore, the wise man is just as interested in the protection of his Mental Freedom as he is in the protection of his physical freedom.

It is ironic that many Christians criticize the world system while, at the same time, they are subtly controlled by its mentality. However, the good news is that no matter how long our thoughts may have been channeled in a negative direction, we always have the power to regain control over our thinking and be mentally free. We always have the power to create better mental channels and to redirect our thoughts, so they can flow in a better direction.

▣ The fifth lesson we learn from the text in John 8:31-36 is: **It is possible for a sincere believer in Jesus Christ to be in Mental Captivity to world system thinking. Believing in Jesus Christ does not automatically set a man free from bondage of the mind.** It's one thing for us to forsake the pull of the world system and sincerely believe in Jesus Christ; but it's another thing to renew our minds to such an extent that the thinking which originated in the world system will completely leave us.

We are trained from childhood to follow the way of the world; and we believe 'that's just the way it is' or 'that's just the way things are'. From childhood, the world system dictates our thoughts and ideas about ourselves, about other people, about life, and about God. We are trained from childhood to think in certain ways which the mini-systems prescribe, so that the world system can easily maintain its influence over us and manipulate us. Our actions will always follow our thinking. Therefore, for thousands of years, the world system has been increasing its control of mankind's actions by increasing its control of mankind's thinking. Technology is now being used to greatly increase this control.

The trick within the threat

One of the most cunning schemes which the world system uses to trick humanity into supporting the agenda of the system is: *The world system keeps creating and promoting threats to our physical freedoms, physical rights and physical wellbeing.*

The world system keeps promoting the idea that there are threats: to our health, to our finances, to our marriage, to our longevity, to our food safety, to our children, to our personal safety, to our retirement, to our environment and to national security, just to name a few. Every day, we see and hear threats of some kind highlighted in media programs, even though the word 'threat' might not be used. We are bombarded with interviews conducted with experts, analysts, advisors, consultants, activists, victims, concerned citizens and other worried or traumatized individuals, all discussing the latest threat that is supposedly out to get us. Media programs sensationalize crime, violence, inhumane acts, economic instability, social instability, conflicts, disasters, marches and protests of all kinds. The world system will even assign celebrities (e.g. politicians, entertainers, actors, religious leaders, preachers etc.) both to promote these threats and to champion the fight against these threats, so that we will focus on these threats and see them as being very frightening. Threat Promoters are everywhere, even in Church. The world system will even go as far as to select special days and create annual events to promote 'threat awareness'.

Whether these threats are real or just seem to be real, there are reasons why the world system wants to keep us preoccupied with threats. They benefit the agenda of the world system in two main ways:

(1) These threats are designed to keep us so concerned about gaining or losing our physical freedoms, and so preoccupied with fighting to protect our physical rights and physical wellbeing, that we never detect that we are living in a state of Mental Captivity to world system thinking. We never discover that we have been deliberately *programed* to focus on threats; and that our actions and reactions in response to these threats are not consciously chosen. We become fixated on the threats to our physical rights and freedoms; so we never realize that we have given away to the world system our fundamental right of Mental Freedom. We are unable to connect the dots and see the big picture of the agenda of the world system, and how we are being manipulated to serve that agenda. Therefore, these physical threats are used by the system as **Distraction.**

(2) The world system uses these threats to our physical rights, freedoms and wellbeing, as a way of triggering extremely negative thoughts and feelings in our minds. We have been *programed* to have a very negative, knee-jerk reaction to threats; so our thoughts and feelings automatically

start to flow in a very negative direction. As long as these negative thoughts and feelings are flowing in our minds, the negative mental channels, which the world system had already created in our minds since our early childhood, will widen and deepen. As a result, our negative reaction to these threats gives the world system an even tighter control of our thinking, and tighter control of our actions and reactions. Therefore, these physical threats are used by the system as **Bait.**

So, we see that all physically free people *(such as individuals; communities; religious congregations; voting blocs; the base of any political party; religious/political/social/racial/ethnic groups; certain demographics in society; even entire free nations)* can be easily manipulated and controlled without them ever knowing it. This is easily done by *creating and/or promoting the right kind of threat which will cause people to react in a specific way.* This is mental manipulation on a mass level.

The world system is fully aware of the great importance of Mental Freedom. The world system knows that people are not truly free unless their mind is free. The world system is also fully aware that as long as people are distracted by these physical threats, they never have a chance to detect that they are mental captives. It knows that as long as people are focused on these *external* threats, they will be unaware of the only true threat to their freedom, their rights and their wellbeing. The one true threat is the *internal* threat of Mental Captivity to world system thinking; and the world system is fully aware of this. By contrast, people in general are totally unaware of the great importance of Mental Freedom. They don't know that they are not truly free until their mind is free. They don't know that the one true threat is Mental Captivity. So they never suspect or care that the real purpose of a physical threat is to give the world system tighter control of their thinking. You may wonder: *Why is the world system so determined to control my thinking?* It's because anyone or anything which controls your thinking controls you.

You will notice that many of these physical threats to our rights, freedoms and wellbeing are used: (1) to divide us into rival groups; (2) to promote a strong feeling of animosity between these groups; and (3) to lock us into an 'us versus them' mindset. You may wonder: *How does this benefit the agenda of the world system?* Here's the answer: As long as we are divided into groups which are opposing each other and seeing each other as 'the enemy', we are too distracted to recognize that *all* the groups are being mentally manipulated by the world system. Thoughts and feelings of anxiety and strong animosity are then encouraged and fueled by the appointed Threat Promoters, in order to pit one group against another. Therefore, each group is baited into thinking ever more strongly in a negative direction in order to protect itself from the supposed threats posed by the opposing group. This is a prime example of how physical threats are used as Distraction and Bait.

These negative thoughts and feelings lead to Group Reactions such as: fear, outrage, hatred & conflicts; angry protests & marches; getting a desired election result; giving big profits to a particular mini-system; mayhem & murder; and war & genocide, just to name a few. These Group Reactions can be seen all over the world and throughout history. The world system uses physical threats to manipulate all groups into thinking and reacting negatively. By doing so, the system easily achieves its true goal of robbing us of our Mental Freedom, and dictates our actions and reactions with our full support.

'Divide and Conquer' is the oldest trick in the world system's book. That is how the world system has kept millions and even billions of people under control. That trick has been successfully used against humanity for thousands of years, and people are still blindly falling for that trick today. Here's something to remember: *Anyone or anything which divides us into opposing groups, and gets us thinking with an 'us versus them' mentality, is serving the agenda of the world system.*

The world system plans to eventually change its tactic from 'Divide and Conquer' to 'Unite and Conquer'. It will promote unity as the solution to the conflicts which it has deliberately fostered on the Earth. It plans to use highly advanced technology to speed up and intensify our mental conditioning to such an extent that we are quickly completely mind controlled. Then we will be allowed to unite as mindless captives of world system thinking. We will behave like bees in a beehive. That's the world system's ultimate endgame.

In the meantime, the world system ensures that these external, physical threats keep coming at us relentlessly, as a permanent distraction and as enticing bait. Therefore you will notice that whenever some threat to our physical freedoms, rights and wellbeing seems to be addressed by the system, the same threat will crop up again in some other form; or a new threat will quickly be created to take its place. It never, ever ends; even though there are obviously more than enough financial, political and intellectual resources readily available to permanently end all of these 'threats'. This is why, as the saying goes, the more things change, the more they remain the same.

Now, men are natural-born protectors. A man recognizes that his ability to protect himself, and to protect whomever and whatever he loves, is of great importance to his sense of duty, power and masculinity. Therefore, men are especially sensitive and reactive to anything which seems to be a threat, and will instinctively go into protective mode. The world system is expert at targeting men's minds. It knows that the more a man is stressed out because of physical threats, the less able he will be to think calmly, clearly, analytically, lovingly and peacefully.

So, here are some suggestions as to how you can: (1) be a protector; (2) hold on to your sense of duty, power and masculinity; and (3) hold on to your Mental Freedom, all at the same time:

- ▣ From now on, notice how often media programs of all kinds (even advertisements) focus on and sensationalize threats.

- ▣ Every time you see or hear the promotion of any threat to the freedom, the rights or the wellbeing of yourself, your loved ones, your 'group', other people, your nation or humanity in general, pause and recognize the cunning trick within the threat. Always remember that the threat is both a Distraction and Bait. Ask yourself: *"How is this 'threat' designed to make me feel and react?"* Then, using your common sense, consciously choose how you will feel; and consciously decide what response, if any, is necessary.

▣ Calmly identify the Threat Promoters when you see and hear them. Never get emotionally attached to any Threat Promoter. Never believe that a Threat Promoter is either against you or is on your side. View all Threat Promoters with cool detachment.

▣ Don't allow any threat (any so-called 'hot button topic') to push your emotional buttons. Stop yourself from having that knee-jerk reaction. Refuse to take the bait.

▣ Let this be your permanent mental attitude: *Nothing and no one has power over my thinking.*

▣ Refuse to get into an 'us versus them' mentality or a 'me versus him/her/it' mentality. Regardless of the 'threat', choose to keep a calm, positive and loving attitude within yourself, toward all people everywhere, and toward life in general. Focus on all the goodness which still exists in the world. The Bible tells us: *"God has not given us the spirit of fear; but* [He has given us the spirit] *of power, of love and of a disciplined mind". (2nd Timothy 1:7)* By choosing to be a calm, loving man who has a disciplined mind, you are superior to any threat, and you are a powerful protector of all that is near and dear to you. You will then be able to calmly choose what attention, if any, you should pay to a 'threat'; or whether you can ignore it completely.

What are some of the negative mental channels which these threats are designed to deepen and widen in our mind? They are channels of: worry, fear, anxiety, terror, panic, perplexity, uncertainty, fatigue, anger, rage, hatred, strife, violence, revenge, irritability, discord, criticism, judgment, suspicion, prejudice, hostility, insensitivity, pride, victimization, grief, frustration, helplessness and hopelessness. Can you identify any of these channels in your thinking? Are there any 'threats' which are causing your thoughts to flow along these channels?

If you notice that your thoughts and feelings have been flowing along negative mental channels such as worry, fear, anxiety etc., here's a suggestion: Take time out to make a list of any threats which are directing your thoughts and feelings along these channels. A negative thought or feeling is always a reaction to a perceived threat of some kind. It can even be a 'threat' in a personal or a workplace relationship. So ask yourself: *'What is the threat that I am reacting to now?'*

Here's another suggestion: Rather than focusing on threats, focus on deepening and widening your positive mental channels such as: understanding, optimism, faith, patience, perseverance, peace, harmony, open-mindedness, flexibility, discernment, intelligence, compassion, joy, gratitude, love, enthusiasm, cheerfulness, creativity, ingenuity, resilience, tenacity, courage, self-belief, ability, success, progress and power. The more you flow your thoughts and feelings along these positive mental channels, the deeper and wider they become. You are always free to choose to have Truth Awareness rather than threat awareness in your thinking.

Are you conforming or transforming?

The directive of the world system to mankind can be summed up in one word: "CONFORM!" (i.e. comply; obey; follow convention, custom and tradition; fit in; be similar; keep up with society; join the group; follow the crowd; go with the flow; fall in line; follow celebrities; follow fashion and trends; 'follow' whatever is 'trending'; follow your feelings; go along with whatever is popular; focus on external things and keep looking 'out there'; accommodate, tolerate and accept the world's way). Therefore, the world system will never, ever teach us the Truth which will set us mentally free from world system thinking. Its agenda is to protect itself and its own interests by keeping our minds tightly chained and shackled.

The world system teaches us to focus on external things and to conform. By contrast, the directive of Truth to mankind can be summed up in one word: "TRANSFORM!" (i.e. take back control of your mind; free your mind from world system thinking; think for yourself; revolutionize your thinking; renew your mind; change the direction in which you flow your thoughts; stop serving the agenda of the world system; change your mind; think differently; look within yourself and focus internally; know yourself; know the Truth, follow Truth, live the Truth; be your Ideal Self).

Now, the wise man doesn't see the world system as 'the enemy', and he doesn't try to fight the system. A man measures his lifespan in decades; but the world system measures its lifespan in millennia. The system can afford to be patient and play the long game, because it knows that it will outlast its opponents. So, the wise man recognizes that there are positive things and negative things in the system. He never gets into the state of mind of resisting the system, and neither does he just go with the flow. Rather, he liberates his mind from world system thinking; and he does this by knowing the Truth.

Therefore, as truth-seekers, our goal is *not* to fear, to fight, to flee from, to fuss about or to fix the world system. Rather, our goal is to know the Truth which the world system cannot teach us. By doing so, we free our minds to such an extent that, even though we are in the world, we are not mental captives of world system thinking. We can then interact with those mini-systems and get maximum benefit from them, without allowing them to dictate to us how we ought to think.

Mind Renewal is not automatic

When we believe in Jesus Christ, we don't automatically escape that subtle, negative mental conditioning to which we have been exposed from childhood in the world system. In living at the level of freedom of the mind, there are certain core beliefs which we will unlearn. There are also certain higher levels of divine truth which we will learn. This is why Jesus Christ taught these believers that the only way to be truly free is by 'knowing the Truth'.

Physical Captivity is easy to identify because the chains and shackles, which hold the captive in bondage, are visible. Mental Captivity is hard to spot, because the chains and shackles, which hold the mentally captive man in captivity to world system thinking, are invisible. Nevertheless, those invisible chains and shackles are just as effective in controlling the man. The **'chains and shackles'** used in Mental Captivity are **thoughts and ideas** which hold us back from living victoriously over world system thinking. These thoughts and ideas became firmly attached to our minds while we were growing up in the world system. We are not immune to these thoughts and ideas. However, we have the power and the authority to clear them from our minds. This is why the Bible teaches us: *"Don't be conformed to this world* (i.e. don't continue to think in the way that the world system taught you to think), *but be transformed by the renewing of your mind..." (Romans 12:2)*

'Mind Renewal' is not automatic. It is a process of investigating how we have been programed to think. It is also a process of making adjustments in how we choose to think from now on. This process will require the complete and conscious participation of the man who sincerely desires to experience transformation in his life. Any man who is in Physical Captivity is fully aware of it. However, a man, (even one who is a sincere Christian), can be in Mental Captivity to world system thinking and be completely unaware of it. This is why Mental Captivity is so subtle.

The text tells us that these believers in Jesus Christ were restricted and controlled in their thinking, and yet they were completely unaware of it. Therefore they were offended when Jesus told them that

Truth would make them free. In order to free our minds, let's be perceptive enough to realize that we have all been mentally conditioned; bold enough to investigate this mental conditioning and its restrictive effect on our lives; and open-minded enough to know the Truth which will set us free.

Mental Freedom is your gift to yourself

So we understand, from the text, that when Jesus said: "the truth will make you free", He was speaking of experiencing Mental Freedom, which is freedom of the mind to think in ways which are different from world system thinking. We are not truly free until our mind is free. We will experience Mental Freedom when we give ourselves unconditional permission to think differently about ourselves, about other people, about life and about God. If we chain and shackle ourselves to our current level of thinking, we will be limited to that level. Every time we attempt to progress spiritually and to live victoriously above world system thinking, we will be held back by those thoughts and ideas which chain and shackle us. We will be stuck, despite our strong desire to advance.

In order to be mentally free, let's be willing to examine our thoughts and ideas honestly. Then we can see if they have been helping us to live victoriously or if they have been hindering our progress. If we find that any of our thoughts and ideas have been holding us back, let's honestly identify such thoughts and ideas as what they are: mental chains and shackles which keep us under the control of world system thinking. By identifying these mental chains and shackles, we give ourselves permission to think differently; to renew our mind by being open and receptive to truthful thoughts and ideas. Once we make up our mind to think differently, the mental chains and shackles will release their grip. They will eventually fall away and we will be mentally free.

Jesus Christ never submitted Himself to world system thinking.

This is why the religious system of His day fiercely opposed Him; and this is also why He is qualified to teach us the Truth which the world system cannot teach us. The fact that you have been intrigued by a book which is titled *Feeling Free To Be Like Christ,* may indicate that you feel that there is some sort of restraint which is preventing you from being like Christ. If there is such a restraint, it exists in just one place: *in your thinking.* It is not external; it is internal. That's good news, because anything which is in your mind is under your control. Perhaps you have now decided to identify and get rid of that restraint once and for all, so you can think like Christ and be like Christ. If you have, there is information in this Men's Bible Study for you.

Mental Freedom is a gift which you give to yourself. No one else can give this gift to you; for you are the only person who is thinking your thoughts. You are the only person who really knows what is going on in your mind. To *'know the truth'* means *'to become fully conscious and fully aware of the Truth'.* This truth is not just any ordinary kind of truth. This truth is Higher Spiritual Truth; i.e. a higher level of spiritual knowledge which is above world system thinking. However, before a man can know the Truth, he has to be willing to know the Truth. Are you willing?

What is the image of God?

So, Mental Captivity happens because we harbor in our minds certain thoughts and ideas which act as mental chains and shackles. These thoughts and ideas hold us back from living powerfully, masterfully and victoriously. By contrast, Mental Freedom happens when we let go of such thoughts and ideas. We become truly free from world system thinking when we give ourselves unconditional permission to be fully conscious and fully aware of the whole Truth of who we really are. Then, we protect our Mental Freedom by thinking in alignment with the Truth which has set us free. Once we know the Truth and consistently think the Truth, we can then live the Truth in our daily lives. Once we start to think differently, it will be easy to act differently;

for our actions follow our thoughts.

So, in order to be mentally free, let's be willing to become fully conscious and aware of the Truth of who we really are. Let's be willing to know the Truth of our real identity. This is a truth which the world system has tried desperately to hide from us. And what is this Truth which we will come to know about ourselves? The Bible makes it clear. *We are created in the image of God.*

"Created in the image of God": This is an expression which most Christians have already heard in Church, but it conceals a very high Truth which many Christians do not yet know. It's one thing to hear the truth in Church or to read the truth in the Bible; but it's another thing to be fully conscious and aware of the truth. Many Christians have never paused to ask: 'What is the image of God? And what does it really mean to be created in the image of God?' Therefore, many have never taken the further step to renew their minds to express this image.

Genesis 1:27 says: *"So God created mankind in **His own image**; He created **them** in the image of God; He created **them** male and female."* Now, human males and human females do not have identical physical bodies; but yet Genesis 1:27 says that both males and females are created in the image of God. Therefore, hidden in this verse is this truth: **The image of God is not a physical image or a physical body. It is something other than physical.**

We are created in the image of God. This is a truth for all time; for God has never removed the image of God from mankind. The ultimate purpose of mankind is to express the image of God in which we have been created. So then, what is the image of God? In order to answer that question, we may be required to re-examine our ideas about God. Many people are mentally chained and shackled by thoughts and ideas about God which got attached to their minds in the world system. However, Jesus Christ taught us this Truth: *"God is a Spirit; and those who worship Him must worship Him in spirit and in truth."* (John 4:24). (Please read this verse a second time before moving on. Let it sink in.)

Since God is a Spirit, we have further proof that the image of God is not a physical image. Rather, it is a spiritual image which contains the qualities, character, essence and attributes of God. The 'image of God' is referred to in the Bible as "the divine nature". The Bible also tells us that we are designed to express this divine nature. *(See 2nd Peter 1:4)* This image of God, this divine nature, has never been removed from mankind. It is hidden within mankind; but it is always there. When our divine spiritual nature becomes our personal truth, only then can we really worship God "in spirit and in truth".

Now you may be wondering: *"Since God is a Spirit and has no physical image, how is it that we refer to God as "He" and "Him"? How is it that we call God "Father"? What about those people mentioned in the Bible who saw visions of God as having a physical form? Weren't they telling the truth?"* All of these questions will be answered from the Bible later on in this book. Remember, we are going step by step.

The image of God is not a physical image. Therefore we do not see God's image when we look at our physical body in a mirror. Nevertheless, this inner spiritual image, this divine spiritual nature, this divine spiritual essence in which we are created, is just as real as our physical body but it is hidden within us. This divine nature is the truth of who we are right now, although we do not see it physically and we may not yet be experiencing it. We are created in the divine image of God. Therefore, we are designed to outwardly express in our daily lives that inner divine image.

The victorious, all-prevailing power of Infinite God is within that inner divine image. 'All That God Is' can be found within that inner divine image. Therefore, we have been equipped by God, from birth, to live powerfully, masterfully and victoriously in this present world; and that is very good news. However, before we can experience and express this divine nature which is within us, we are required to first become conscious and aware that, in addition to our Human Identity, we have a Divine Identity. The 'image of God' within us gives us that Divine Identity. The world system knows of our dual identity even though we may be unaware of it. For example, our dual identity is hinted at in the well-known saying: "To err is human; to forgive is divine."

The world system does everything to ensure that we never become fully conscious of our inner Divine Identity. World system thinking is designed to keep us focused on external things. As long as we are focused on external things, we will never discover the true divine spiritual identity and the awesome divine power which are within the inner divine image which we already have. We will be looking for answers 'out there', when all the answers are already within us. With this understanding, we clearly see why the world system has subtly programed us to believe that "the truth is out there."

In order to truly express the inner image of God, our understanding of God must be clear and truthful. God is not a creature. God is not a man. God is not 'the Man upstairs'. God is not an entity. God is not in any way a physical being. God is not alive; rather, God is Life itself. Spirit-God does not just fill the universe. Truthfully, what we call 'the universe', with its billions of galaxies, is just one tiny speck within the bottomless, surface-less, boundless Ocean of Power, Intelligence, Love and Life which is Infinite Spirit-God. Infinite Spirit-God is The Spirit of Infinity.

We are not able to fully define The Infinite because our comprehension of The Infinite is limited. However, for the purpose of this Bible Study, we will start with this working definition: *God is Divine, Invisible, Infinite, Eternal Spirit.* This means that God is a Spirit who: (1) is totally divine in nature and essence; (2) cannot be seen; (3) has no limitations or boundaries or form or shape; and (4) has no beginning or ending of existence. *(See Numbers 23:19; 1st Timothy 1:17 & 6:16; Colossians 1:15; Psalm 90:2)* We may ask: What is the true significance of being created in the 'image' of Divine, Invisible, Infinite, Eternal Spirit?

Here's the answer:

(1) God is a Spirit. Since we are created in the image of God, we are created in the image of Spirit; and since we are created in the image of Spirit, we are spirit-beings. Our physical body is the 'house' in which we live temporarily as spirit-beings. Our physical body is the 'light bulb' through which the inner, spiritual, divine Light of God is supposed to shine and impact the world. Our physical body is the means by which we are to radiate and outwardly express the inner, divine spiritual image and the inner, divine spiritual power which we carry. Our body is our interface with this physical world which we are visiting temporarily.

(2) As spirit-beings, we are more than human; more than mortals; more than flesh and bones. Truthfully, we carry in our spirit the divine nature and essence of God. Our divine spirit, which comes directly from God, is invisible to our natural eyes. Our spirit is also infinite and eternal. Our spirit is like a droplet within the boundless Ocean which is Infinite God. So, God is in our spirit; and our spirit is in God. Therefore, the All-ness of God is within our spirit. Our divine spirit is always one with God; so it has no limitations, no boundaries, no beginning and no ending.

(3) We are neither physical beings nor earthly beings. Truthfully, we are *Divine Spirit-Beings* who are created to be a perfect reflection of the divine glory, the divine nature and the divine power of Spirit-God. This is what it means to be created in the 'image' (i.e. the 'manifestation') of God. The inner divine image is our Ideal Self. It is the highest expression of our Divine Identity. (Please read these three paragraphs a second time before moving on. Let this Truth sink in.)

This is a profound Truth, and may seem strange at first. If you are feeling any resistance to this Truth, it's because the mental conditioning and the programing which you received in the world system have taught you the opposite about yourself. Any resistance, which you may be feeling in your mind, is the pull and tug of the restraint of mental chains and shackles which want to hold you back and prevent you from knowing this divine Truth about yourself.

Now you may be wondering: *"Since we are created as Divine Spirit-Beings, what is the significance of man's physical body being "made from the dust of the earth" as stated in the Bible?"* The story of creation, recorded in the Bible in the Book of Genesis, is written in mystical language which must be deeply studied in order to be clearly understood; and we will do so at Level 3 of this Men's Bible Study. Genesis 1:27, which we have just read, tells us that we are created in the image of God. Later, in Genesis 2:7, the Bible speaks mystically of man's physical body being made from "the dust of the earth". In mystical language, the Bible then tells us that God 'breathed' into that physical body the spirit-being which He had created in His own image. Then man became a 'living being' which is both physical and spiritual. So, that 'living being' has power to enhance his personal non-physical identity which is otherwise called 'a soul'. So your spirit and your soul are *not* the same. We will study this Truth from the Bible later on in this book, and in great detail at Level 3 of this Men's Bible Study.

Know the Truth or just accept ideas

So, we are Divine Spirit-Beings whose origin is Infinite Spirit-God. We are a manifestation of Divine Life. Let's now compare this Truth with the ideas taught by the world system:

▣ If we are atheists or agnostics, the world system has taught us either that there is no God or that, if God exists, it is impossible to know for sure. It has taught us that God is an invention of religion. It has taught us that a man is only a physical body and is just another animal. It has taught us that we are either an accident of nature or we were 'intelligently designed' by extraterrestrial creatures. If we believe in these ideas, it's because we have forgotten that although science has helped mankind in many ways, and although science has many theories to explain the existence of matter and the material world, science has no explanation for Life itself. Science cannot answer the question: 'What exactly is Life?' That's because Life transcends the natural realm of matter. Life is from the spiritual realm. Infinite God is Life itself; therefore Infinite God cannot be an invention of religion. Before religion ever existed, The Infinite was The Infinite, and Life was Life.

▣ On the other hand, if we are non-religious but we believe that there is a higher power which is greater than the physical world, the world system has taught us either to ignore the teachings of Jesus Christ, or to see Him as just one in a long line of teachers. It has taught us that, by our own devices, we have to somehow qualify so that we can reach up to the divine state someday in the very distant future. It has taught us that we are just lost souls and spiritual orphans.

▣ Last but not least, if we are religiously inclined or are firm believers in some concept of God, the world system has taught us that God has some physical or human form and/or that God is an old man with grey hair sitting on a throne, and that He lives far away in the sky. It has taught us that, whoever God is, He is very angry with us; and so we have to find ways to appease Him. It has taught us that God has no reason to love us, for we are only human. It has taught us that, at the core of our being, we are nothing more than evil, wretched sinners, all unworthy of the least of God's goodness. It has taught us that we are all separated from God, and that none of us has any innate God-connection. It has taught us that if we want to have a relationship with God, we have to become God's 'adopted child'; and only then will we be granted admittance into God's family.

When we compare the truth of our Divine Identity with all of these 'ideas' about our identity which are taught by the world system, there is a question which every man will have to answer for himself and within himself at some point in his life; and that question is: **'Who do you think you are?'**

As seekers of Truth, the more we study the Bible with an open mind, the more we come to realize that all of these 'ideas' are exactly opposite to the Truth hidden in the Bible. The world system will give us many ideas, but it will never tell us Truth; because it knows full well that Truth will set us free from the influence of the world system. If we are holding in our minds any thoughts or ideas which tell us that we are less than Divine Spirit-Beings who are already created in the divine image of The Infinite Source, such thoughts and ideas are contrary to the Truth. If we cling to those thoughts and ideas and refuse to let them go, we cannot know the Truth which will set us free. By holding on to those thoughts and ideas, we will not be free to express the divine truth of who we are. We will block the divine Light from shining through us. Whichever of these 'ideas' we may believe now, we were not born believing them. Somewhere along the line, our beliefs about ourselves and about God were programed into us by the world system. The good news is that we always have the power to take our minds back to the state of having an un-programed mind. Let's give ourselves unconditional permission to let go of all the misinformation which we were taught in the world system, and go back to being conscious of our Divine Identity. We carried that consciousness in our spirit before we were ever born (and we will investigate this at Level 2 of this Men's Bible Study).

When we make room in our minds to accept the whole truth of our Divine Identity, we give ourselves freedom to understand our inner divine nature. When we regain control over our thinking, our mind will be free from the inferior self-identity which the world system has imposed upon us. We will be free to express our true spiritual identity. We will at last know the truth of who we really are: Divine Spirit-Beings who are created to express the divine nature and the divine power of Divine Spirit-God.

Aiming for the target

Since we are created to express outwardly through our physical bodies that 'inner divine image of God' which we already carry, we are required: (1) to become fully conscious and aware that we already carry God's divine image in our spirit; and (2) to be perfectly aligned with that image. *Outwardly expressing the inner divine image of God* is the target at which we are aiming. We can either be hitting that target or missing that target. We can either be in alignment with the divine image or we can be out of alignment and living contrary to the divine image. When we are conscious and aware of our identity as Divine Spirit-Beings, we are on target. However, when we get to the place where we are fully expressing outwardly the inner divine nature and the inner divine power, we are hitting bull's eye.

Having grown up in the world system, we would not know what the image of God is like and what it means to express that image. We would not know whether we were hitting the target or missing the target. So Infinite God, in divine mercy, provided us with an outward, visible representation of the inner, invisible divine image so that we could have a pattern to follow. That pattern is Jesus Christ. This is why Hebrews 1:3 tells us that Jesus Christ is the "express image" (i.e. the exact expression) of God.

As we know, the Bible is a collection of 66 Books divided into two sections known as 'the Old Testament' and 'the New Testament'. As we also know, the books of the New Testament were written in the Greek language and then translated into the English language. The Greek word which is translated as "express image" literally means 'an engraved stamp which produces an exact copy'. So the man Jesus Christ was the complete, outward, visible expression of the inner, invisible, divine nature and divine power. He was the invisible image of God in complete expression.

As was said before, the image of God is not a physical image. It is an inner, divine, invisible, infinite, eternal, spiritual image, bearing the qualities, the attributes, the essence and the character of God. In fact, the Greek word which is translated as "express image" is the origin of our English word 'character'. Therefore, since Jesus Christ is the invisible image of God in expression, the only way we can truly hit the target of being in the image of God is to *be like Christ.*

Who was Jesus Christ? Jesus Christ was a divine, invisible, infinite, eternal Spirit-Being disguised by an outward, human appearance. The Bible refers to Him as "the Son of God", which means that He was the image, the reflection, the manifestation of Infinite Spirit-God. The Bible, in speaking of Jesus Christ, says: *"God was in Christ..."* *(2nd Corinthians 5:19)*. In other words, God who is 'Divine Light' was in the 'Light Bulb' of Jesus' physical body. The Bible also describes Jesus Christ by saying: *"God was manifested in flesh..."* *(1st Timothy 3:16)*. So, the man Jesus Christ is called 'Son of God' because He was the 'Manifestation of Spirit-God'. The word 'son' means 'manifestation'.

Since we desire to be like Christ, let's first come to know the truth that, just like Jesus Christ, we are Spirit-Beings in the image of Spirit-God, but we are disguised by our human appearance. We are divine spirits wearing a human disguise. This spirit is not the same as our 'soul'. This spirit, which is the truth of who and what we are, is completely of God and from God. It carries encoded within it the pattern of Truth which our soul, mind and body are supposed to follow. This is why it is so necessary to wake up to the truth of our divine spiritual identity, and to walk the spiritual path in accordance with the Truth which is available in the Bible.

Some persons believe that they are just bodies of flesh and bones, and that spiritual matters are either silly or foreign to them. Other persons believe that they are lost souls trying to get to Heaven, or to Paradise, or to Nirvana. As long as we hold such beliefs, we will not know the Truth of who we really are, and we will not be mentally free. The claws of world system thinking will therefore keep their grip on our mind.

However, when we are conscious and aware that we are Divine Spirit-Beings who are here to express the divine nature of Spirit-God, we begin to think truthfully about ourselves for the very first time. Spiritual things will then become our comfort zone. The true essence of Infinite God is power; and the true nature of Infinite God is love. If we reject or resist the truth of our spiritual nature, and if we reject or resist our own innate, spiritual God-connection, we will struggle in our human attempts to express divine power which is governed by divine love.

Now at this point someone may say: *"But won't the Holy Spirit cause us to express the divine nature?"* Yes, that's true. However, as we shall see from the scriptures later on in this book, the Holy Spirit (who is 'Spirit-God in action and in communication') will directly connect and communicate with our own spirit only, and not with our human aspect. It's a Spirit-to-spirit connection.

Are you 'only human'?

The target at which we are aiming is: to outwardly express the complete, inner, divine nature (the Ideal Self) which is in our spirit. That inner divine nature is the divine image of God. However, if we lack a conscious awareness of our own spiritual identity, we will struggle to express the divine image. Our body, soul and mind will not be free to express the glory of God which is in our spirit. We will live in a manner which is contrary to our Divine Identity. We will be off-target in our mind, and we will consistently miss the target of the divine image in our daily life.

As was said before, the New Testament in the Bible was translated from the Greek language to the English language many centuries ago. During medieval times in England, if an archer shot an arrow but did not hit the target, spectators would say: "He sinned". To a person living in medieval England, to 'sin' simply meant 'to miss a target'. Consequently, when the early translators of the New Testament came upon the Greek word which literally means 'to miss the mark; to fail to hit the target', they translated that Greek word as *'sin'*. Remember, our target is: The complete, outward expression of the inner, divine image of God (the Ideal Self) which we already carry. The more we hit that target, the less we 'sin'.

If a man is unaware that the divine nature is already within him, he is going to struggle to express the divine nature. That's because, even if he seeks for the divine nature, he is seeking for it 'out there'; outside of himself. A man, who is unaware that he has already been created as a Divine Spirit-Being in the image of Divine Spirit-God, is not yet thinking truthfully about himself. Such a man is not free to express the divine image, because he does not yet know the truth of his own divine, spiritual identity. He is not aware that the image of God has never been removed from mankind. Therefore, he does not consciously know that the divine nature of God, for which he is seeking, is already within him. He examines his thoughts and his actions, and he doesn't really see a reflection of God's divine nature, divine wisdom or divine power. So he settles for the limitations of his human identity, and he assumes that God either doesn't exist or is an absent stranger.

How does the world system respond to the man's lack of knowledge of his own Divine Identity? The world system takes full advantage of his lack of knowledge, and teaches him to settle for an identity which is less than spiritual and less than divine. He is unaware of his divine nature; and so, from childhood, the world system mentally conditions him to believe that he is nothing more than a slave to human nature. He is taught to focus on, to accept and to believe in human nature and his human body as being the reality and the totality of who he is. This is why human nature and body obsession are heavily promoted in the popular songs of the world system, and also saturate all forms of popular entertainment and culture.

A man, who is deceived by the world system, gradually comes to believe in this dangerous lie: *"I'm only human"*. This is a belief which Jesus Christ never accepted about Himself; and that's another reason why the religious leaders of His day fiercely opposed Him. A man distances himself from his Divine Identity whenever he accepts this inferior self-identity of being 'only human'. If a man sees himself as being only human, he 'sins' in his thinking. He mentally 'misses the target' of his Divine Identity. His own concept of his identity falls short of the glory of God which is already within his divine spirit. The world system does everything to ensure that this inferior self-identity is then reinforced in his thoughts and ideas about himself. Those thoughts and ideas are then outwardly expressed more and more in the 'sinful' behavior of his physical body.

The world system knows that if men ever knew the truth of their Divine Identity and divine power, they would break free from the domination of the system. Therefore, the world system is designed to mentally program men either to ignore spiritual things, or to pay mere lip service to spiritual things, or to accept a worldly version of spirituality which does not recognize the absolute sovereignty of Infinite God and of Divine Spiritual Truth. Men are taught that God either doesn't exist or that He is an absent stranger who is "watching us from a distance". Men are *not* taught that the divine ability and nature of God are actually within them. Men are programed to become mental captives to world system thinking. Therefore, these 'conformers' live a 'sinful' life; a life which misses the mark of God's inner divine image; a life which falls below the level of their Ideal Self. Over time, their minds become mentally conditioned to 'sin'. It feels normal to them to live contrary to the Truth of their Divine Identity.

Even if they become devoutly religious, men are then programed to aim for a type of religious godliness while denying their true Divine Identity, their true Godlike-ness. Therefore, they never feel good enough. They always feel that there is a gap of separation between themselves and God which they keep trying to close. They feel that if they could just obey all the religious rules, observe the religious rituals, finally get everything right and be a better person, then they would be more worthy of God's love. So, they sincerely try (and fail), by religious efforts, to live above 'sin'. No matter how hard they try, they never feel as if they are measuring up to the standard of who they 'should' be as a 'good Christian'; and they end up chasing this elusive goal of Christian perfection, but to no avail. They hide their failings, and pretend to be okay, just so they can fit in with their religious group. Then they exist in a constant, secret struggle with their failings, their shame, their guilt and their self-condemnation, never feeling right about themselves. They don't realize that the goal of spirituality is not human perfection; but rather, the goal is *to **feel** whole and complete within yourself*. They will never truly feel whole and complete until they know the Truth that they are already Divine Spirit-Beings who lack nothing. They lack nothing because everything for which they are seeking, The All-ness of God, (the Ideal Self), is already within them.

Due to a lack of knowledge of their true divine, spiritual identity, all mental captives eventually surrender to Mental Captivity. They live in mental subservience to 'sin' in some way. They resign themselves to 'missing the target' and make excuses for their behavior. As the years progress, they become slaves to 'sin'. The only thing which will release these mental captives from the grip of world system thinking is the renewing of their mind.

This is why the Bible encourages us: *"Don't be conformed to this world* (i.e. don't continue to think in the way that the world system taught you to think about yourself), *but be transformed by the renewing of your mind so that you can know what is that good and acceptable and perfect will of God (the perfect plan, desire and design of God for you)"* *(Romans 12:2)* God's perfect will for us is to live as the whole and complete divine beings we truly are. The more we know it, the more we experience it. So, we have a choice. We can continue to conform to the ideas which the world system has taught us about ourselves and about God, or we can transform by allowing our mind to be renewed in accordance with the Truth. If we are not transforming, we are conforming.

Understanding Mental Captivity

Let's go further in our analysis of the main text, and understand more of what it means to be a slave to 'sin'. *"They answered Him: 'We are the descendants of Abraham. We have never been anybody's slaves! So how can you say that we will be set free?' Jesus replied: 'I tell you this timeless truth: Anyone who lives a sinful life is a slave to sin'." (John 8:33-34)*

You may still be wondering whether a man who truly believes in Jesus Christ can really be in Mental Captivity to world system thinking. You may be asking: *Can a man, who is a sincere Christian, really be a mental captive without being aware of it?* Sadly, the answer is 'Yes'. However, the text also gives the solution to this situation. It says that when believers in Jesus follow His teaching, they will make the mental shift from being 'believers' to being 'disciples'. (John 8:31) This is what we are becoming aware of in this Bible Study. We are becoming aware of how to follow His teaching as a disciple; how to truly *be* like Christ.

Jesus Christ knew that He was a Divine Spirit-Being with a divine nature concealed in a human disguise. There was not a doubt in His mind about this truth. Similarly, you are created in the image of Divine Spirit; therefore right now you are a Divine Spirit-Being and you have a divine nature, but you are concealed within a human disguise. That is the truth, regardless of how strange and unbelievable it may sound at first. Can you imagine the positive and powerful impact this truth would have had on your life if you had been mentally conditioned to know it from your early childhood? Can you imagine the impact this truth would have had if it had been taught to you at the beginning of your Christian life?

A mental captive does not know this truth about himself, and so he does not see himself as a Divine Spirit-Being with a divine nature. Even if he is a committed Christian, a mental captive sees himself as only human. He sees himself as a natural, physical, flawed, mortal, earthly being who is: (1) trying his best to be good; (2) trying to have a relationship with God whom he regards as being completely opposite in nature to himself; (3) trying to imitate the character of Christ; and (4) hoping against hope that his best efforts will be good enough. Do you somehow see yourself in this way?

By being unaware of the truth of his divine, spiritual identity, the man who is in Mental Captivity to world system thinking is mentally chained and shackled to an earthly, human identity which is inferior to his true identity. He is a spiritual prince living as a spiritual pauper because of a mistaken identity. He is living in opposition to his Ideal Self. He unwittingly entertains thoughts and ideas which are contrary to the divine truth about himself. Despite his best intentions, he is ruled and dominated by these contrary thoughts and ideas. Mental conditioning has chained and shackled him with habitual thoughts and ideas which keep his daily life out of harmony with the inner divine image. His contrary thinking leads to contrary actions, *"...for as a man thinks..., so is he". (Proverbs 23:7)*

If we are in Mental Captivity, we are out of alignment with Divinity. Our own misguided thoughts and ideas about ourselves trap us and hold us in the condition of constantly missing the mark of divinity. Time after time, whenever we aim at acting like Christ, we fall short. Whenever we try to be good, we fail, and act worse. Whenever we attempt to make spiritual progress, we are restrained and held back. Has this been your experience? We experience this because we are trying to live in a manner which is opposite to our thoughts and ideas about ourselves. We are trying to portray externally a divine image which we sincerely believe we don't carry internally.

The mentally captive man is bound, shackled, restricted and ruled by the condition of always 'missing the target' of the divine image of God in how he thinks about himself. He enslaves himself to that mental state, and becomes a slave to 'sin'. As a result, the mentally captive man will struggle to hit the target of the divine image in his daily life. Any man, who sees himself as being less than a Divine Spirit-Being who has a divine nature, is missing the mark of the inner divine image in his thinking. He is a captive servant, a 'slave', to an inferior idea of himself. Even if he is a devout Christian, his idea of himself is: "I'm a sinner who is trying/working/fighting/struggling/hoping to someday live as a saint." He is unconscious and unaware that he already carries the divine image, and that the divine image is his true identity.

A man cannot truly express the divine image unless he knows that the divine image is who and what he already is. The mental captive becomes mentally free when he realizes that right now he is a Divine Spirit-Being who is already carrying divine attributes. He is a Divine Spirit-Being because he is created in the image of God who is Divine Spirit. He becomes conscious and aware of this truth about himself even if, at present, he sees no outward evidence of it in his daily life.

The true definition of 'sin'

Many Christians struggle with the issue of 'sin' because they have been misinformed as to what 'sin' is. **If a man does not know the truth that he is already a Divine Spirit-Being who already carries within himself a Divine Ideal Self which is to be projected and expressed outwardly, he is mentally 'missing the target' of the inner divine image in how he thinks about himself. So, he 'sins'. That is the only true definition of 'sin'. Truthfully, 'sin' is a misguided way of thinking. This misguided way of thinking causes a man to live at a level which is less than his Ideal Self and to live under circumstances which are less than his ideal circumstances. Therefore, 'sin' is more than 'wrongdoing'. The activities which are commonly regarded as 'wrongdoing'/ 'sin' / 'sinful' are just the end-result and the outward projection of a man's misguided understanding of himself.**

The deeper a man's lack of awareness of his divine spiritual identity, the deeper he sinks into misguided thinking (i.e. into 'sin'). Any man who does not know the truth of his own Divine Identity is in fact living a 'sinful' life, regardless of how outwardly religious he is. This is so because, in his thinking, he has 'missed the target' of his Divine Identity.

By mentally distancing himself from the divine image (the Ideal Self) that is within him, he has 'missed the mark'; he has 'sinned'. If he continues to do so, he will become 'a slave to sin'; i.e. a captive servant to this inferior, negative mental state. His thinking will be controlled and dominated by thoughts and ideas about himself which are opposite to his divine, spiritual nature. Those thoughts and ideas will rule his life like a slave-master, and will manifest themselves in his actions and habits, no matter how much he struggles against them. His actions will follow his 'sinful thinking'; and he will not be free until his mind is free.

Even if he is a devout Christian, his mind will be trapped in a constant struggle to silence his 'sinful' thoughts. He will struggle to control his 'sinful' actions and habits. He will desire freedom, but he won't experience it; because he cannot be free until his mind is free. Mental Captivity to thoughts and ideas which deny his divine status will cause him to keep missing the target of outwardly expressing the inner divine image of God. With this understanding, we see clearly what Jesus meant when He said: "Anyone who lives a sinful life is a slave to sin." Here's something to remember: 'Sinful' thoughts and feelings cannot be conquered. They can only be *transformed.* Transformation occurs when a man becomes fully conscious and aware of the Truth of his Divine Identity.

Those Jews, to whom Jesus Christ was speaking, were very religious. They obeyed the religious rules, and they were proud of their religious heritage. They congregated in the places of worship on specific days. They were diligent students of the scriptures. They were also sincere, committed believers in Jesus Christ. Nevertheless, at the very same time, they were living a 'sinful' life as slaves to 'sin' because they did not know the Truth of their own Divine Identity. They were ignorant of the divine nature within their spirit.

▣ Therefore, the sixth lesson we learn from the text in John 8:31-36 is: **It is possible for a man to be a devout, sincere, committed believer in Jesus Christ and yet be 'a slave to sin'.** He is a 'slave to sin' if he is habitually 'missing the target' of the divine image in how he thinks about himself. He will continue to be a 'slave to sin' until:

(1) he knows the Truth of his own status as a Divine Spirit-Being who has a Divine Identity; and

(2) he permanently holds that Truth in consciousness to such an extent that he outwardly expresses the power of the inner divine nature.

It is therefore possible for a man to be devoutly religious in his outward actions and yet, at the very same time, be living 'a sinful life' as a mental slave to 'sin'.

A mental slave to 'sin' is any man who is mentally trapped in the condition of seeing himself as only human. A mental slave to 'sin' is any man who does not know the truth that he is a Divine Spirit-Being with a divine nature temporarily disguised in a human appearance. He is a servant in mental bondage to misconceptions about his true identity. He is serving world system thinking.

Aligning with God's definition of you

By contrast, the man who is mentally free has allowed himself to fully accept in his mind that, although he wears a human disguise, he is a Divine Spirit-Being. He fully accepts that he already carries within his spirit the divine nature of God. He knows that the All-ness of God is within the divine image (the Ideal Self) which is already within him. He fully accepts this truth, regardless of what the outer circumstances of his life may appear to be at present. The deeper he accepts this truth, the more easily he will express it in his daily life. The mentally free man, the true disciple, knows that he already carries the divine image within him. Even though he wears a human appearance, he knows that he is a Divine Spirit-Being. This is true Christ-like thinking.

Despite the limitations (and even the faults and failings) of his physical body, he is consciously aware that he is not his body. He knows that he is a Divine Spirit-Being right now, because he is created in the image of Divine Spirit-God. He knows that he is a Divine Spirit-Being living temporarily in a limited physical body. He knows that this is the truth of who he is, regardless of how he may have been mentally conditioned to think about himself in the past.

The mentally free man has broken from his mind all the chains and shackles forged by habits of world system thinking. He is completely free from all inferior definitions of his spiritual identity. He has completely rejected the mental conditioning which tells him that he is only human, and he no longer sees himself in any way as a slave to human nature.

He does not define himself as a natural, physical, flawed, mortal, earthly being who is trying his best to be good and who is trying to imitate the character of Christ. He knows that he is more than just an animal, more than just a body, more than just a mind, and more than just a soul. He knows that he is a divine spirit with a divine nature. He also knows that all his faculties are designed to yield to this divine nature and to be victorious over world system thinking, so that he can live powerfully, masterfully and victoriously in this present world.

The mentally free man has re-aligned his mind completely with Infinite God's definition of who he is. He has taken back control of his mind. He is thinking correctly about himself. The thoughts and ideas in his mind are in complete alignment with the truth of his Divine Identity. He knows the truth that he is created in the image of Divine Spirit. He knows the truth that he is therefore a Divine Spirit-Being with a divine nature housed temporarily within a physical body. More and more, he lives his daily life from the ever-unfolding, conscious awareness of this truth.

The mentally free man is on target in his mind. He is hitting the target in his mind, hitting the mark of the divine image which he is created to express. Every day, he aligns his thinking more and more to harmonize with his Divine Identity. His powerful, successful right-actions flow easily out of habits of right-thinking. He is in harmony with

Divinity because he is free to think with the Spiritual Mind which is within his own spirit. Even if he is not yet hitting bull's eye, he is mentally on target.

The mentally free man understands that he is *not* a physical being who is trying to be in a relationship with God. Rather, he knows that he is a Divine Spirit-Being in right relationship with Divine Spirit-God. The mentally free man has no need to imitate Christ. Rather, he is free to be like Christ because he is thinking correctly about himself. So, he is free to be much more than just a believer in Christ. He is free to be a disciple of Christ; *he is free to be as Christ is.* He has no thoughts and ideas which can chain him, shackle him and hold him in Mental Captivity to world system thinking. The Truth about his own divine spiritual identity has made him free. Do you see the difference?

Think like a son

Now let's go a little deeper into the main text. In the second part of the text, Jesus speaks of "a slave" and "a son". What do these expressions mean?

Jesus said: *"I tell you this timeless truth: Anyone who lives a sinful life is a [mental] slave to sin. A **slave** has no permanent place in the family, but a **son** belongs to the family forever." (John 8:34-35)* What does this mean? In this passage of scripture, the words 'slave' and 'son' are used as symbols to represent two opposite types of identities which a man may choose to express here on Earth. 'Slave' is the identity of captivity. 'Son' is the identity of freedom.

A physical slave can be defined as a servant who is held in Physical Captivity. However, when Jesus uses the word "slave", He is not speaking of a physical slave but of a mental slave. A mental slave is a servant who is held in Mental Captivity. *What is a mental slave serving?* A mental slave is serving an inferior definition of his identity. *Where did he acquire this inferior definition of himself?* He acquired it while he was progressing from childhood to adulthood in the world system. *What definition of himself was he taught in the world system?* From childhood, he was mentally conditioned to believe that he is only human. He was programed to believe that he is nothing more than: (1) an animal; (2) a body of flesh and bones; (3) a slave to human nature; (4) a member of 'Adam's fallen race'; and (5) a wretched sinner who is separated from God and who is unworthy of the least of God's goodness.

Due to a lack of knowledge of the truth of his Divine Identity, he accepted this inferior definition of himself without question and began to serve it. Over time, he bowed to its demands and conformed to it; obeying it in his thoughts and in his actions.

A mental slave is unaware of his true divine spiritual identity; this is because, from childhood, he has been mentally chained and shackled to an inferior self-identity which is less than Divine Spirit-Being. Since this inferior identity is all he has ever known, he is completely unaware that he is in Mental Captivity. He does not know that this inferior self-identity is a slave-master. Therefore, he has no concept of freedom, and no desire to be free.

This inferior definition of his identity is indeed a slave-master; controlling and dominating every aspect of his life. It holds him captive in his thinking. It blocks him from believing that Mental Freedom is necessary, let alone possible. As long as he continues to define himself as less than a Divine Spirit-Being who already carries God's divine nature, he is not free to express the divine image. It is his conscious awareness of the truth of his own Divine Identity which will set him mentally free. The mental captive, the 'slave', is not free to be a true disciple of Christ, because he does not yet know the truth about his own Divine Identity. Therefore, the most he can be is a believer in Christ.

By contrast, when Jesus uses the word 'son', He is speaking of a man who is living daily from the permanent, conscious awareness that right now, in spirit, he is the image, the reflection, the expression, the manifestation, the spiritual offspring, the spiritual child, the divine, free-born, spirit-son of Infinite God, who is his own Source and Spirit-Father.

A 'son' is a person who has broken free from the mental programing which taught him that he is just an animal, or just a body, or only human. A 'son' has broken free from the idea that he is nothing more than a slave to human nature. A 'son' has broken free from the mental conditioning which taught him that he is nothing more than a member of 'Adam's fallen race'. A 'son' has let go of the idea that he is just a wretched sinner who is separated from God. A 'son' no longer believes that he is unworthy of God's goodness. A 'son' no longer believes that he is a lost soul, a spiritual orphan or a spiritual adoptee.

A 'son' knows the truth that, from eternity, he is a Divine Spirit-Being with a divine nature. He knows the truth that, from birth, he is created in the image of Spirit-God. Therefore, he is free to express the divine nature more and more in his daily life. He has unchained and unshackled himself from every perception, thought and idea about himself, and from every definition of himself, which is contrary to this truth. He is hitting the target of the divine image and going ever closer to hitting bull's eye. A 'son' is a person who is mentally free. He is free to be more than just a believer in Christ. He is free to be a disciple of Christ. He is free to be what Christ is.

So, every man has a choice. He can either choose to be ignorant of the truth of his Divine Identity, or he can choose to know the truth of his Divine Identity. He can either choose to live in the darkness of ignorance, or he can choose to live in the light of awareness of the Truth of who he really is. He can think that he is a human 'slave', or he can know that he is a divine 'son'. However, at some point in his life, whether consciously or unconsciously, he will choose an identity. His choice will then answer the question: 'Who do you think you are?'

▣ We therefore learn the seventh lesson from the main text: **Every man is required to choose whether he will think as a mental 'slave'**

to world system thinking or whether he will think consciously as a divine 'son'. He can either choose to think like a servant in Mental Captivity (i.e. he can choose to be a mental 'slave'), or he can choose to think like a beloved, free-born, spirit-son of his Divine Spirit-Father (i.e. he can choose to think and be like Christ).

If a man chooses to think like a servant in Mental Captivity, he will be controlled, restricted and dominated by 'sin'; for 'sin' is a way of thinking. He will be habitually 'missing the mark' of the divine image; first in his thinking and then in his daily life. However, if a man stops thinking like a mental 'slave', and chooses to think like a beloved, divine, free-born, spirit-son of Spirit-God, he will know the truth of his Divine Identity. This truth will set him free by mentally positioning him to experience and express **'Divine Sonship'**; first in his thinking and then in his daily life.

By being like Jesus Christ the Son of God in his thinking, and by accepting that right now he is a beloved, free-born, spirit-son of God, he will be free from thoughts which are contrary to truth. By being (not acting) like Jesus Christ, he is truly saved from sin. He is saved from mentally missing the target of the divine image (the Ideal Self) which he carries within him. He is free to be like Christ the Beloved Son of God, because his mind is now free from every other concept of his own spiritual identity except beloved, free-born, spirit-son of God. He knows that, from birth, he is in a family relationship with Infinite God; because Infinite God has never removed the divine image from mankind. He is no longer thinking like a mental captive. That's because he is now conscious that, as a spirit-son of God, he is in a family relationship with Jesus Christ the Beloved Son of God. The Son has set him free mentally, and he is free indeed. Do you see the difference?

Being in the Divine Family

Jesus said that: *"A slave* [i.e. a person who is in Mental Captivity] *has no permanent place in* **the family**, *but a son* [i.e. a mentally free person] *belongs to* **the family** *forever". (John 8:35-36)* What family is this?

When Jesus uses the expression 'the family', He is speaking of The Family of Divine Beings. The Bible teaches us that this Family exists both in heaven (i.e. in the spiritual dimensions) and in earth (i.e. in the natural world). Ephesians 3:14-15 states: *"For this reason I bow my knees unto the Father of our Lord Jesus Christ, of whom the whole family in heaven and earth is named."*

▣ Here is the eighth lesson from the main text: **We are spirit-sons of Spirit-God, and we are designed to be part of the Divine Family (the Family of Divine Beings). As sons of God, we belong to the Divine Family forever. Therefore, our true identity is divine.**

Now, with this understanding of the truth of our divine spiritual identity, let's amplify our main text, and its meaning will become crystal clear:

"Jesus said to those Jews who believed on Him: 'If you follow my teaching, then you are really my disciples [If you follow My teaching, then you are really exactly like Me], *and you will know the truth* [you will be conscious and aware of the whole truth of your spiritual identity], *and the truth* [which you hold in conscious awareness] *will make you* [mentally] *free* [from captivity to world system thinking].'*

They answered Him: 'We are the descendants of Abraham. We have never been anybody's [physical] *slaves! So how can you say that we will be set free?*

Jesus replied: 'I tell you this timeless truth: Anyone who lives a sinful life [anyone who habitually lives a life which misses the mark of the inner divine image, the Ideal Self] *is a* [mental] *slave to sin* [is in mental captivity to an inferior definition of himself because he has missed the mark of the inner divine image in his thinking].*

A [mental] **slave** *[a mental captive to world system thinking]* **has no permanent place in the** *[divine]* **family, but a son** *[a mentally free man who is consciously aware of the truth that he is a beloved, free-born, spirit-son of God and who is expressing the divine image]* **belongs to the** *[divine]* **family forever.**

So if the Son makes you free *[if the outward Manifestation of the inner image of God makes you free from Mental Captivity],* **you are truly free** *[you are truly free to be a son of God expressing the divine image of God; you are truly free to be like Me; you are truly free to be like Christ]'."* (Please read these amplified verses a second time before moving on. Let them sink in.)

It is interesting to note once again that Jesus was speaking to believers; nevertheless they were still mentally ruled, restricted and controlled by thoughts and ideas which are contrary to Truth. Believing in Jesus Christ is wonderful, but it will not be enough to free us from bondage of the mind. There is specific Truth which will make us mentally free, and this will be the focus of this Men's Bible Study series.

Identity determines Experiences

Now, let's dig a little deeper in the main text. *"A slave* [i.e. a man who is in Mental Captivity] *has no permanent place in the family, but a son* [i.e. a mentally free man] *belongs to the family forever. So if the Son makes you free, you are truly free." (John 8:35-36)* Physical enslavement was the order of the day in the Roman Empire. Therefore the Jews, to whom Jesus was speaking, had a clear understanding of the difference between slaves and sons in a family. We see that, by using the words 'slave', 'son', and 'family', Jesus was using the system of physical enslavement as a symbol to illustrate a spiritual and mental principle.

Under the system of ancient physical enslavement, a slave belonged to the family of the person who owned him. The slave was held in physical captivity and bonded to serve that family. A 'slave' was therefore classified as a 'servant in bondage' or a 'bondservant'; (and for the purpose of this Men's Bible Study, we will be using these terms interchangeably.) However, the slave's place in the family was not permanent, for the slave-master could sell or otherwise dispose of that slave at any time. A slave couldn't free another slave. The father in the household had the authority to set any slave free. The son of the father could also free a slave if the father gave his authority to the son.

Under the system of ancient physical enslavement, bondservants and sons lived in the same house. The man of the house was 'master' to his bondservants, but he was 'father' to his sons. Both the bondservants and the sons were an integral part of the family, but a bondservant's position in the family was temporary while a son's position in the family was permanent. Both the bondservants and the sons were required to be obedient and respectful to the man of the house. Both were required to be loyal to the family and to give service to the family which would promote the interests and wellbeing of the household. However, despite these similarities, the experiences of the bondservants were far different from the experiences of the sons. The experiences, the expectations and the privileges of the bondservants and of the sons were determined by just one thing: Their Identity (i.e. who and what they were in that family).

Those who identified themselves as bondservants expected to be treated as bondservants, and so they were. Those who identified themselves as sons expected to be treated as sons, and so they were. The treatment meted out to the bondservants in the house was inferior to the treatment given to the sons in the house. Any kindness shown to the bondservants was due to the goodness of the master's heart; a crumb of kindness falling from the master's table. Sons, on the other hand, received the best from their father by right of birth.

The bondservants in the family were nothing more than servants in bondage to their master, but the sons in the family were completely free from birth, and were in loving relationship with their father.

Bondservants had no permanent place in the family. Their status could change on any given day. They could be sold, traded, given as payment for debts and even executed on a whim. Sons, on the other hand, were part of the family permanently. Their status could never change. So, to sum it all up: *In the family, Identity determines Status, Status determines Treatment, and Treatment determines Experiences.*

Walking in the Light

We have seen the difference between bondservants and sons as it existed under the system of ancient physical enslavement. Let's now personalize this information and see how it applies to us spiritually in the modern world.

You will recall that the captivity of which Jesus was speaking was not Physical Captivity but rather Mental Captivity. You will also recall that Mental Captivity is a misguided way of thinking. It is a disharmonious state of mind. It is a person's inadequate understanding of his Divine Identity. It is a condition of being unaware that he is a divine, beloved, free-born, spirit-son created in the image of Divine Spirit. Mental Captivity is a way of thinking which binds, restricts, blocks, belittles, oppresses and confines a man, and prevents him from being the person whom God created him to be. Mental Captivity hides under the guise of false modesty and self-rejection. It feeds on fear and insecurity. It takes refuge in traditional ideology. Mental Captivity occurs when we do not know the whole truth of who we are created to be, and in our lack of knowledge, we accept and believe in an inferior definition of ourselves; an inferior identity. That lack of knowledge confines and restricts us from expressing the divine image, and blocks us from living powerfully, masterfully and victoriously. The word of God through the mouth of the prophet says: *"My people are destroyed for lack of knowledge..." (Hosea 4:6).*

We are created in the image of God and we are Divine Spirit-

Beings with a Divine Identity. A lack of awareness of this Truth will cause us to walk in Darkness. Our perception of God, of life and of our own selves will not be clear. By contrast, conscious awareness of this Truth will cause us to walk in the Light. Our hearts will be pure and untainted. Our minds will be clear. Our perception of God, of life and of our own selves will be in harmony with God who is Divine Light. When we choose to be mentally free, we mentally position ourselves to be released from Darkness (i.e. Ignorance) and to walk fully in the Light (i.e. Truth Awareness).

Your true identity

The bottom line is: we have a choice. We can either choose to be mental captives of world system thinking or we can choose to follow Jesus' teaching, know the Truth and be mentally free. We can live as mental 'slaves' or as divine 'sons'. What does the Bible say is our true identity? The answer is found in our opening text, our WORD FOR TODAY. It says: *"Beloved friends, right now we are the sons of God..." (1st John 3:2)* From birth, we are created to be divine sons in the Divine Family; for the divine image has never been removed from mankind. (And please note that the term 'sons of God' has nothing to do with physical gender. It is a spiritual description, not a physical one. Therefore, even if some people's physical bodies, their human disguises, are female, they are still sons (manifestations) of God. We are spirit-sons of God. 'Son' means 'Manifestation'. This is an important point. Please bear it in mind.)

"Right now we are the sons of God". This is another statement which many Christians have heard in Church, but it conceals a truth which many Christians do not yet know. We all acknowledge that we are the children of God and that we are part of the family of God. We have heard this in sermons and we have sung this in Church. However, have we ever paused to know the truth of what this means?

"Right now we are the sons of God". Let us think about this for a moment. Let's allow this profound truth to sink deep in our minds. Right now we are the manifestations of Divine Spirit on Earth. We are the spirit-sons of the Divine Spirit-Father. God is our Source, our Origin and our Spiritual Ancestor. We proceeded and came out of God, as a Divine Spirit with a Divine Identity, long before we ever arrived on Earth and assumed a human appearance. Our spiritual DNA comes from God. As God is Spirit, so we are spirit right now. We are more connected and have more in common with Infinite God than with any physical object seen on Earth. Contrary to what we may have been taught, we are not the adopted sons of God. We are not adopted sons in the Divine Family. Truthfully, we are the free-born sons of God from eternity. Remember that Jesus said that sons belong to the Divine Family *forever*. (Later in this book, we will study the truth about 'the adoption of sons' spoken of in the New Testament.)

To sum it all up, being a beloved, divine, free-born, spirit-son of God is your true spiritual identity. You are a Divine Spirit-Being. This is your only identity, even if world system thinking and your human disguise have tried to persuade you otherwise. This is the Truth which you are required to know. This is the Truth which will set you free. You confirm that you know this Truth when you live each day with the ever-unfolding, conscious awareness that you are a divine sprit-son of God created in the image of Spirit-God. "Right now I am a divine, beloved, free-born, spirit-son of God": this is the basic Truth which is the foundation of being in right relationship with your Divine Spirit-Father. When you choose to be conscious of this Truth, you are mentally positioned to break free from every form of mental bondage.

But here's the catch. The only way to fully know this Truth is to give up and disown every opposing definition of who you are. The importance of this requirement cannot be overemphasized. Do you have any beliefs about yourself which are in opposition to your being a Divine Spirit-Being? If so, feel free to permanently evict from your mind those beliefs and definitions. The Bible says that right now you are a son (a manifestation) of God. Are you agreeing with this Truth about yourself or are you denying it?

Giving up the old way of thinking is what many of us find most challenging. Therefore, this is what we will mainly be working on in the 7 Lessons in this book: investigating, unmasking and freeing ourselves from the subtle mental conditioning which has been lying to us for years, and which has been preventing us from living powerfully, masterfully and victoriously. By the end of this book, we will break free from such mental conditioning because we will know the Truth.

So, how have you been defining yourself? Who do you think you are? In your mind, is divine, beloved, free-born, spirit-son of Spirit-God your only identity? When you get to the point where you know this Truth, that right now you are a Divine Spirit-Being with a Divine Identity, you will look back and wonder how you had ever held any opposing opinions of yourself. That is the power of Mental Freedom.

You choose your State of Mind

Jesus Christ walked among mankind as the ultimate Expression of Divine Sonship. Divine Sonship is our spiritual birthright. We position ourselves to experience Divine Sonship: (1) when we know the Truth of who Jesus Christ really was; and (2) when we are willing to follow the pattern of Divine Sonship which He portrayed.

By following the pattern of Divine Sonship, we, the original sons of God, regain our fellowship with our Spirit-Father which was broken by 'sin'. We regain our original status as divine sons in the Divine Family. This is the status which 'sin' stole from us. As we have seen earlier in this Lesson, a man may choose to think like a mental 'slave' or he may choose to think like a divine 'son'. As he thinks, so is he. His thought patterns will create his own self-identity in his own mind. If a believer in Jesus Christ fails to think like a divine spirit-son of Divine Spirit-God, he is still being subtly dominated and enslaved by world system thinking.

▣ Here is the ninth lesson from the main text in John 8:31-36: **A man always has the freedom to choose the identity which he will express in the Divine Family.** The words 'slave' and 'son' represent two different identities available to us. They are two opposite ways of thinking. A man may choose whichever he prefers. He can either choose to miss the mark of the inner divine image and be a mental 'slave to sin'; or he can choose to experience and enjoy Divine Sonship by living as a beloved son of God. It all comes down to how the man chooses to think about himself.

God has given to every man, including you, this freedom of choice: the freedom to select his own state of mind. Whichever state of mind you choose, God will respect your choice. Your chosen state of mind will determine the type of relationship you have with God, and the type of relationship God has with you. If you are in a conscious relationship with God, you can either choose to be in a 'Father-son' relationship with God, or you can choose to be in a 'Master-bondservant' relationship with God. You can either choose to see God as your 'Beloved Divine Spirit-Father' and to see yourself as 'God's beloved divine spirit-son'; or you can choose to see God as your 'Master and Overlord' and to see yourself as 'God's human bondservant'. Your choice will determine your identity which will determine your status which will determine your treatment which will determine your experiences in the Divine Family.

Your habitual thoughts, your state of mind and your level of conscious awareness will determine how you see God and how you see yourself. This is another truth hidden in the main text: As you walk the spiritual path, you get to choose whether you will live as a mental bondservant or as a free, beloved son in the Divine Family. By choosing your state of mind, you get to choose which identity you will express.

Here are the two states of mind available to you as you walk the spiritual path:

(1) If you see God as your Master and if you see yourself as God's human

bondservant, you are thinking like a captive servant, and you have chosen Mental Captivity. You may have picked up these ideas in religion, but they are still part of world system thinking. Many ideas which are taught in religion have their origin in the world system and serve the agenda of the world system. However, Truth was Truth before religion ever existed. This is why it is necessary to know the Truth for yourself.

(2) If you see God as your Beloved Divine Spirit-Father and you are consciously aware that you are a divine, beloved, free-born son of God with a Divine Identity, you are thinking like a divine son, and you have chosen Mental Freedom. As a son of God, you are still in service to God and in service to other people. You still serve in humility in whatever capacity you are called to serve. However, you are in service, but not in servitude. You give humble service, but you are not a 'slave' or 'bondservant'. At all times, you are a son of God giving service.

Character follows Identity

You know that you are mentally free when you are fully conscious and aware that you are a Divine Spirit-Being; a divine, beloved, free-born son of God. This is "the truth that will set you free". When you know this truth, you will be more than an admirer of Christ and more than a believer in Christ. You will be a disciple of Christ. You are truly His disciple when the truth of His teaching transforms you mentally into being what He is.

According to our main text in John 8:31-36, there are two things which will set you free: (1) the truth that you know; and (2) the Son. The New Testament in the Bible teaches us that Jesus Christ is the Son (the Manifestation) of God. *(See Matthew 16:15-16)* You become free when you know the truth that, right now, you are what Jesus Christ is. You are a son (a manifestation) of God. When you know this truth, you are a disciple of Christ and not just a believer in Christ.

◙ Therefore, here is the tenth lesson from our main text: **The only**

truth which will set you free is the truth that you know about DIVINE SONSHIP; i.e. the divine sonship of Jesus Christ and your own divine sonship as a beloved son of Infinite Spirit-God.

Here's how you stop conforming to world system thinking. Here's how you transform from being a 'believer' into being a 'disciple'. Here's how the Son sets you free. Here's how you will be free indeed: *You are free when you are like Christ; first in identity and then in character.*

Character follows Identity. Whenever Identity is first established in the mind, Character can be molded to match it. So if you have been waiting to be like Jesus, the divine Son of God, in character before you become conscious and aware that right now you are a divine son of God in identity, we are sorry to have to tell you that it will never happen.

Rather, it works the other way around. When you are conscious and aware that right now you are a divine spirit-son of God in identity, and you live with that conscious awareness, the Christ in you (the divine nature in you) will spiritually authorize you to become a divine spirit-son of God in character. The human nature will gradually give way to the power of the divine nature. This is why, regardless of any 'weakness' or 'mistakes of the past' or 'issues' which may be challenging you, the truth of your identity still stands: Right now you are a son of God.

When your mental chains and shackles are broken, you are free to be like Christ, because at last your mind is free and open to the whole truth of your Divine Identity. That's true freedom. Right now, you are in the Divine Family; that is true. However, Jesus said that both 'slaves' and 'sons' are in the Family. If you see yourself as a bondservant to 'sin' or as a bondservant to God, you are not yet conscious that you have a permanent place in the Divine Family as a son. However, when you are conscious and aware that you are a beloved spirit-son of God and you are conscious and aware that God is your Beloved Divine Spirit-Father, then you know the truth that you are in the Divine Family forever. It cannot be otherwise.

Only bondservants have a Master

Even as a devout Christian, you have a choice. (1) You can either choose the state of mind of a bondservant, toiling and suffering in servitude to a God who is your Master; or (2) you can choose the state of mind of a divine, beloved, free-born, spirit-son of the one true God, who is your Divine Spirit-Father. Only bondservants have a master. Only bondservants need a master. Mental Captivity causes its captives to need a master.

Some devout Christians try to combine these two opposite states of mind. They try to think as a bondservant and as a son at the same time. That's when they run into problems. The Bible warns us about the perils of being "double-minded" *(See James 1:6-8).* You can't successfully see God as your Master and as your Divine Father at the same time. A choice has to be made. Trying to combine these opposite states of mind will leave you frustrated and confused. This will be discussed in more detail later on in this book. Jesus Christ never said "Master" in speaking to God. He always said: "Father". This is the pattern we follow.

Remember, only bondservants have a master, and only bondservants need a master. If you see God as your Master, you have mentally chained and shackled yourself. You have put yourself into servitude; and you can expect to be treated as a bondservant, experiencing suffering and harsh punishment. However, if you see God as your Beloved Divine Father only, then you are mentally free. You have put yourself into divine service as God's beloved son. You can expect to be treated as a beloved, free-born, spirit-son of God, receiving the best that the Divine Spirit-Father has for you as your divine right, mixed in with loving training and divine discipline.

So, in the Divine Family, *Identity determines Character; and it also determines Relationship.* It's not enough to be in a relationship with God. All bondservants have a relationship with their master, but it's tough on the bondservants. The aim is to be in right relationship with God; and the only right relationship with God is the Father-son relationship. This is why Jesus Christ taught us so much about our "Heavenly Father" and taught us to pray: "Our Father..." *(See Luke 11:1-4)* By teaching to us this prayer, Jesus Christ was telling us: 'You and I are sons of God (manifestations of God) in the same Divine Family. He's our Father'.

God is willing to be a Father to you, but God will not force you. It is your divine destiny to experience and express Divine Sonship. Therefore, be willing to live as God's son and not as a mental 'slave'. That requires you to remove from your mind every idea which is opposite to your being a beloved, free-born son of God. It all comes down to your chosen state of mind. Only bondservants have a master.

Now in case you are wondering: *"What about that verse where Jesus told His disciples that they were right to call Him 'Master'?"* Well, let's look at that verse which is found in John 13:13. Jesus said: *"You call Me 'Master' and 'Lord', and you are right, for so I am".* What was He saying?

In this verse, the Greek word which is translated **"Master"** means "Teacher" (not slave-master). It is translated as "Teacher" in modern versions of the Bible. The 'Master-Teacher' is recognized in the Eastern traditions as a spiritual teacher who teaches his disciples how to be just like the Master. Jesus said: *"The disciple is not above his master (teacher); but everyone who is just like his master (teacher) is perfected".* *(Luke 6:40)*

The word **"Lord"** is a title which denotes respect for authority; and in Eastern custom it was used by members of a family when addressing 'the man of the house'. The Bible records that Sarah used to call the patriarch Abraham "Lord", even though he was her husband. *(See 1st Peter 3:6)* It was done out of respect for his authority as the head of the household. It does not mean 'overlord'. Jesus is the Lord in control of His own house. He is 'the Man of the House', and we will see the full significance of this in future Lessons.

The State of Mind of a Christian mental captive

Now let's take a close look at how Mental Captivity exists within organized Christian religion. It is essential to understand this information, even though you are unlikely to ever hear it spoken of in Church. This information is brought to your attention so that you can see it clearly, analyze it and decide whether or not you will choose this particular mentality for yourself. This information is not intended to criticize, judge or condemn you or anyone else.

We have seen that under the system of ancient physical enslavement, slaves and sons had different experiences because of their different identities. The same thing happens in the Divine Family. As a follower of Christ, your chosen identity will determine your experiences. So, in the Divine Family, it is not God who determines how you are treated; it's you.

All sons of God are called to "walk in the light". What does this mean? The Bible is written in symbolic language. Many ordinary words in the Bible are used to represent spiritual concepts. In the New Testament, 'light' represents 'complete conscious awareness of divine Truth'; and 'darkness' represents 'ignorance of divine Truth'. By keeping this understanding in mind when you read the New Testament, you will get very deep insight into the scriptures which speak of darkness and light. *(e.g. See John 8:12 & John 12:46)*

'Light' = Truth Awareness. When a devout Christian is living daily in the complete, conscious awareness of the truth that he is a beloved, free-born son of God, a divine spirit-son of the Divine Spirit-Father, that person is walking in the Light. He is not living anymore in the darkness of ignorance of his Divine Identity. Such a person finds it easy to see everyone else as his true brothers and sisters, regardless of how much they appear to be to be 'missing the mark' at present. He sees them all as being the human manifestation of the spirit-sons of his Divine Spirit-Father. In Church, when he calls another believer 'brother', he is not paying lip service to the idea. He means it from his heart.

Therefore, in whatever way you truly see yourself, you will see others in the same way. Your chosen identity determines your relationship with God. It also determines your relationship with other persons. This is why the Bible says: *"...God is light, and in Him there is no darkness at all. If we say that we have fellowship with Him, yet we are walking in darkness* [i.e. living in ignorance of our divine status], *we are lying, and we are not doing the truth. But if we walk in the light as He is in the light, we will have fellowship with each other..." (1st John 1:5-7).* (Please read these verses a second time before moving on. Let them sink in.)

These verses are telling us that when we walk in complete conscious awareness of the divine Truth that we are indeed the spirit-sons of God, and when, in our minds, there is no area of ignorance at all concerning our real identity, we will find it easy to have fellowship with each other in Church.

However, when a believer in Christ is in religious servitude, and sees himself as a human bondservant to God his Master, then he sees all other believers in Christ as being human bondservants, and as being potential rivals for the Master's favor. Remember, Jesus said that a slave's position in the family is always uncertain. Therefore, to the eyes of a religious 'slave', every other religious 'slave' looks like a threat to his position, his status and his prospects in religion. This is why, in organized Christian religion, you will unfortunately sometimes see character traits of envy, rivalry, jockeying for church positions, character assassination, abuse of vulnerable persons, strife and false pride manifested among some Christians. These character traits show up whenever Christians have a Bondservant's Mentality.

By contrast, the position of a beloved, free-born, spirit-son of God in the Divine Family cannot be threatened by anyone. Persons, who have chosen the 'son of God' state of mind, belong to the Divine Family forever, and they know it. Sons of God are never insecure.

So, let's investigate further. In organized Christian religion, what are some of the experiences of those of us who are in religious servitude, those of us who are just believers but not disciples, those of us who see God as our Master and see us as God's human bondservants?

◨ THE EXPERIENCES OF RELIGIOUS BONDSERVANTS are: chronic uncertainty and insecurity regarding their position in the Divine Family; uncertainty about their status with God; a feeling of separation from God; pressure; religious stress; self-hate; self-rejection; self-criticism; self-condemnation; harsh punishment; the use of religious rituals and suffering and sacrifice as means of trying to 'appease God'; struggle; burdensome obligations; feeling restricted from enjoying the privileges of Divine Sonship; fear and intimidation; envy of the success and the status of other persons in the Divine Family; the willingness to promote themselves to the detriment of the Divine Family; misuse and abuse of spiritual power and religious position; and manipulation to suit their own agendas.

The 'super Christians' & the 'not good enough Christians'

In organized Christian religion, the bondservant's mentality is usually manifested in a Christian in one of two ways, and they are: (1) The 'Super Christian' Mentality; and (2) The 'Not Good Enough' Mentality.

◨ THE 'SUPER CHRISTIAN' MENTALITY: Mentally captive Christians always have a deep, lingering doubt about their status in the Divine Family, although they may not admit it. Inwardly and secretly, they are plagued by fear and insecurity. As a result, some mentally captive Christians tend to overcompensate. Due to their feelings of insecurity, they feel that they must prove that they are 'closer to God' than other Christians and that they are somehow better than or superior to other Christians in some way. They feel that they have to pass themselves off as a 'super Christian'. So they fall into the trap of arrogantly promoting themselves, belittling other believers, abusing vulnerable persons, exploiting those who look up to them, and acting 'more spiritual' than other believers in order to receive status, recognition, acclaim, applause, prominence and fame in Christian religious circles and eventually in the secular world.

'Super Christians' *need* to have other Christians as their 'followers'. They inflate their religious image and their ego by feeding off the energy of these followers. The 'super Christians' keep their followers spellbound, enthralled and in awe of them as they bask in the limelight. The followers of the 'super Christians' are also kept in a state of dependence on the 'super Christians', both spiritually and mentally. Therefore, these followers are always learning but never able to come to the knowledge of the truth. They never become aware of the truth which has the power to set them free; the truth of their own Divine Identity. These followers are never allowed to get to a state of spiritual maturity and self-mastery, for if they ever got to that state, it would threaten the super Christians' façade of superiority.

Fear and insecurity cause the 'super Christians' to crave religious promotion in order to validate their position, their status and their worth. They have a driving ambition to be 'Chief Bondservant' in some way, and they will manipulate anyone or anything to get there. Whenever religious titles and religious promotions are bestowed on the 'super Christians', they will feel self-satisfied for a while. However, they will also feel that they must guard and defend these positions of religious status at all costs. No matter how highly the 'super Christians' are promoted or how famous they become, their insecurity and fear never go away. Anyone whom they see as a threat to their position and prominence will be fair game for a vicious attack; and they will use lies, innuendo, slander, treachery, character assassination, manipulation, intimidation and even 'spiritual weapons of warfare' to carry out that attack. 'Super Christians' are held captive by their own mentality. They can choose freedom at any time; but they will never be free until their mind is free.

◙ THE 'NOT GOOD ENOUGH' MENTALITY: Not all mentally captive Christians act as 'super Christians.' Sometimes the opposite happens. Some Christians living under the bondservant's mentality tend to cower, to shrink, to hide, to engage in self-pity, self-loathing, self-deprecation, self-criticism, self-condemnation, self-persecution and self-humiliation. Some will even subject themselves to abuse, disrespect, hardship and generally horrendous conditions, all the while believing that they are practicing patience and humility.

Just like the 'super Christians', these Christians have a deep, lingering doubt about their status in the Divine Family. Inwardly and secretly, they too are plagued by fear and insecurity. They never truly feel good enough or spiritual enough; so they look around in Church for anyone who seems to be 'better' and 'more spiritual' than they are, so that they will have someone to blindly follow. However, since they have not yet developed their own deep fellowship with the inner, living Christ, they are unable to tell whether the person whom they are following is truly following Christ. They have not yet developed keen spiritual discernment. They are searching for Christ, but they are searching for Christ 'out there'. They are not yet consciously aware of the divine image of God which is within them; and so they look to the celebrity image portrayed by the 'super Christians'. By doing so, they end up being merely 'followers' who live in religious servitude to the 'super Christians'. They laud the 'super Christians' while speaking and thinking negatively about themselves. They gravitate towards whatever is the latest fad in religious circles, trying to find what they feel they are lacking. They are always looking 'out there' for the answers to their questions, because they are unaware of the wholeness and completeness of the divine image of God which is already within them.

Christians, who have the 'not good enough' mentality, will blindly follow 'super Christians'; because they never feel good enough within themselves, and they do not trust that Christ, who is the Power of God and the Wisdom of God, is within their own spirit. *(See 1ˢᵗ Corinthians 1:24)* The 'not good enough' Christians keep searching for a religious 'father figure' because they are mentally disconnected from their Spirit-Father, and they are unconsciously trying to fill that void. They will sometimes go from church to church or from preacher to preacher, seeking for someone to be their spiritual mentor. A mentor can teach only what he knows. Therefore, the 'not good enough' Christians, who are mentored by a 'super Christian', will end up joining the ranks of the 'super Christians'. They will then feel superior to other Christians, and will temporarily relax in the self-satisfaction that they have somehow arrived. Yet, truthfully, all they have done is to exchange one expression of mental bondage for another. The 'not good enough' Christians are held captive by their mentality. They can choose freedom at any time; but they will never be free until their mind is free.

Now, neither of these expressions of the bondservant's mentality will ever be the mentality of a disciple of Christ who is consciously aware of his own Divine Identity as a spirit-son of God. So, while all of this is going on in religious circles, the sons of The Infinite, who know their true identity, just look on and smile quietly to themselves while shaking their heads in amazement and dismay. The sons of The Infinite have nothing to prove to anyone. Their position in the Divine Family is permanent and secure. They walk in true humility and in divine confidence. They know the truth of their Divine Identity, and the truth has set them free.

Here's a suggestion: If you can identify either the 'super Christian' mentality or the 'not good enough' mentality in yourself or in others, don't criticize, judge or condemn yourself or anyone else. God has given to every person absolute freedom to choose his or her own mentality; and the exercise of that freedom deserves respect. As you participate in organized Christian religion, simply be aware that you don't have to participate in these expressions of the bondservant's mentality. You can choose to live mentally free as a beloved son of God regardless of what others do. Choose for yourself; and allow other people to choose for themselves.

The 'son of God' State of Mind

Now, as a comparison, let's examine some of the experiences of disciples of Christ who have chosen the state of mind of a spirit-son of God in the Divine Family; the sons of God who are mentally free.

◙ THE EXPERIENCES OF THE SONS OF GOD are: the Fruit of the Spirit as recorded in Galatians 5:22-23: i.e. *divine love, joy, peace, patience, gentleness, goodness, faith, humility and self-control;* divine protection; divine provision; divinely ordered promotion in the family of God; divine confidence; divine guidance; divine wisdom; true spiritual discernment; divine authority to become the sons of God in character; God-directed power; authenticity; true humility of heart; divine training and discipline; willing obedience to God; surrender of self to God; the desire to promote oneness and harmony in the family of God; equal respect for all the sons of God regardless of religious position; seeing every son of God as valuable in the family; genuine love for all sons of God; deep love for the Divine Father from the heart of a loving son; and complete assurance of their permanent position in the Divine Family. There is no fear, no insecurity, no rivalry, no backstabbing, no envy, no scheming, no manipulation and no arrogant self-promotion to be found in the sons of God.

◙ Spirit-sons of God are in harmony with Divinity. They are one with God. There is no separation between them and the Spirit-Father. Just like Jesus Christ, they know this truth about themselves: *"I and my Father are one"* (John 10:30). Therefore, while they recognize and honor God-appointed leaders in the Church and while they recognize and honor every person's natural and spiritual gifts, they never see themselves as being 'less than' anyone else; neither do sons of God see themselves as being 'greater than' anyone else, for all sons of God are in divine oneness. Spirit-sons of God maintain a high level of self-respect even while submitting to authority; and they calmly ensure that they are treated respectfully by religious leaders and by others in authority, and that the divine essence within themselves is always recognized, respected and honored.

◙ Spirit-sons of God love the truth above all else. Sons of God know the truth of their Divine Identity, and their knowing of this truth has made them free mentally and spiritually. They know that their status with God cannot be challenged, and so they are never insecure or fearful. They do not exalt themselves above the sons of God. They walk in love and in true humility, no matter how gifted they are.

◙ Spirit-sons of God know that they are in the Divine Family forever, just as Jesus said. They have nothing to prove. While they appreciate accolades, praise, commendation or recognition, they do not crave or depend on these things for their self-worth. They do not flaunt their spiritual status. They do not use spiritual power and influence to promote their own personal agendas. Their ministries are for service, not for show. They do not chase fame or recognition. They are not in servitude to God or to man. They have a spiritual inheritance bestowed on them by divine right. They know that they are the free-born, spirit-sons of Spirit-God from eternity, and that will never change. Do you see the difference?

The origin of Mental Captivity

Now, you may be wondering: *'How does a man get a bondservant's state of mind in the first place? How does he come into mental bondage?'* It comes from the time in his life when he had absolutely no submission to spiritual truth, but was content to live his life as he pleased. This was a time when he lived completely under the domination of world system thinking, completely alienated from God in his mind, completely 'missing the mark' of Divinity. He lived according to the demands of his body and the dictates of human nature, and was not conscious of his Divine Identity or his divine nature. This is when he developed the identity of being a 'sinner'; a complete and total mental 'slave to sin'. Remember, 'to mentally miss the mark of the inner divine image (the Ideal Self)' is the true meaning of the word 'sin'. 'Sin' is a misguided way of thinking.

No one is born with the sinner identity established in his mind. That is an identity to which a man increasingly conforms over the years. By being more and more mentally conditioned to disregard the divine life of God which is in him, he grows to become more and more conformed to world system thinking.

We were created in the image of God, created to express Divinity, created as one with God. However, because of a lack of knowledge of who we were created to be, we all got separated from God in our minds. We had no awareness of the truth of who we are. Instead of allowing our thoughts to be obedient to the Divine Mind of Infinite God which is within our spirit, our 'sinful' thoughts became our masters and we became their slaves. We became bondservants to inferior ideas about ourselves. These low, wretched definitions of ourselves ruled over us and controlled our actions. We became mentally enslaved; chained and shackled to a base self-identity which is inferior to our Divine Identity.

Gradually, our character conformed to that inferior identity; for Character always conforms to Identity. We became slaves to our negative thoughts and feelings, slaves to our self-will, slaves to our past experiences, slaves to our moods and emotions, slaves to our bad habits, slaves to our addictions, slaves to our needs, slaves to our desires, slaves to our pleasures, slaves to fashion and trends, slaves to technology, slaves to peer pressure and slaves to the dictates of society, just to name a few.

The problem with enslavement is that, after a while, enslavement becomes the mental comfort zone of the enslaved man. If a man stays in enslavement long enough, he can't function without a master. He will have a *need* to be intimidated, dominated and manipulated by someone or something.

Men who have lived for years as complete and total 'slaves to sin' have been mentally conditioned to be ruled by a master. Their minds have been conditioned to be dominated by someone or something. When these men later become believers in Jesus Christ, many of them don't give up their ties to mental enslavement. Instead, they just switch masters. 'Sin', brought about by world system thinking, was once their master; dominating, controlling and using them. Now they see God as their Master; dominating, controlling and using them. They will even sing gospel songs and hymns begging God: "Use me, Lord!" Do you sing such songs with the idea that God should use you as a master uses a bondservant? If so, you can adjust such thoughts, and see yourself instead as a tool being used by a master craftsman to create a beautiful world.

As a result of not giving up mental enslavement, mentally captive Christians continue to see themselves as some type of a sinner, even though they are sincere believers in Jesus Christ who came to save them from sin. *(See Matthew 1:21)* They cling to the old, inferior, sinner identity which they adopted while living as complete slaves to 'sin'. As long as they think that they are some type of sinner, (such as a former sinner, a reformed sinner or a sinner saved by grace), their character will want to go the direction of 'sin'. The mental link to 'sin' has not been broken. They are not complete slaves to 'sin' anymore, but they are still not completely free. They are not fully seeing themselves as divine, free-born, spirit-sons of Spirit-God. They are not yet consciously aware of their original Divine Identity.

Now here's something to remember. God's Divine Family Inheritance is designed for God's sons. Near the very end of the Bible, we see the ultimate destiny of the sons of God. Revelation 21:7 says: *"The man who is victorious shall inherit all things; and I will be his God and he shall be my son."*

Mental Captivity originates from a time when you were a complete slave to sin, completely missing the mark of the divine image, being controlled by inferior thoughts which originated in the world system and which are out of harmony with divinity. That old mentality still has links and ties to 'sin', its old master. It wants to keep you in a state of mental bondage. It knows that, even though you are a son of God, if it can keep you thinking like a sinner or a bondservant, it still has power over you. The good news is that you have the power and the authority, through the Christ in you, to break free once and for all, and live victoriously as the free-born, spirit-son of God you were created to be.

Symptoms of the Bondservant's Mentality

What are some of the symptoms of the bondservant's mentality? We have already seen some of them, but let's examine a few more.

1.   *A man with a bondservant's mentality will find himself in a constant battle with 'sin'.* Any man who is a mental captive is mentally 'missing the target' of the divine image (the Ideal Self). Even if he is a devout Christian, his self-identity has not really changed. He used to see himself as a 'sinner'; now he sees himself as a 'saved sinner'. He believes that he is still some type of a sinner but now he is trying to live as a saint. He has not yet fully reclaimed his single, original, eternal identity which is 'son of God'. His two opposite self-identities (i.e. 'sinner' & 'son of God') will pull his character in two opposite directions at the same time. As a result, the memories and the pull of the old life will haunt him. He will find himself struggling, since he is constantly: fighting with his 'weaknesses'; feeling separate from God; doing his best to 'make it in'; being in fear of hell and damnation; trying and failing to act like Christ; having trouble 'getting past his past'; having difficulty breaking unwanted habits; being haunted by unpleasant memories; and searching high and low for that secret ingredient so he can finally feel good enough.

2.   *A man with a bondservant's mentality will have a habit of speaking negatively about himself, and will also belittle himself in the religious*

songs he sings. Many mentally captive men have a habit of speaking negatively about themselves. Some do it because they actually feel badly about themselves. Others do it because they mistakenly believe that it is a sign of humility. Jesus Christ always spoke positively about Himself. He is the pattern for all sons of God. Any man who has the habit of speaking negatively about himself is responsible to set himself free. God will not do it for him. As soon as a man breaks free from Mental Captivity, he will automatically stop bad-mouthing himself.

A mentally captive Christian feels comfortable referring to himself as: a poor sinner; an outcast; a beggar asking for the crumbs from the table; unworthy God's blessings to receive; a wretch like me; a worm as I; weak; vile; and even a child of hell. Believe it or not, these are quotes of lyrics found in some Christian religious songs. Now we can identify the mentality behind such words, and it has nothing to do with Christ. It is the bondservant's mentality.

Do you sing such songs? Do you use such words to describe yourself? Are you comfortable referring to yourself in this manner? Do you believe that the use of such words to describe yourself is a sign of humility? Do you feel that it pleases God when you speak of yourself in this way? If you answered *'Yes'* to any of these questions, then you have fallen into Mental Captivity. It's not your fault. You were trained to think this way. However, it's easy to take back control of your mind and retrain yourself to think differently. Here's a suggestion: From now on, examine carefully the lyrics of the songs you sing in Church and the lyrics of the songs you hear other Christians sing. See if these religious hymns and gospel songs are the songs of bondservants or the songs of free-born, spirit-sons of God. You will be amazed at how many hymns and gospel songs contain lyrics which promote the bondservant's mentality.

We urge you never, ever to sing any songs which deny or oppose your status as a son of God, or which deny that you are already created in the image of God. This is not about finding fault with songs or criticizing songwriters. It's about being sensitive and conscious as to what you are singing, and being selective as to which songs are helping and which are hindering your spiritual progress. Songs are very powerful mental conditioners. They program your mind. So, choose your songs wisely. Feel free to be silent when the lyrics of any song, which you are singing in a congregation, are promoting the idea that you are less than a son of God. When you get to that part in the song, just stop singing.

3.   *A man with a bondservant's mentality will feel comfortable believing in condemnation, punishment, suffering and struggle.* He will feel comfortable living in self-loathing, and he will have the habit of judging and condemning himself and others. (Please note that a feeling of self-criticism and self-condemnation is one of the deadliest feelings which a believer in Jesus Christ can entertain, and must be avoided at all costs.) If he makes a mistake, he will find it difficult to truly forgive himself and to accept forgiveness. He will find it difficult, if not impossible, to truly forgive others. He will live in fear of God's 'punishment' and in fear of 'hell and damnation'. He will believe in suffering and struggle. He will believe that, in order to be a true Christian, he has to go through hell on earth in order to get into heaven. He will sing songs which reinforce these negative beliefs. He will accept burdensome religious obligations as normal. He will go through life toiling spiritually under religious servitude. Once these ideas and attitudes dominate his mind, he will gravitate towards religious teachings which reinforce these ideas.

Do you have any of these symptoms of Mental Captivity? If you do, you can easily free yourself from them. Remember, God punishes bondservants but He gives loving training to His free-born, spirit-sons. Bondservants will settle for the crumbs from their Master's table; but spirit-sons have a permanent seat at their Father's table, and get the best from their Spirit-Father by divine right. A man's chosen identity will determine his experiences.

4.   *A man with a bondservant's mentality will be plagued by fear and*

insecurity. He will always be ill at ease in his mind, because he sees himself as a bondservant, and his place in the Divine Family is doubtful. He will be in constant fear that his soul can be 'lost'. He will be fearful of hell, of evil and of all the turmoil in the world today. He will be fearful of the future, and extremely fearful of the 'end-times' that we hear so much about. He will gravitate towards religious beliefs and teachings which feed his fears. He sees God as his Master; and so he will be afraid that God may hurt him, abuse him, overlook him, turn against him, demote him, reject him or cut him loose at any time. He will feel terrified of God, and he will feel threatened by the other 'bondservants' whom he sees around him.

He will not be conscious that he already carries divinity within him. Therefore, he will look externally for validation and self-worth. Anyone who gets promoted in the Church will look like a threat to his position and future prospects. He will be jostling others in order to get validation, recognition, positions and titles in his religious group. All of these are signs of insecurity, a symptom of mental bondage.

5.   *A man with a bondservant's mentality will believe that God is a benevolent tyrant.* A benevolent tyrant is a controlling person who will be very good to you if you are in his good graces, but if you displease him in the slightest way, he will turn on you like a monster. This is how the mentally captive man defines God. Furthermore, since God is his Master, he will expect God to be harsh, to be selfish and to use him because this is how masters treat their bondservants. He will see God's love for him as conditional, based on his behavior. He will believe that if he were a 'better person' he would be 'more worthy' of God's love. Do you have these ideas anywhere in your mind?

If you believe that God is a benevolent tyrant, you have opened yourself up to being intimidated, dominated and manipulated by people who are benevolent tyrants. You are especially vulnerable to being abused, if the benevolent tyrants in your life are religious authority figures whom you regard as being 'God's representatives'. Ironically, you might even start acting like a benevolent tyrant in your relationships with other persons. Always remember this: You are God's beloved son in whom He is well pleased. Identity is everything.

Now here is the worst symptom of Mental Captivity-

6.   *A man with a bondservant's mentality will see Jesus Christ as being someone who is far different and separated from himself.* He will relate to Jesus Christ as someone whom he admires from a distance and someone to whom he is in servitude, but not as someone who is family to him. Jesus Christ is the "express image" of God. Therefore, the mentally captive man, by feeling separated from Jesus Christ, is also separated from the divine image he was created to portray. The character, the attributes and the essence of God will be things for which he is reaching but never attains. The mentally captive man has not come to terms with his own identity as a divine son of God with a divine nature; so, he cannot *be like Christ.* Therefore, he will try to make do with a poor substitute. He will try to *act like Christ,* but without success. Then he will try to hide his failure by pretending, and by looking around for other bondservants who are somehow 'worse' than he is, so that he can feel better about himself.

Do any of these symptoms of the bondservant's mentality sound familiar to you? If you identify any of these symptoms of Mental Captivity in yourself or in other people, please don't be upset and don't criticize yourself or them. You have brought these symptoms out into the light of your awareness. They can't hide from you in the darkness anymore. They can't take power over you any longer. Now you can identify the root of the problem, and that root is Mental Captivity as manifested by the bondservant's mentality. These symptoms of Mental Captivity may be hard for a believer in Jesus Christ to face and acknowledge at first. No man likes to admit that anything has taken power over his life. However, before any man can make spiritual or mental progress, he has to be honest with himself about what the root problem is.

Here's a suggestion: In the privacy of your own mind, look at your life and ask yourself these questions: Is God my Master or is He my Divine Father? Am I seeing God as both my Master and my Father? What is my mentality? How do I really see myself, and how do I really view God? Do I see God as my loving Divine Father, or is my God a benevolent tyrant? Do I have the 'super Christian' mentality? Do I have the 'not good enough' mentality? Do I have any of the symptoms of the bondservant's mentality? Answer yourself honestly. There is nothing to fear from being completely and totally honest with yourself.

Removing the yoke

Now that we have seen the symptoms of Mental Captivity and of Mental Freedom, these questions arise: *"Which side is Jesus really on? Does He desire that those who believe in Him should be in some form of mental captivity and servitude, or does He really want them to be totally mentally free?"*

We find the answer in the well-known passage of scripture recorded in *Matthew 11:28-30* where Jesus says: *"Come to Me, everyone who is toiling and is forced to carry heavy [mental] burdens, and I will give you rest. Take My yoke upon you and learn from Me, for I am gentle and humble in heart, and you will find rest for your souls. For My yoke is easy and my burden is light."* (Please read these verses a second time before moving on. Let them sink in.) The condition of toiling and being forced to carry heavy burdens speaks of a condition of enslavement; and we now know that this is mental slavery to world system thinking and not physical slavery.

The word 'yoke' in this passage of scripture has a double meaning; here is the first. Under the system of ancient physical slavery, there were two types of yokes. One type of yoke was a metal pole with a 'collar' at each end which would be shackled to the necks of the slaves. These yokes were used to keep slaves in line as they walked single file.

The length of the poles would keep the slaves separated from each other as they walked together, but the devices shackled to their necks would ensure that they were still bound together. These yokes were designed to restrict their movement and prevent their escape. The other type of yoke was a heavy, curved, wooden beam to which heavy burdens would be attached at each end. The slave would be forced to carry this yoke and its burdens across his neck and shoulders.

If we are either complete 'slaves to sin' or if we are believers in Jesus who are living under the bondservant's mentality, we are wearing mental yokes. These mental yokes keep us in line and under control. These mental yokes force us to conform to world system thinking, and prevent us from being truly free in our mind. These yokes also keep us bound mentally to like-minded people who are also mental captives. Ironically, we are bound to each other by our shared mentality but yet we feel disconnected from each other. There is no divine oneness. Mental yokes also cause us to bear heavy mental burdens which we don't need to carry. We labor and toil needlessly even though Mental Freedom is available. Do you see the parallel?

Jesus Christ offers freedom from these yokes of bondage, when we give up world system thinking and become completely free in our minds. So the Bible tells us to *"stand firm in the freedom by which Christ* (the inner Christ; the divine image) *has made us free, and never again be entangled in the yoke of slavery". (Galatians 5:1)*

When we make the conscious decision to give up the yokes of Mental Captivity, and to accept no other definition of ourselves except the beloved, free-born, spirit-sons of Spirit-God, we have taken the first step to Mental Freedom.

We then take the further step; we take on the yoke of our Master-Teacher, Jesus Christ the Son of God, and learn from Him. We follow His teaching to the point where we transform from being His believers to being His disciples. It's the only way that our souls will enter into true rest. That is the second meaning conveyed by the word 'yoke' in this passage. In Jewish tradition, a rabbi or spiritual teacher would refer to his teachings as his 'yoke'. Each disciple would have to be willing to take on the yoke of his teacher, by fully learning, following and embodying his teachings. This would ensure that the disciple is just like the Teacher.

The world system has put us under the yokes of world system thinking. This has put us into mental servitude to human nature. Jesus Christ offers us freedom from those yokes when we follow Him and acknowledge our Divine Identity.

So it's a grand exchange which has to be made. We exchange the yokes of Mental Captivity for the yoke (the teaching) of Divine Sonship. The yokes and burdens of Mental Captivity are heavy to bear, and we have struggled under these things for years. The yoke (the teaching) of Jesus Christ is easy to bear and His burden is light. His yoke is **The Truth of Divine Sonship;** not just His divine sonship but our divine sonship as well. His burden is the burden of taking the time to lift the load of Mental Captivity from our minds.

If we desire to transform from being believers in Jesus to being disciples of Jesus, let us be willing to learn, follow and embody the teachings of the Son of God. Let us be willing to be like Him, *be a divine son of God,* even if it means that we will go against the grain of what is popularly believed and accepted as truth.

Freeing yourself

The bottom line is, if we see God as our Master, we will never fully be like Christ. In order to be like Christ, let's be willing to be what He is. Jesus Christ is our perfect pattern. He is the template of what we are created to be. Jesus Christ once asked His disciples: *"Who do you say that I am?"* to which Peter accurately replied: *"You are the Christ, the Son of the living God"* (See Matthew 16:15-16).

'Feeling free to be like Christ' simply means 'feeling free to be a son of the living God'. In order to get to that point in consciousness, the negative mental conditioning and mental programing, to which we have all been subjected, have to be set aside.

We are not truly free unless our mind is free. Therefore, let's be willing to free ourselves from mental bondage and to step out of servitude. Nobody can do this for us. Let's be willing to disentangle our minds from every thought that God is our Master. Let's be aware that we are not God's adopted sons, but as the Bible teaches, we are God's sons from eternity. Let's accept that right now we are what God created us to be: the divine, beloved, free-born, spirit-sons of Spirit-God. Let's be willing to accept 'Divine Spirit-Being' as our personal identity, to the exclusion of every other definition of ourselves.

Let every son of God be willing to think of Jesus Christ and to say from his heart: *"By the grace of God, what He is, I AM."* When we affirm this truth, we are not speaking of the physical side of ourselves. We are speaking of our true selves, the Divine Spirit-Being who lives in our physical body. Doubts may arise in our minds and tell us that it is not possible, but *1st John 4:17* tells us that *"...as He is, so are we in this world."* Let's come to know this and accept this as the absolute truth.

This book is designed to serve you in your personal spiritual development as an individual. The lessons in this book are designed to empower you to get to the place mentally where you can accept this truth and live victoriously. So just be willing to purify your mind of every trace of mental bondage to which you have been subjected under the world system.

Now, you may have read in the Bible where some of the writers of the epistles of the New Testament [i.e. the book of Romans through to the book of Jude] refer to themselves as 'slaves' or 'bondservants' depending on what version of the Bible you are reading. And, you may have read where these same writers tell us that we are the 'sons' or the 'children' of God. You may be wondering about this seeming contradiction; but it will become very clear when we study *the Mirror Secret of the Bible* here at Level 1; and crystal clear when we get to Level 3 in this Bible Study series. So, please don't let this puzzling question be a roadblock to your spiritual progress. Remember, we are going step by step. For now, just set your heart and mind to receive this truth which Jesus Christ taught regarding the difference between slaves and sons in the Divine Family.

The Son of God; the Servant of Humanity

Like Christ, you are to be the son of God and the servant of humanity. This is exactly what is being taught in this well-known passage of scripture recorded in Philippians 2:5-8. Let's look at verses 5 through 7 and then we will examine the rest in later Lessons:

"Let this mind be in you which was also in Christ Jesus, who being in the form of God [the image of God] *did not think that it was robbery to be equal with God, but He* [i.e. Christ Jesus] *made Himself of no reputation* [i.e. He humbled Himself], *and assumed the appearance of a servant..."* (Please read this passage of scripture a second time before moving on. Let it sink in.)

This passage from the Bible is one of the most crucial for you to understand in order to know the truth of who you really are. It is also one of the most misunderstood passages in the New Testament. *What is this text saying to us?* It is giving us direct instruction to have in us the same state of mind which Christ had.

And what is that state of mind? Christ, being the Son (the Manifestation) of God, did not deny His divine status. He did not think that He was robbing God by being conscious and aware that He was expressing the image of God. He did not see it as diminishing God in any way by knowing that He was the Son of the Divine Father. Yet He humbled Himself and accepted the role of *'the Son of God giving service'.*

This is the state of mind which the Bible instructs us to have.

Let us alert you at this point. Some modern translations of the Bible translate these verses to state that Jesus gave up His divine status and became a slave. However, you will realize that this is not so at all, when you read the statements which Jesus made concerning Himself as recorded in The Four Gospels (i.e. the Books of Matthew, Mark, Luke and John in the New Testament). Jesus never denied that God was His Divine Father, and Jesus was never a slave.

Consider this for a moment: If Jesus were a slave, He would have had no power and no authority to set anyone free. A slave cannot free another slave; but a son, acting under the father's authority, can free any slave. This is why, at the beginning of Jesus' earthly ministry, His identity was made crystal clear when the Divine Voice proclaimed: *"This is my beloved Son* [not slave] *in whom I am well pleased." (Matthew 3:17).* The man Jesus Christ was the Son acting under the Divine Father's authority; so He had divine authority to set mental slaves free.

Therefore, at the beginning of His service to humanity, Jesus Christ outlined His own divine Mission Statement when He said: *"The Spirit of the Lord is upon me, because He has anointed me to preach good news to the poor. He has sent me to heal the brokenhearted, **to announce freedom to the captives**, and the recovering of sight to the blind; **to set at liberty those who are oppressed**" (Luke 4:18).* At all times in His earthly ministry, Jesus Christ was the Son of God giving service to humanity. He was never in servitude.

As a son of God, you still give service to God and also to humanity. As a son of God, you are still called upon to do spiritual work and also secular work. However, doing so does not make you a bondservant or a slave, and it does not make God (or anyone else) your Master. It does not put you into a state of servitude. There is a world of difference between 'giving loving service' and 'living in servitude'. No son of God is called to be in servitude to anyone or anything. So when we say that you are not a bondservant, it means you are not in servitude to God. Rather, as a divine spirit-son, you give your loving service to your Divine Spirit-Father. Do you see the difference? Even while serving, you do not ever deny your divine status. Never in any way deny that God is your Divine Father. This is a very crucial point. Always be mindful of it.

Now, here is a verse which teaches another facet of service. In *John 12:26* it is recorded that **Christ** said: *"If any **man serves Me**, let him follow Me* [let him be My disciple; be what I am; think as I think; have the same mind that I have]; *and where I am* [in consciousness], *there shall also My **servant** be* [in consciousness]: *if any **man serves Me**, My Father will honor him."*

This verse teaches us that our human nature (i.e. 'man') is called to *serve* our inner divine nature (which is also known as 'Christ') by obeying the Mind of Christ, which is the divine mind. This type of service lifts us above world system thinking. (If necessary, re-read this paragraph until you see this hidden meaning clearly.)

In this instance, the Greek word translated 'servant' is the same as 'waiter'. It is a person serving a guest of honor who stays in his house. It does not mean 'slave' or 'bondservant'. At all times, you are a son of God. You are simply a son of God giving service to the Christ in you, from a heart of love and not from fear or insecurity. At all times God is your Divine Father. This is the state of mind of all sons of God who know the truth of who they are.

Now just in case you are thinking that you do not yet see that divine image (that Ideal Self) fully portrayed in yourself, please understand that when you let go of the sinner identity which the world system imposed on you, and when you know that right now you are an original son of God, you have taken the first major step towards Mental Freedom. Remember, your character follows your identity; and your character will always conform to your identity. The more you continue in this truth, the more you will conform to the inner divine image that you already carry.

The Bible instructs us to have the same state of mind that Christ Jesus had. In order to do so, we are required take back the control of our minds which we gave up to the world system. We are required to reposition ourselves mentally, where we see ourselves in the same way that Christ Jesus saw Himself: as 'SON OF GOD'. When we do so, we will know the whole truth of who we really are, and this truth will set us free to be like Christ.

Right now we are the sons of God

The WORD FOR TODAY tells you that right now you are a divine son (a divine manifestation) of God. This is your only true identity; not when you get everything right, not when you 'fix' your past mistakes, not when you are 'perfect', not when everybody loves you, but right now. You are a free-born, spirit-son of Spirit-God and you are in His family forever. This truth is the foundation of a right relationship with God. It is the secret ingredient to living a life which is victorious over world system thinking. The key to freedom comes from being fully conscious and aware of this truth.

So you can make your choice. Do you see God as your Master or do you see Him as your Divine Father? Are you a human bondservant or a divine son in His family? Have you chosen to be in servitude or have you chosen to give loving service? It all comes down to how you think and how you see yourself. So then, who do you think you are?

Being a beloved, divine, free-born, spirit-son of Spirit-God starts inwardly with conscious awareness of your divine spiritual parentage, and then it works its way outwardly and is manifested in your character and physical behavior. Mental Freedom comes when you realize that you are not a human body trying to 'act spiritual'. Rather, you already are divine spirit. It is futile to try to be like a divine son of God on the outside if you don't first know the truth that, because God is your Divine Spirit-

Father, you are already a divine spirit-son of God on the inside.

"And you will know the truth, and the truth will make you free." Here's the truth which you are required to know: 'Right now I am an original son of God. I am in the Divine Family forever.' The truth that you *know* is the only truth which will set you free. It's not enough to hear this truth, or to understand this truth, or to mentally accept this truth on an intellectual level. It is not even enough to believe this truth. You can do all of those things and still be shackled by world system thinking and the bondservant's mentality.

However, when you get to a level in consciousness where you are fully conscious and aware of the truth that you are a beloved, divine, free-born, spirit-son of Spirit-God, and that you are one with God, you position yourself mentally to be free to be like Christ. By the grace of God, if you are not yet at that level of consciousness, you will get to that level by the end of this book.

'Knowing' is higher than 'Believing'. What does this mean? We will answer that question and many, many more in our next Lesson. Have you ever wondered whether there is an effective way to develop your faith and to get your faith to really work for you? That question will also be answered in our next Lesson. See you then. Be sure to read the Supporting Scriptures, Affirmation and Review which follow this Lesson.

Supporting Scriptures

Galatians 4:6-7: "And because you are sons, God has sent forth the Spirit of His Son into your hearts, saying, 'Father, our Father'. Wherefore you are no longer a slave, but a son. And since you are a son, you are an heir of God through Christ."

Galatians 5:1: "Christ has set us free so we may enjoy the benefits of freedom. Stand firm in that freedom, and never again put yourself under the yoke of bondage."

Affirmation

Let's now take back control of our thinking by regaining our original, divine mental channels:

They told me that God is my Master; and that I am just God's human slave;
They told me that I'm just a sinner; wretched, condemned and depraved;
They told me that I'm only human; just a body of flesh, bones and blood;
They said I'm a spiritual orphan, with no inborn connection with God.

But now I know God is a Spirit, and I am God's own spirit-son,
And God is my own loving Father, and I and my Father are one;
My divine sonship cannot be challenged, for I was God's son long before birth;
My connection with God is much stronger than with anything seen on the earth;
For I am in kinship with Jesus, and our Family ties nothing can sever;
I'm God's son in God's own divine image; and I'm in the Divine Family forever!

Review

Q. What are the ten lessons we have learned from the text in John 8:31-36?

A.
1. It is possible for a man to study the Bible and to be well-versed in the scriptures and yet not know the Truth.

2. It is possible for a man to be a sincere believer in Jesus Christ and yet not know the Truth.

3. It is possible for a man, who is a sincere believer in Jesus Christ, to be restricted and controlled by the same things which used to restrict and control him before he became a believer; because so long as a believer does not know the Truth, he is not free.

4. It is possible for a man to be physically free but yet, at the same time, be restricted and controlled in his thinking, without ever being aware of it.

5. It is possible for a sincere believer in Jesus Christ to be in Mental Captivity to world system thinking. Believing in Jesus Christ does not automatically set a man free from bondage of the mind.

6. It is possible for a man to be a devout, sincere, committed believer in Jesus Christ and yet be 'a slave to sin'.

7. Every man is required to choose whether he will think as a mental 'slave' to world system thinking or whether he will think consciously as a divine 'son'.

8. We are spirit-sons of Spirit-God, and we are designed to be part of the Divine Family (the Family of Divine Beings). As sons of God, we belong to the Divine Family forever. Therefore, our true identity is divine.

9. A man always has the freedom to choose the identity which he will express in the Divine Family.

10. The only truth which will set you free is the truth that you know about Divine Sonship; i.e. the divine sonship of Jesus Christ and your own divine sonship as a beloved son of Infinite Spirit-God.

Q. What is the definition of a mentally captive man?
A. A mentally captive man is any man who does not know the truth of his own divine status; a man who is separated from his own Divine Identity in his mind; a man who believes in an inferior definition of himself; a man who is not yet conscious that he is one with God.

Q. How does a man become a captive in his thinking?
A. A man becomes captive in his thinking when he habitually thinks thoughts which are out of harmony with Divinity. By persisting in such thoughts, the man becomes more and more alienated from the truth of his own divine self and cannot perceive his true identity as a divine being. Gradually these ungodly (un-Godlike) thoughts take control of the man's mind and actions and start to rule the man. He loses sight

completely of his true identity and becomes enslaved to inferior ideas of who he is. This is Mental Captivity.

Q. What is the definition of a man who is living in Mental Freedom?
A. A mentally free man is a man who is *not* separated from Divinity in his mind. Such a man knows that he is one with God; that he is created in the image of God; that he is a Divine Spirit-Being in the divine category; and that he is a spirit-son of God who is his Divine Spirit-Father. He lives his life in accordance with this truth that he knows. He lives in harmony with Divinity and in harmony with his Divine Identity.

Q. When we say that Jesus Christ is the Son of God, and when we say: 'I AM a son of God', what does the word 'son' mean?
A. The word 'SON' means 'MANIFESTATION'. (We will study this truth in depth at Level 2.)

Q. Does the term 'sons of God' refer to male persons only?
A. No. The term 'sons of God' has nothing to do with physical gender. It is a spiritual description. Female persons are also 'sons of God'. We will study this truth in detail at Level 3 of this Bible Study.

Q. What is 'sin'?
A. To 'Sin' is "to miss the mark" or "to miss the target" of our own Divine Identity, our inner Ideal Self, the inner divine image of God. That "missing of the mark" is first done in our thoughts when we are unaware of and reject our own divine status. Then we see ourselves as being 'only human' and as being slaves to human nature. We assign to ourselves and accept a lower definition of who we are. Therefore, 'sin' is a misguided way of thinking.

'Sin' causes us to choose an Identity which is not on target with our Divine Identity. The thoughts, which then proceed from our minds, are not completely in harmony with Divinity. Over time, our thoughts become *'ungodly'*; (i.e. they become 'un-Godlike' or 'unlike God' or 'not divine'). This causes us to become ungodly in character, because our character always follows our identity. These disharmonious thoughts are then expressed in our ungodly (un-Godlike) actions.

Q. What is the world system?
A. The world system is the overarching framework which organizes, governs and controls civilization on Earth. It is made up of many mini-systems such as: the political system, the financial system, the banking system, the law enforcement system, the military system, the education system, the sport and entertainment system, the technological system, the commercial system and the financial system, just to name a few. Over thousands of years, these mini-systems have become ever more integrated and sophisticated, and they impact the lives of nearly every person on Earth.

Q. What is 'world system thinking'; and how are 'threats' used by the world system to dominate mankind?
A. The fundamental agenda of the world system is to protect itself, to protect its own interests and to control every person on Earth by dictating how each person will think, act and react. By doing so, the system ensures that people distance themselves from their Divine Identity in their way of thinking.

The aim of the world system is to keep people in Mental Captivity, living as 'slaves to sin', blindly serving their human nature and being unaware of their divine nature. Physical 'threats' to people's rights, freedom and wellbeing are created and/or promoted by the world system to distract people from their state of mental captivity to 'world system thinking', and to bait people into permanently having extremely negative thoughts, feelings, actions and reactions in response to these 'threats'.

Q. How can we truthfully describe God?
A. God is Divine Invisible Eternal Infinite Spirit.

Q. God is a Spirit and does not have a physical image. So how is it that the Bible says we are created in the image of God?
A. The image of God is a spiritual image which expresses the nature, character and essence of God. We are created as Divine Spirit-Beings because Divine Spirit is our source. Our divine spirit is invisible to our natural eyes, yet it is real. The divine nature within us is infinite, because it comes from Infinite God and is also one with Infinite God. Truthfully, we are Divine Spirit Beings even though we wear a human appearance.

Q. What are the two ways in which I can perceive God, and are they compatible with each other?
A. You can see God as your Master, or you can see God as your loving Divine Spirit-Father. These two perceptions are not compatible with each other. Therefore, make a clear choice in your mind between the two. As a son of God you do not have a master. Only bondservants have a master.

Q. When the disciples called Jesus 'Lord' and 'Master', what do these expressions mean?
A. In Eastern custom and tradition, 'Lord' is a term of respect used by family members to address the head of the household. 'Master' means 'Teacher'.

Q. At some future date am I supposed to be a son of God and be like Christ?
A. No. The Bible teaches that we are sons of God right now. So once you break any chains of Mental Captivity which may have bound you, you will be free to be like Christ. You will have authority to become a son of God in character because you consciously carry the divine image inwardly.

Q. When Jesus Christ said: "...Take My yoke upon you, and learn from Me", what is that 'yoke'.
A. His 'yoke' is the Truth of Divine Sonship. He teaches us how to express the divine nature as divine sons of God so we can be like Christ.

Q. Jesus said: "You will know the truth, and the truth will make you free".
What is the truth which will set me mentally free?
A. In the passage of scripture from which that quote is taken, Jesus explained the difference between 'slaves' and 'sons'. The truth is that right now you are a Divine Spirit-Being with God's divine nature. You are a spirit-son of God and not a bondservant to God. You are required know this to be your true spiritual identity to the exclusion of all else. By doing so, you will experience Divine Sonship. As a son of God, your status in the Family of Divine Beings is not in question. You are part of His family forever. You are required to know the truth of the divine sonship of Jesus Christ and the truth of your own divine sonship as a spirit-son of God. Then you can reclaim your Divine Identity which world system thinking has tried to steal from you.

Q. As a son of God, I am not a slave or a bondservant. Do I still serve God
and others?
A. Yes, you do. However, at all times, you are a son of God giving service from a heart of love, and not out of fear or insecurity. You are in divine service, not in servitude.

Q. In what two ways does the bondservant's mentality usually manifest
itself in organized Christian religion?
A. It manifests itself as the 'Super Christian' Mentality and as the 'Not Good Enough' Mentality.

Q. What state of mind does the Bible instruct me to have?
A. The Bible instructs you to have the same state of mind which was in Christ Jesus. It is the state of mind which causes you never to deny your divine status. It is the state of mind which knows that God is your Divine Father. It is the state of mind which does not see it as robbing or diminishing God in any way when you say that you are one with God.

With this state of mind, you walk this Earth as a son of God in the disguise of a human. You are a son of God giving service to God and humanity from a heart of love. You are not in servitude. This is the state of Mind which Christ Jesus had. *There is also another facet of service:* The human side of you is called to serve your inner divine nature. This service is simply your obedience to the divine mind which is already within your divine spirit. This is the mind of the Christ in you.

Lesson 2: You don't need to believe what you know

WORD FOR TODAY: "I know the One in whom I have believed, and I am certain that He is able..." (2nd Timothy 1:12)

God will not interfere with your State of Mind

Now let's pick up where we left off in our last Lesson. We were looking at the difference between seeing ourselves as God's human bondservants and seeing ourselves as the divine, free-born, spirit-sons of Infinite God. We came to understand that only bondservants need a master. Sons of God have no master; for God is their Divine Father only. We saw that 'bondservant to God' and 'son of God' are two opposite states of mind, and we also saw how these two states of mind will affect our relationship with God and our relationships with other people. We also saw that we cannot successfully operate both the state of mind of God's human bondservant and the state of mind of God's son at the same time. So, let's not be reluctant to choose Divine Sonship. If we are 'double-minded', we will be unstable in all our ways. It is God's will that we live as His sons and that we will allow Him to be a Father to us, but He will not force us to do so. God will never interfere with our state of mind. We are free to choose our thoughts, and by doing so we will be choosing our experiences. Now let's go deeper in our study.

How your State of Mind works with your Faith

In our last Lesson, we started to focus on the importance of being in the correct mental attitude and of having the correct State of Mind. We saw the importance of freeing our minds from 'world system thinking'. You may still be wondering: *"Why is my State of Mind so important?"*

As we saw in Lesson 1, having a State of Mind which is captive to world system thinking will cause a man to have incorrect thoughts and ideas concerning who he is. These thoughts and ideas will cause him to develop an identity which is inferior to his Divine Identity. By persisting in these thoughts and ideas, he will eventually develop a low State of Mind. This low State of Mind has 'missed the target' of Divinity. It has fallen below the level of the person whom he was created to be; below his Ideal Self. It will block him from expressing the inner, divine image of God which he already carries. This will negatively affect his relationship with himself, with other people, with God and with life in general. It will prevent him from living powerfully, masterfully and victoriously in this present world.

Having a low State of Mind will also restrict a man from having faith in God. Now at this point, someone reading this may say: *"Well, I'm not really a religious man, so I don't think that this stuff about faith applies to me."* However, the truth is that faith is not some spooky religious concept. Everybody on Earth lives by faith. Every morning, you and billions of other people wake up having complete confidence that there will be enough air to breathe. When you sit on a chair, you do so with complete confidence that it won't collapse. When you flip a light switch, you do so with complete confidence that you will have light. You are using faith, but you are doing so unconsciously. When you start to pay attention to your spiritual aspect, you learn how to take the same faith which you use unconsciously every day, and start using it consciously in a more expansive way. The Bible teaches us how to use our faith consciously and how to have faith in Infinite God.

Christians are aware that Faith in God is essential. With Faith in God, we can connect directly to the power and ability of The Infinite. Therefore, we can accomplish things which are beyond our natural, human resources and abilities. We know that without Faith it is impossible to please God *(Hebrews 11:6)*. Consequently, you will hear a lot being said in Christian religious circles regarding Faith, Faith, Faith. This is good and beneficial. Unfortunately, you won't hear as much being said about having the right State of Mind.

Your State of Mind and your Faith are your helpful friends. They are always working for you. Your State of Mind and your Faith are also friends with each other, and they work together. Here's how: *Your **State of Mind** determines what things you get, the quality of the things you get and the circumstances under which you get them. Your **Faith** determines when you are ready to get these things.* (Please read this statement a second time before moving on. Let it sink in.) Therefore it is futile to try to increase your level of Faith while neglecting the development of your State of Mind.

The Bible says: *"Now faith is the **substance** of **things** hoped for..."* *(Hebrews 11:1).* The Greek word which is translated 'substance' literally means 'support from beneath'. So, this verse is saying that your Faith has the job of supporting the process which will bring into reality the ideal 'things' which you are confidently expecting to receive. Therefore, when you start out by having complete confidence that you will receive some definite, ideal 'thing', your Faith can do its job; because you have given your Faith some 'thing' to support. The ideal 'thing' is clearly defined and held firmly in your mind. It is not wavering, fleeting, hazy or nebulous. It is not a wish.

Once you have a settled hope (i.e. a solid expectation) to receive some definite, ideal thing, Faith will automatically show up to give the thing support. You know that Faith is working when you can mentally see and feel that the thing already exists and is already yours. Therefore, even though you can't yet perceive the thing with your natural eyes or hold it in your physical hands, you receive it **now.** It is already real to you. You start to enjoy the ideal thing before you physically get it. You feel a sense of relief because, in your mind, it's a done deal. This is why Jesus said: *"...Whatever **things** you desire, while you are praying* (i.e. while you are harmonizing your mind with those ideal things) ***believe that you receive them*** (i.e. mentally receive them), *and you shall [physically] have them." (Mark 11:24)* (Please read this verse a second time before moving on. Let it sink in.)

When you mentally receive the ideal thing which you desire, you have the assurance that the thing is already yours. This inner assurance, this inner conviction that the ideal thing already exists and that you have already received it, indicates that Faith is working. It also indicates that you are *ready* to accept the object of your desire into tangible reality. You get the witness in your spirit which says: "IT IS DONE!"

Identifying that ideal thing

So, the Bible says that in order to consciously get your Faith to work for you, you first have to be expecting to receive some definite thing. Now, this world is full of millions and millions of things of every description. *So, what is it that will cause you to select one particular ideal thing from the millions and millions of things which are available, and reject all the others?* It is your State of Mind which will cause you to make the selection.

Your State of Mind is determined by your habitual way of seeing, feeling and thinking about 'things'. Your State of Mind will cause you to have an attraction to certain things and to have an aversion to other things. It determines what things you like and what things you dislike. Your State of Mind also determines what things you regard as possible and what things you regard as impossible in your life. Therefore, your State of Mind will include and accept certain ideal things, and will exclude and reject other things. No two men have identical States of Mind. This is why all men don't like or desire or expect or receive the same things.

Therefore, it is your State of Mind which chooses and limits the ideal thing which your Faith will bring into reality; because it is your State of Mind which determines your choice of your one-in-a-million ideal thing which you expect to receive. If you truly desire an ideal thing but you feel that it is impossible to have it, that ideal thing does not yet exist within the boundaries of your current State of Mind. You desire it, but you don't feel that it's possible for you to have it. The ideal thing feels impossible because your State of Mind has excluded it and rejected it. You have no real expectation to get that thing. Therefore, your Faith cannot bring this ideal thing into reality even though you truly desire it. Why can't Faith work in this case? *Because your State of Mind has not given your Faith any 'thing' to support.* Since you desire to receive that ideal thing, you are the one who will deliberately include that ideal thing within your State of Mind and believe that it is possible now. Then your Faith can support that thing and bring it into reality.

Your State of Mind also determines the circumstances under which your Faith will give you your ideal thing. Do you believe in suffering and hardship? Do you generally believe that life is against you and is unfair? If you have these beliefs in your State of Mind, you will tend to obtain your ideal thing under unpleasant circumstances.

It's Now or never

So, how will you know if you have included an ideal thing within your State of Mind? If in your mind you cannot see and *feel* yourself being, doing, having and enjoying that ideal thing right now, then that thing is not yet included in your State of Mind. Until the ideal thing is included within the boundaries of your State of Mind, you will never form a solid expectation to receive that ideal thing even though you may truly desire it. You desire it but, mentally, you haven't received it yet. Your mind has not yet harmonized with the ideal thing. In your mind, you can't see it and feel it and accept it and enjoy it as part of your reality as yet. The ideal thing is still mentally excluded, and it still feels distant and impossible. Therefore, your Faith can't support it.

In order to expect to receive whatever ideal thing you desire, you are required to ignore your present circumstances, ignore any failed attempts to obtain the ideal thing, and include the ideal thing within the boundaries of your current State of Mind right now. Faith can only support and produce what you expect right now. So if you don't have a solid expectation to receive the ideal thing **now**, your Faith cannot do its job. Therefore, never, ever put yourself into a mental position of 'waiting' for the thing.

Many Christians spend fruitless years of their lives in the mental attitude which is mistakenly called *"waiting on the Lord"*. By doing so, they mentally keep pushing the ideal thing away from them and into their future. They keep waiting for the ideal thing to show up 'someday when God gets ready'. They tell themselves: "If I can just hold on and wait, in God's good time, I will have that ideal thing and my change will come". By contrast, *"God says: 'I heard you at the right time and I helped you in the day of salvation'. Behold, NOW is the right time! NOW is the day of salvation!" (2nd Corinthians 6:2)* As the saying goes: *It's NOW, or never.*

'Seeing' and 'feeling' create expectation. If that ideal thing which you desire *feels* far above or far beyond what you deem to be possible now, or if you *see* that ideal thing as being somewhere in your future, then you are not seeing yourself being it now, doing it now, having it now, experiencing it now and enjoying it now. If the ideal thing is still not close enough mentally for you to see it, feel it, expect it and enjoy it **now**, it still exists outside of the boundaries of your current State of Mind.

Your Faith can only truly connect with whatever falls within the boundaries of your current State of Mind right now. If the ideal thing exists outside of your 'now State of Mind', your Faith has no connection to it. So, your **Now Faith** can only support the ideal thing which exists in your **Now State of Mind.** Simply put, if in your imagination, you can see it, and feel it, and touch it, and taste it, and hear it, and smell it, and enjoy it as your reality right now, then it is proof that the ideal thing already exists in an intangible state within your Now State of Mind and within your Ideal Self. It is the job of your Now Faith to take that intangible thing and bring it to you as a tangible thing; and Now Faith is very good at its job.

Your Faith is your friend; and it is always looking within you for some ideal thing to support. However, *your Faith is looking nowhere else except within the boundaries of your State of Mind.* Your Faith can be active; or your Faith can be inactive. If your desired thing exists outside of the boundaries of your Now State of Mind, your Faith cannot see that thing. Therefore, your Faith remains inactive as far as that thing is concerned; because *Faith can only support what it can see.*

What Faith sees is what you get. Therefore, when you place your desired thing solidly within the boundaries of your Now State of Mind, and when you mentally accept and feel the ideal thing as being *'yours right now'*, your Faith now **sees** the thing. Faith then changes immediately from being Inactive Faith to being Active Faith, and springs into action to bring that thing into physical reality. It changes from 'Faith' to 'Now Faith'. *'Now Faith'* can therefore be defined as: *'Active Faith which produces and materializes whatever 'thing' your current State of Mind is seeing, experiencing, enjoying and feeling as possible now'.*

The Bible speaks about 'Now Faith'. However, when Christians read Hebrews 11:1, we usually put the emphasis on the word 'faith'. So the verse comes out sounding like this: *"Now FAITH is the substance of things hoped for..."* By reading the verse in this way, we miss out on the principle of 'Now Faith'. In order to understand the principle of 'Now Faith', here's an experiment for you to try. Read the verse Hebrews 11:1 again, but this time, put equal emphasis on the words 'now' and 'faith'. Pause after the word 'faith'. Try it and see: *"NOW FAITH ...is the substance of things hoped for..."*

Do you see it? The only faith that works is 'Now Faith'. Hebrews 11:1 says, "Now Faith is..." (i.e. Faith is now!) That's Active Faith. Your level of Now Faith is limited by the level of your Now State of Mind. It is limited by the level of intensity of your inner vision and your inner feelings in your State of Mind right now. Now Faith requires that you convince yourself of this one thought: *"My ideal thing is possible right now!"* Whenever your ideal thing which you desire fits comfortably within your Now State of Mind with such intensity that you can comfortably see it and *feel* it as yours in the here and now, then your Faith will produce it for you; because you have a solid expectation to receive it now. It looks and feels possible for you right now. Therefore, your Faith clearly sees it, and so your Faith becomes powerfully active.

Let's look at a practical example. If a man defines himself as having a weakness (i.e. a habit or desire which he thinks he cannot break), his Faith will support that weakness. Faith will always support whatever thing it sees in a man's State of Mind, whether that thing is positive or negative. He will not be free from that weakness until his mind is free from that weakness. That weakness is nothing more than an idea which he has accepted about himself. He will transform when he removes the idea of weakness from his State of Mind, and sees himself in his mind as being powerful, victorious, whole and complete right now. He does this by practicing a vision in his mind where, right now, he acts and feels like someone who does not have that weakness. He comes to the realization that total freedom from that weakness is possible now. In his mind, he enjoys freedom from that weakness now, not later. As soon as the ***idea of weakness*** is permanently excluded from his State of Mind, he will be feeling free from that weakness. Faith no longer *sees* a weakness within him; and so there is no weakness in him for his Faith to support. Instead, new ideas of power, victory, wholeness and completeness are permanently included in his State of Mind now. For the first time, Faith can now *see* power, victory, wholeness and completeness within him. His Faith now springs into action, and becomes Active Faith. It becomes Now Faith. It begins to support his new inner vision of power, victory, wholeness and completeness. That new vision will ultimately express itself outwardly and permanently in his actions. *"Where there is no **vision**, the people perish..." (Proverbs 29:18).*

A man's present circumstances are nothing more than his past ideas expressing themselves in a tangible, physical manner. Therefore, whenever he looks at the present he is actually seeing the past. If he desires new and better things, they will be created out of his new and better ideas which he enjoys mentally right now.

Truthfully, the only things which exist in our State of Mind are *Ideas*. When an Idea finds a place in our minds, we call it a *Thought*. When an Idea influences our emotions, we call it a *Mood*. When an Idea creates pictures and scenes in our minds, we call it *Imagination*. When an Idea influences how we see ourselves and how we see life, we call it *A Point of View*. When an Idea influences our daily actions and experiences, we call it a *Mindset*. When an Idea becomes habitual and ingrained, we call it a *Mentality*. When an Idea becomes so deep-rooted that it is part of our Identity, we call it a *Belief*. However, it's always just an Old Idea. There is only one thing which can cause Mind Renewal, and that one thing is: *A New Idea*.

The ability of our Faith to produce good results is limited by the quality of the Ideas which exist in our State of Mind right now. Only Ideal Ideas will produce Ideal Results. Our current State of Mind sets the boundaries, the limits of possibility, within which our Faith can operate. Therefore, let's forget the past, ignore the present, lose all concerns about the future and take action now. Let's believe that our Ideal is possible now. It's NOW, or never. Our God-given power, to experience and enjoy ideal things, is already working within us right now.

Do you know why nothing is impossible for Infinite God? It's because the State of Mind of Infinite God has absolutely no boundaries! Infinite God is Infinite Mind and Unlimited Thought. The word 'impossible' does not exist in the vocabulary of The Infinite. God does not accept and believe in the Idea that anything can be impossible. God is not limited by Time; so there is no concept of past, present or future in the Mind of Infinite God. God is in the Eternal Now; and in that Eternal Now, all things are possible and are happening right now. God's 'Now' is totally different from what is known as 'the present'. God's 'Now' is the point of transformation. God's 'Now' is where supernatural Power lives and functions. So, let's mentally step out of Time, enter into God's Now and "wait on the Lord" there.

Buying the Orchard

This question arises: *What exactly is a State of Mind?* Our State of Mind is not a fleeting thought or a temporary feeling about our ideal thing. It is not a desire to have the ideal thing. Rather, our State of Mind is our total identification with the ideal thing; an identification which is so focused, untainted and single that the ideal thing becomes our dominant thought; our personal truth; the truth of who we are; our permanent state of being. It is the mental state which permanently knows "I AM..." and permanently adds to that "I AM..." whatever the ideal thing is. When we are in process of adjusting our State of Mind, our new State of Mind is: Our New Definition of who we are right now even as we physically await its inevitable outward expression.

How do we bring a new ideal thing within the boundaries of our State of Mind? The good news is that we don't have to pull that thing toward us mentally and then to try to force it to fit into our current State of Mind. Rather:

(1) We remove all mental limitations and restrictions which we may have placed on ourselves and on God where that ideal thing is concerned. World system thinking will always try to convince us how impossible things are. That 'idea of impossibility' is a major mental chain and shackle used in Mental Captivity. However, *"With God **all things** are possible" (Mark 10:27).* As sons of God, we are always with God, and God is always with us. Whatever our ideal thing is, it's possible and it is already ours.

(2) With this level of confidence, we expand the boundaries of our State of Mind to such an extent that it includes the ideal thing which we desire, and accepts it as ours right now. So the aim of the mental game is *Mind Expansion:* that is, expanding our level of acceptance of the ideal thing.

We let go of all mental resistance against the ideal thing and completely harmonize our mind with the ideal thing. We let go of all the reasons why we won't or can't or shouldn't have this ideal thing which we desire. We let go of whatever didn't work out in the past. We stop thinking and feeling: 'It's too much / too good for me'. We stop wanting, we stop yearning, we stop complaining, we stop blaming, we stop worrying and we stop feeling sorry for ourselves. We mentally accept the thing **now.**

(3) We identify strongly with the ideal thing until we can *feel* it connect. That certain shift in *feeling* indicates that the ideal thing, (which was once excluded), is included in our State of Mind right now, and our Now Faith is supporting it. At this point, it's a done deal.

In order to make this process crystal clear, let's look at a practical example. If you owned a property next door to a valuable, fruitful orchard, and you were eager to own that orchard and to feast freely on its fruits, would you buy one tree at a time? Would you then drag each tree onto your property, transplant each tree, and hope that each tree would survive the transplant, would fit into the available space on your property and would then bear fruit? No, you wouldn't. Rather, you would purchase all the land on which the orchard grows. Then the boundaries of your property would immediately expand to include the orchard and its fruits. The trees would remain exactly where they were before, but since your property boundaries have expanded, every tree is now yours and every fruit in the orchard is now yours for the taking.

Similarly, your State of Mind is your 'mental property', your 'mental territory'. Any 'thing' which is included within the boundaries of your State of Mind is yours. By expanding those boundaries to include whatever ideal things you desire, there is no need to forcibly try to 'transplant' those ideal things into your experience. Do you see it?

So, what do we use to make the 'purchase' of the 'orchard'? In working with Faith, our Ideas (our thoughts, feelings, inner vision, imagination, point of view, mindset, mentality and beliefs) act like money. Our Ideas are mental money which we use to purchase the ideal things which we desire. Once we mentally feel, see, experience and enjoy these ideal things as being already ours, and we do so with persistent intensity, it is an indication that the boundaries of our State of Mind have expanded to include these things. Mentally, they are *already* bought and paid for. We have purchased the orchard and everything in it. The feeling of 'already' is a mental signal that "All is ready!"

Whenever you think about your desired ideal thing, if you feel tense, nervous, fearful, despondent, exhausted, angry, powerless, burdened, frustrated, worried, hopeless, anxious or doubtful, you are trying to 'transplant trees'; but if you feel joyful, expectant, excited, lighthearted, thrilled, relaxed and relieved, and if you feel that your world just got bigger and brighter, you are 'buying the orchard'. Therefore, keep checking on your feelings. The ideal thing is yours as soon as you can connect with the *feeling* that it's yours.

So, whatever ideal thing you choose, whether physical thing, material thing, mental thing, behavioral thing or spiritual thing, you are required to purchase it now with your intense thoughts, feelings and inner vision. You are also required to expand the boundaries of your State of Mind to comfortably include the ideal thing which you have 'purchased', and to include it **now**. Then that thing will automatically become yours. With this understanding, it is clear what the Bible means when it says: *"All **things** are **yours**... All of them belong to you."* (1st Corinthians 3:21, 22) Always remember this: The boundaries of your current State of Mind are moveable. You can expand them at any time to include more.

The secret of working with Faith is: *The only 'thing' you can get is the 'thing' that you already consciously have.* Faith can only give you the thing which you already have and already possess in your State of Mind. If, in your State of Mind, you don't already have it now, you can't get it. Also, if you lose anything mentally, if it slips out of your State of Mind, you will eventually lose it physically. This is what Jesus meant when He said: *"The man who* [mentally] **already has, more** *shall be given to him* [physically]*; but the man who* [mentally] *does not* **already have**, *even that which he* [physically] *has shall be taken from him" (Mark 4:25).* As soon as we mentally possess and enjoy the ideal things, our Now Faith will bring them to us physically. Then, once we get our ideal things physically, we maintain strong mental boundaries, and keep holding on to them mentally, so we don't lose them. This applies to all ideal things, even good health.

To sum it all up, it is self-defeating for a son of God to mentally feel and say: "I lack...", "I need..." or "I want...", because it is the same as mentally feeling and saying "I don't already mentally have..." Therefore, the Psalmist says: *"The Lord is my Shepherd;* **I shall not want**." *(Psalm 23:1)*

Fear says: *"I lack..." Poverty* says: *"I need..." Envy* says: *"I want..."* But *Now Faith* says: *"I already have..."* So, instead of feeling "I lack...", "I need..." or "I want...", ignore all appearances and mentally step over the line from 'wanting' to 'enjoying'. Get into the feeling of: *The ideal thing is already mine, and I'm enjoying it now!"* When you become proficient in the use of the Mind Renewal Technique which will now be shared with you, you will recognize that you can enjoy something long before you get it physically. The Bible gives us the formula: *"**Meditate** upon these [ideal]* **things; give yourself completely to them** [i.e. immerse yourself in the Ideal State of Mind with intensity until you fully identify and connect with it], *and everyone will see the progress you make." (1st Timothy 4:15)*

Expanding your State of Mind

Mind Expansion is the aim of the mental game. An easy way to expand your State of Mind is to use the following Mind Renewal Technique to practice the ideal vision of yourself and your life. This powerful Technique can be used to change your Ideas, change your attitudes, improve your moods, break bad habits, transform a 'weakness', solve your problems, supply your 'needs' and bring about whatever other natural, mental or spiritual improvements you want to enjoy now. The Technique may seem simple. However, never underestimate its power. This Technique was taught by Jesus Christ, but He taught it in mystical language; so many of us pass over this Technique in the Bible without really seeing it. At Level 2 and Level 3 of this Men's Bible Study, we will study this Technique from the Bible; but you are encouraged to get into the habit of this daily practice in the meantime. You will reap tremendous benefits from this three-step process.

STEP 1: Choose your 'thing'. Know exactly what ideal thing you desire.

STEP 2: Whether you desire a physical thing, a mental thing or a spiritual thing, recognize that Infinite God is the only Source. Infinite God is the Limitless Storehouse of every ideal thing which you can ever choose for yourself. As a son of God, no 'thing' is too good or too much for you to enjoy, for this is your Father's world. *"The earth is the Lord's, and the abundance thereof; the world and everyone in it." (Psalm 24:1)*

Every tangible thing, which you see around you, first existed in an intangible state either within the imagination of The Infinite or the imagination of mankind. Then afterwards, it became tangible. Understand that your ideal thing already exists now in an intangible state within Infinite God. It is a Divine Idea within Divine Mind. This is easy to understand, now that we are conscious that Infinite God is Infinite Spirit, Infinite Mind and Unlimited Thought. By becoming conscious and aware of the inexhaustible Storehouse which is Infinite God, you recognize also that this Storehouse is now within you; because your divine spirit is one with God's Divine Spirit. So your ideal thing is not somewhere out there. Rather, it is already within you in an intangible state. It is part of the divine image, part of your Ideal Self, and it is already freely given to you by Infinite God. *"...God richly gives to us all things to enjoy". (1st Timothy 6:17)* You don't need to wait for further permission or for better timing to have this ideal thing. It is already yours, and it's ready when you are ready. You indicate that you are ready when you completely harmonize your mind with the ideal thing.

Therefore, be conscious that all ideal things are already created, prepared and awaiting your selection. It's just like being an honored guest at a grand buffet. As a guest, you are not required to beg for food; and nobody passes judgment on you for your choice of food from the buffet table. The chef has already freely and lavishly prepared for your selection all the fabulous, mouthwatering dishes which heart could ever desire. The only thing you are required to do is to select whatever you desire from all the available dishes, and place it on your personal plate. A chef is honored when you enjoy his food; God is honored when you enjoy ideal things. That ideal thing, which you have been waiting for, is actually waiting for you. It is waiting to become a tangible thing through your conscious awareness that it already exists in you and for you. *All is ready.* Your inner vision and State of Mind create the pattern which will determine the form, shape, quality and circumstances which the intangible thing will ultimately take on when it shows up in your physical world. So, remove from your mind any idea of struggle, and don't waste any time in focusing on things that you don't desire.

STEP 3: Each night, just before you fall asleep, while you are in that totally relaxed, almost sleepy state and in a state of inner and outer peace, release all tension, close your eyes and *create a vision* where you are seeing, hearing, smelling, tasting, touching, and enjoying the ideal thing right now with *feeling.* Make the vision real enough so you feel that you are actually in the situation looking through your eyes. You are right there in the situation being, doing, having, experiencing and enjoying the desired thing right now, without effort or strain. Create a vision which suggests that the thing has already happened or is already yours and that you are completely in harmony with it. Let your thought be: *"This is who and what I AM."* Never contemplate why you 'need' the thing or the circumstances which created this 'need'. Rather, see the thing as a done deal. Know that, by using the Technique, the transformation has already happened. Feel as if you are remembering something which has already happened rather than trying to make something happen. View your world from the viewpoint of someone who is already enjoying the ideal thing. In your imagination, see other people reacting favorably to this 'new you'. Hear them congratulate you. Hear yourself speaking about how much you are enjoying this ideal thing. Touch and hold the objects in your vision, and feel their weight and texture. Feel that it is real. Feel thankful to Infinite God for the victory. Feel thankful that people all around the world who are expecting a similar ideal thing are also receiving it. Hold this feeling of relaxation and enjoyment for at least five minutes (or more if you can). Then in that state of harmony, acceptance and enjoyment, joy, gratitude and happiness, fall asleep.

You can also slip into this State of Mind throughout the day, even with your eyes open; however, practicing the Technique immediately before sleeping is most effective. Make this State of Mind your comfort zone. If you think about it, the only reason you will ever desire anything is so that you can feel relief. You don't need to wait on the physical thing; rather, feel relief right now.

Feel the thrill of the feeling. How would you feel if every ideal thing you desire suddenly happened to you? Capture that same feeling and hold it, even when you are not consciously using the Technique. Keep your mind in a harmonious state by avoiding all discord, quarrels, anger and other disturbing elements. Practice this Technique deeply especially around midday (if possible) and also every night immediately before sleeping. Practice this all the time until it feels natural, effortless and real. Give quality time to this practice. Make it a point to enjoy practicing this Technique. Joy creates Expectation. Keep that state of mind of Enthusiastic Joyful Expectation during all of your waking hours. Do you remember, as a child, being so excited to receive something or to go somewhere that you could hardly sleep the night before it happened? That's the feeling of Enthusiastic Joyful Expectation. Once you practice that feeling, you will be divinely guided into the right course of action to bring your vision into reality; for *"faith without action is dead"*. *(James 2:26)*

The Bible says of your inner vision: *"For the vision awaits an appointed time* (and that 'appointed time' is 'NOW'). *It hastens towards its goal, and it speaks truthfully about its end-result. If it is not fulfilled right away, wait for it [physically]. It will surely happen. It won't be late."* (Habakkuk 2:3) Your inner vision also speaks directly to you in mystical language through the words of Jesus Christ and says: *"...**I go to prepare a place for you.** And since I go to prepare a place for you, **I will come again** and receive you unto myself that, **where I am, there you will be also**." (John 14:2-3)*

Remember that the ideal thing already exists in an intangible state, for All Good already exists within Infinite Mind. All you are doing is personalizing this Good by including it within the boundaries of your Now State of Mind, and inviting your Now Faith to support it. The more you persist in enthusiastically and joyfully practicing this new vision of yourself and the good feelings which go with it, the more permanent will be your positive transformation. *"...Be transformed by the renewing of your mind." (Romans 12:2)*

The purpose of this Technique is to expand the boundaries of your State of Mind so that the ideal thing which you have chosen will fit comfortably within your State of Mind right now without any feeling of resistance on your part. If you can comfortably see it, feel it, experience it and enjoy it **now**, you will recognize that it is real right now. The thing is included into your definition of who you are right now, not in the future. That is an invitation for your Now Faith to kick in and start to work on your behalf. You start to expect it.

As you practice this Technique, your Now Faith looks into your Now State of Mind and says: *"Okay. I clearly **see** a new 'thing'. Let me get to work and support it."* Your Now Faith takes over and gives the support and the assurance to bring the thing into being. Once you get to that point, the thing, which once seemed so distant and unattainable, has been brought within the boundaries of your Now State of Mind. You are now seeing it as yours. It is within the boundaries of your Now State of

Mind, and your Now Faith is giving it full support. Suddenly, you know that it is inevitable, even though you might not yet know exactly how it will happen. At that point, it's a done deal. The unexpected way in which your thing will then show up physically in your life may surprise you.

Don't worry about the 'how'

Here are some suggestions: Never believe that you specifically require the cooperation of a particular person to fulfill your vision or to give you whatever ideal thing you desire. Infinite God has infinite ways to get things done. The Bible says: *"...His ways cannot be figured out..."* *(Romans 11:33)*. Most times, The Infinite will give you something much better than you desire; so don't limit The Infinite with your list of demands. Never plan out, or project, or try to manipulate, or think about, or wonder about, or worry about **how** the ideal thing will happen or show up in your life. Your work is simply to get into the State of Mind of **now**. God's work is to organize the **how**.

Infinite God has ways to make things happen that you could never imagine in your wildest dreams, and Infinite God will guide you into taking divine right action. So, don't insist on things happening your way. As you relax and trust Infinite God, you will be guided into the fulfillment of your vision. God will position you at the right place at the right time, allow you to come into contact with the right people, bless you with the right information and transformation, open the right door of opportunity, place the right angels around you, give you right understanding and make a way where there seems to be no way. Just keep feelings of animosity, criticism, discord and resistance out of your mind. Don't even criticize the situation that you want to be changed. Rather, bless it, thank it and release it with love.

As you persist in using this Technique, your Now Faith will grow more and more powerful and active. Through the power of God, your Now Faith will create all the circumstances necessary to materialize the ideal thing. The thing will actually show up in your life in a physical, material and tangible way which you could not imagine or create on your own. So let go of the **how**, and focus on uplifting your State of Mind **now**. Once you get into the feeling of **now**, the word 'impossible' will automatically vanish from your State of Mind. Consider this: The only reason you will ever believe that the ideal thing which you have chosen is impossible, is because you can't see **how** it could happen **now**. So, let go of **how**, and focus on mentally enjoying the thing **now**. Make the Technique joyful and fun! Enjoy the ideal thing even before you physically have it.

Bearing all of this in mind, we understand that when the Bible says: *"This is the victory which overcomes the world [system], even our faith" (1st John 5:4)*, we are being told to mentally position ourselves for victory by first expanding the boundaries of our Now State of Mind. Then Now Faith will *see* in our minds the ideal things which we expect to receive, and Now Faith will work to give us the victory. Many times we deny ourselves the victory because we are trying to 'transplant trees'. We are trying to force things into our reality by using the methods of the world system. Instead, as sons of The Infinite, let's buy the orchard by expanding our mental boundaries joyfully and expectantly.

As you use this Technique, please remember this: Overuse of your outer vision will greatly reduce your ability to create a clear inner vision. The habit of watching a lot of 'programs' (e.g. movies, drama series, sports, video games, newscasts etc.) on noisy electronic devices weakens your ability to imagine clearly in your own mind. If you are serious about using the Mind Renewal Technique successfully, you will find it helpful to greatly reduce the time spent watching such programs while you are using the Technique.

This Technique is actually Visual Prayer; and it is a Technique which Jesus Christ both taught and used. The Bible records that on many occasions, just before Jesus Christ prayed a spoken prayer, He "lifted up His eyes". Traditionally, we have been taught that this means that Jesus

Christ looked up into the sky before praying; and you will even see pictures and paintings depicting this. However, truthfully, when Jesus Christ "lifted up His eyes", He was using this Technique of visualizing and harmonizing His mind with a desired result. His spoken prayer, which followed afterwards, did not ask for anything. It just confirmed what He had seen in His visual prayer. *(e.g. See John 11:40-44)* So feel free to be like Christ and lift up your eyes by making use of this powerful Technique. (We will study more about Visual Prayer when we get to Levels 2 and 3 of this Bible Study.)

Here's something to remember about prayer. 'Getting into the feeling of Now' is not about making a childish, impatient demand of The Infinite. Rather, it is a relaxation into the mental acceptance of the ideal thing right now. Truthfully, Prayer is not about convincing God to do or to give us something. The Infinite has already given us all things to enjoy. The work is already done. True Prayer is about getting our minds into a totally non-resistant state where we are totally open to receive what has already been done and given. That's the purpose of the Mind Renewal Technique (i.e. Visual Prayer).

Similarly, the purpose of spoken prayer is not to beg God for something. Rather, we use spoken prayer to confirm that we have already received the ideal thing seen during our Visual Prayer. If we pray Begging Prayers, we are praying from a mental state of lack. We have been doing this because this is what the world system has taught us. However, if we stop praying Begging Prayers, and practice praying 'Thanksgiving, Receiving and Blessing Prayers' only, (i.e. thanking God that we have already received the ideal thing, and pronouncing a blessing on the ideal thing even before we physically get it), we'll get better results from spoken prayer. The sons of The Infinite don't beg.

Moving from Desire to Manifestation

Now, a 'thing' can be anything. It can be a physical thing, a mental thing or a spiritual thing which we desire. Nevertheless, whether it is physical, mental or spiritual, Now Faith works in the very same way and the Mind Renewal Technique works in the very same way. So, the process is exactly the same if the ideal thing which we desire is the character of a son of God. This character, like all ideal things, already exists in an intangible state within Infinite God, and already exists in an intangible state within the divine image (the Ideal Self) which is already within you. It is a Divine Idea.

If we desire to be like Christ, we don't need to get more faith. All we need to do is to upgrade and expand our State of Mind so that we decide to be like Christ. All we need to do is accept the Idea of ourselves expressing the character of a son of God right now. As our State of Mind expands, our Faith will automatically grow to keep up with it, so that it can give adequate support.

So, if being like Christ feels too big, too great, too wonderful, too hard, too impossible or too far in the future for our Now State of Mind to accept, then our Now Faith cannot bring it into reality. That's because deep down within, even though we desire to be like Christ, we haven't yet decided to be like Christ. Faith doesn't produce the ideal things we desire. Faith produces the ideal things that we have *decided* to be, do and have. Faith produces the ideal things which we are *joyfully expecting to experience.* Faith produces what it can **see** in our State of Mind right now. Faith supports the Ideas which exist in our current State of Mind. Remember, when we are adjusting our State of Mind, our new State of Mind is our chosen definition of who we are now, even as we physically await its inevitable outward expression. By faithfully using the Mind Renewal Technique, we will shift our State of Mind from 'desire' to 'decision', and from 'decision' to 'joyful expectation'. So the process is: DESIRE → DECISION → EXPECTATION → MANIFESTATION.

'Right now I have within me the character of Christ'. If this truth cannot fit within our current State of Mind, then it is a truth which our State of Mind has excluded; because we can't see **how** we could be that

now. Therefore, this Christ-like character falls outside of the boundaries of possibility, and our Now Faith cannot see it and has no connection with it. So, we will be trying and failing to act like Christ, and victory will be out of reach. Please know that our challenge is <u>not</u> to increase our faith. Our challenge is to upgrade our concept of God from 'Master' to 'Loving Father'. Our challenge is to upgrade our Idea of ourselves from 'wretched sinner' and from 'God's human bondservant' to 'beloved, divine, free-born, spirit-son of Infinite God'. By doing so, we expand the boundaries of our State of Mind so that this truth can fit comfortably within it: *'Right now I am a divine, free-born, spirit-son of God in the Divine Family. I have the character of Christ already within me'.*

Even as a committed Christian, if being a divine spirit-son of God, being like Christ and having the mind of Christ feel too big, too great, too wonderful, too hard or too impossible for our current State of Mind to accept right now, then we won't get there. If we see these things as being somewhere in the future, we won't get there. If we see them as separate from us, we won't get there. That's because deep down within, even though we desire these things, we are mentally excluding them. When these Ideas fit comfortably within the boundaries of our current State of Mind, our Faith can see them, support them and bring them into expression. So let's feel free to use the Mind Renewal Technique.

Your Faith always says 'Yes!' to your State of Mind

A man goes to a carpenter and asks him to make a pedestal to support a baby's crib. The man later changes his mind and asks the carpenter to make a pedestal to support a king-size bed. Since a king-size bed is much larger and heavier than a baby's crib, the carpenter automatically knows that he must increase the size and strength of the pedestal. The type of item being supported will determine the size and strength of the support. And so it is with Faith.

Therefore, the good news is that we don't have to try to increase our Faith. When we simply expand our State of Mind to the point where it comfortably includes greater 'things' which require more support, our Faith will automatically increase in size and strength in order to provide the necessary support. When we form the solid expectation in our State of Mind to receive greater things, bigger things, more substantial things, more empowering things, higher quality things, ideal things, our Faith will automatically increase. Faith is the support for things joyfully expected. So, it's not about increasing Faith. Rather, it's about expanding the boundaries of our State of Mind to the extent where we joyfully identify with 'more'. Mind Expansion is the aim of the mental game. Just like the carpenter making the pedestal, once there is an expectation of 'more' to be supported, Faith will automatically increase to provide the necessary support.

Your State of Mind is the Boss. Your Faith is the obedient Employee. Your Faith always says just one word to your State of Mind; and that word is **"Yes!"** Whatever 'thing' your State of Mind commands, your Faith will support it 100% without question and bring it into being. Your Faith will always agree with whatever Ideas exist in your State of Mind. This principle applies whether your State of Mind contains positive Ideas or negative Ideas or a combination of both. Your Faith will say 'Yes!' to the positive things and 'Yes!' to the negative things. Your Faith will always unconditionally support whatever it sees in your State of Mind.

Here's a practical example: Let's suppose that you *expect* to receive a good 'thing' but at the same time you *feel* that you don't deserve to have it, and you *believe* that "Good things don't last". How will Faith respond to your State of Mind? Faith will say 'Yes!' to your positive expectation, 'Yes!' to your negative feeling and 'Yes!' to your negative belief. Faith will support your expectation to receive the good 'thing', and will create all the circumstances to give it to you. Then, once you get the good 'thing', Faith will support your feeling that you don't deserve to have that thing and will support your belief that 'good things don't last'. Therefore, Faith will create all the circumstances to ensure that you lose that good 'thing' somehow. So, if you have ever felt that you are taking one step forward in life, only to take three steps backward, now you know why this has been happening. This is why it is necessary to use the Mind Renewal Technique to remove from your State of Mind *all* resistance to your good 'thing' and to flood your mind with Ideal Ideas.

If you have a positive, harmonious and liberated State of Mind, your Faith will support it. If you have a negative, disharmonious and captive State of Mind, your Faith will support it. If you expect to be treated as God's human bondservant, your Faith will support this. If you expect to enjoy the divine rights and privileges of a divine, free-born, spirit-son of Spirit-God, your Faith will support this. If you expect to receive positive things, your Faith will support this. If you expect to receive negative things, your Faith will support this. If you expect to have the abundant life, your Faith will support this. If you expect to suffer, your Faith will support this. If you expect to be like Christ, your Faith will support this. If you expect to struggle spiritually and to be in a never-ending battle with 'sin' and with self-condemnation, your Faith will support this. With this understanding, you can clearly see how dangerous and self-defeating it is to be in Mental Captivity, and to have incorrect Ideas controlling your State of Mind. Now you see why it is crucial to let the same State of Mind be in you which was also in Christ Jesus. You win the mental game when you allow your mind to be in complete harmony with your Ideal Self and Ideal Ideas. You win the mental game when you elevate your mind above all mental cross-currents. Therefore, feel free to let go of all ideas of disharmony and discord which now exist between you and life, or between you and God, or between you and circumstances, or between you and other people, or between you and yourself.

The Character of Christ

So you don't need to get more Faith. When a man gives up thinking, feeling and seeing himself as a bondservant and starts thinking, feeling and seeing himself as a beloved son of The Infinite, he automatically has higher expectations. He expects things of a higher quality. He enthusiastically expects more. His elevated State of Mind will command his Faith to produce greater things for him; and his Faith will always answer: 'Yes, State of Mind!'

The be all and end all of the spiritual path is: *expressing the Character of Christ from within.* This is the predominant requirement in a relationship with our Divine Father. It is the reason why we study the scriptures; it is the reason why we pray; it is the reason why we pursue self-knowledge and practice self-discipline. *The Divine Father only recognizes the Divine Son.* This recognition does not come by examining our face. Rather, it comes when the Divine Father examines our character and recognizes the character of the Divine Son in us. Character follows Identity. The Character of Christ is already within us, but it exists as a divine seed. When we create the right mental and spiritual conditions by choosing Ideal Ideas, this divine seed will germinate, grow, mature and produce fruit in our lives.

▣ *What are some of the hallmarks of the Character of Christ?* A totally relaxed mind and perfect self-mastery; self-control even when under pressure; tremendous inner strength; peace even in the midst of challenges; inner satisfaction; feeling whole and complete within yourself; never again feeling like a victim; being self-forgetful in order to be a blessing to others; clear thinking; compassion; sensitivity to the feelings of others; being truthful with yourself and with others; authenticity; sincerity; gentleness without weakness; choosing to overlook offences for your own peace of mind; obedience to the principles of truth and love; endurance; patience; perseverance against all odds; love for yourself and for others; and deep and abiding love for the Divine Father. This is not an exhaustive list. All of these traits already exist within us in seed form. More and more of His character will unfold within us as we walk the spiritual path and gently release our attachment to world system thinking.

So, here's how Faith works in the context of being like Christ in character:

1. Your State of Mind chooses this definite 'thing': *to be like Christ and to live as a divine, free-born, spirit-son of God.* You recognize that this divine character already exists within the divine nature of your divine spirit, and so you fully identify with this divine character. You decide to express this divine character.

2. You give up your efforts of 'transplanting trees'. You stop trying to get more faith, get more love, get more grace, get more peace, get more trust in God, get more forgiveness etc. to fit into your current State of Mind.

3. Instead, you faithfully use the Mind Renewal Technique. In your mind, you start 'buying the orchard'. You start thinking and visualizing and living in that inner vision and *feeling* of yourself as being a divine son of God. You practice it mentally every day. If there are weaknesses or 'secret sins' in your character, you mentally practice saying and doing the exact opposite with ease. You expand the boundaries of your State of Mind to the point where you know the truth that you *already* are a son of God in identity. You do this until it the New Idea feels real to you. This identity becomes yours. You have a solid, joyful expectation to be like Christ and to live as a divine son of God right now, for you are already enjoying this State of Mind.

4. Your Faith **sees** this new 'thing' and becomes active. It kicks in to support this new 'thing' which it now finds in your State of Mind. You feel through Faith that right now: God is your Divine Father; you are a divine son of God; you are in the image of God; and you are in the Divine Family forever. You see yourself this way clearly in your mind.

5. Your character increasingly conforms to your new identity. Your moods and desires start to change. The negative things which used to intrigue or delight you, now disgust you. The attributes and the character of Christ ultimately show up in your moods, feelings, attitudes and actions. You outwardly express the inner Character of Christ.

Remember, your Now State of Mind will produce Now Faith. Now Faith is Active Faith which produces now whatever Ideas your current State of Mind can grasp now. This is why the Bible teaches us that: "...**right now** we are the sons of God" (1st John 3:2).

If you have the 'son of God mentality', if you deeply feel that right now you are a divine spirit-son of God, you will expect to live as a son of God. Your Faith will support this expectation, and will produce in you the character to match. However, if you have the 'sinner mentality', if you deeply feel that right now you are a some type of a sinner, you will expect to be in a constant battle with 'sin'. Your Faith will support this expectation, and will produce in you the character to match. Your Faith always says 'Yes!' to your State of Mind. The way you truly *feel* about yourself is fundamental to walking in victory, because your true feelings about yourself determine what Ideas you will allow in your State of Mind. We will study this topic extensively at Level 2.

So, to sum it all up, whatever 'thing' you choose, your only work is to get the Idea of that thing to fit so comfortably in your State of Mind that you can **feel** it as being yours right now with absolutely no resistance. Instead of seeing it as something that you want to happen, see it as something which has already happened. Once you do that, it's a done deal. It's yours; and it's yours to keep.

The Parable of the Sycamine Tree & the Mustard Tree

Now let's look at Jesus' teaching about how our State of Mind and our Faith work together. Let's analyze this well-known passage of scripture found in Luke 17:5-6:

*"And the apostles said to the Lord, 'Increase our faith'. And the Lord said, 'If you had **faith as a grain of mustard seed**, you **might** say to this sycamine tree, 'Be plucked up by the root and be planted in the sea', and it **should** obey you."* (Please read this passage of scripture a second time before moving on. Let it sink in.)

Notice the words 'if', 'might' and 'should' in these verses. Jesus said this is what should happen if faith is given a chance to work. Jesus said that when faith as a grain of mustard seed is at work, we can tell the sycamine tree to be plucked up by the root and be planted in the sea and it should obey us. What does all of this mean? Once again, Jesus is illustrating what happens in a man's State of Mind.

Our mind is like fertile soil. Our Ideas are like seeds planted in the soil of our mind. Once those 'mind seeds' become part of how we *truly feel*, they 'germinate'. They come to life and are ready to grow. Those Ideas will then grow and produce outer conditions and outer circumstances in our daily life which precisely match whatever 'mind seed' was planted. This principle is seen clearly in the natural world. If we plant a handful of corn in fertile soil, they stay hidden in the soil for a while. We allow those seeds to remain in the soil long enough to germinate and produce plants which are visible. Once those plants have produced a harvest, we will reap corn and not peas. So when we want to truly change what's happening outwardly in our lives, let's first change the Ideas, the 'mind-seeds', we are planting. Then, let's allow these new 'mind-seeds' to stay planted long enough to transform how we truly feel about ourselves and to manifest outwardly in our experiences.

We all know that when seeds are planted in fertile soil, they don't remain as seeds for long. They become seedlings, then plants, then mature plants. If those seeds are capable of producing trees, after a while those tiny seeds will grow into massive trees. Similarly, when Ideas are planted in the soil of our mind, whether they are positive or negative, they don't remain in their seed-like state. After a while these mind-seeds become established ways of thinking, and habitual ways of feeling. They become 'mental trees' growing in the soil of our mind. These 'mental trees' take root in the soil of our mind. They flourish to maturity. They become well established. They produce fruit in the form of situations, circumstances and experiences in our life. Over time, these mental trees become towering, deep-rooted patterns of thought, vision and feeling. They become our Mentality and our Beliefs. They become predominant in our State of Mind.

Jesus Christ teaches us, in this parable, that we always have the power to decide which mental trees we want to have in the garden of our mind. We have the power and freedom to plant new trees. We also have the power and freedom to uproot any unwanted tree and cast it out of our mind. We always have the power to be victorious over world system thinking.

Now, at a casual glance, this parable which we just read seems to be speaking of only one tree, that is, the sycamine tree. However when we read carefully, we see that it is speaking of two trees: the sycamine tree and the mustard tree. The sycamine tree is already growing and well established in the soil, but the mustard tree is still in seed form and has not yet been planted. The sycamine tree is standing deep-rooted in the place where the mustard tree ought to be. The mustard seed cannot be planted and cannot release its potential to become a mighty tree until the sycamine tree is rooted up and removed out of its way. So, before we can plant, in the soil of our mind, new Ideas which align with Truth, it is necessary to take the time to root out and remove the old established way of thinking which is out of harmony with Truth. World system thinking has to be uprooted first.

The followers of Jesus had just asked Him to increase their faith. In response to their request, He told this parable. The parable makes no mention of the size of the mustard seed, because the size of the seed is not the issue here. Rather, it is the *purity,* the *all-ness,* the *wholeness,* the *completeness* of the mustard seed. A mustard seed is just a mustard seed. It is not mixed with anything else. It does not have a dual purpose. The only thing it can do is produce a mustard tree. Similarly, our Faith cannot have a dual purpose. We can't believe in success this minute and believe in failure the next minute. We can't have faith mixed in with doubt. Whenever our Faith is so pure and so focused on the 'thing' which we have selected until success is *all* that we can think of and manifest, we have 'mustard seed Faith'.

Uprooting the Bondservant's Mentality

All of us at some time have planted and tended Ideas in our minds which are contrary to Divine Truth. We have been mentally conditioned to accept many teachings and opinions without questioning them. If we have developed a bondservant's mentality, it is because of how we were traditionally taught.

Over time, we accepted Ideas of Inferiority, Self-Loathing, Self-Disapproval, Self-Condemnation, Self-Rejection, Low Expectation, Fear, Insecurity, Guilt, Shame and Separation from God, just to name a few. Some of these mind-seeds were planted in our minds by the authority figures in our lives. Some of these mind-seeds were planted in us by the programing done by the world system. Some of these mind-seeds we planted ourselves, in our own minds. We accepted all of these Ideas as truth, without really examining them, and without taking thought of what they would produce in us once they were planted. Over the years these mind-seeds have become well established trees in our minds. They have become our Ideologies, our Mindset, our Comfort Zone, our Mentality, our Beliefs, and our Feelings about ourselves. They have matured into Mental Captivity. These are our well-tended and flourishing 'sycamine trees'; and they are standing in the way of our mental and spiritual progress.

The good news is that no matter how long you may have

maintained any negative Ideas, you can clear your mind of them. No matter how large that negative mind-tree is, and no matter how deep-rooted, you have the power to uproot it. You have the absolute freedom and the absolute power to examine every tree in your mind: every mindset, every mentality and every habit of thinking and feeling. If any habitual way of thinking or feeling is not helping and supporting you, and is not producing victory in your life, it is a 'sycamine tree', and you have the absolute freedom to uproot it and cast it from your mind.

For example, if you hold thoughts in your mind such as: *"I can't win"*, *"I'm a born loser"*, *"I've made too many mistakes"*, *"I'll never make it"*, *"God doesn't love me"*, *"I am unworthy"*, *"I am a sinner"*, *"I am weak"*, *"My faith is weak"*, *"I am a broken vessel"* and *"I don't deserve the least of God's mercies"*, these are signs that you have a sycamine tree in your mind that you need to root up and cast out of your consciousness. These are the thoughts of a man who is in Mental Captivity. These thoughts originate from the time in your life when you were not conscious that you were a son of God. Notice that, in the parable, the sycamine tree grows *first* and becomes deep-rooted.

However, there is another mind-tree that wants to take the place of the 'sycamine tree'. The new mind-tree is going to grow out of a new mind-seed: *the mustard seed of Faith.* This is Faith in your single Divine Identity which is not mixed with anything else; Faith that the Ideal Self is in you and is the real you; and Faith in New Ideal Ideas. This mind-tree will produce fruit in your life: love, true Godlike-ness, truth, victory, success and power. All good things come from having the 'son of God' State of Mind. *All Good* is waiting for you, waiting to be manifested out of the mustard seed of Faith which you already have.

This parable teaches that before the divine 'son of God' mentality can grow in our mind, it is necessary to first root out the bondservant's mentality. The sycamine tree of Mental Captivity and the mustard tree of Faith in your Divine Identity cannot occupy our mind together. They can't co-exist. The parable says that the sycamine tree of Mental

Captivity has to be uprooted and *"cast into the sea"*. *What does the 'sea' represent in this parable?* At a different level of meaning, the *'sea'* as referred to in the Bible is a symbol which represents *the people who have conformed to the world system.*

We picked up the bondservant mentality when we were drifting in the 'sea of un-Godlike-ness'. However, Jesus Christ, the 'Great Fisher of Men', has pulled us out of that 'sea'. That bondservant's mentality has to go back to the 'sea', back to where it originated. It cannot remain in us once we choose to be free. So, let's be willing to send it back to the 'sea of un-Godlike-ness' and allow the 'son of God' state of mind take its place. Only then will we be transformed by the renewing of our mind.

The power of your Inner Conversations

Now the question arises: *How exactly does a man get rid of this unwanted mind-tree?* Notice that the parable says *you* are the one who will get rid of any unwanted mind-tree. You have the power to throw the bondservant's mentality out of your mind. You are the only one who can do an inventory of your thinking, and identify any 'sycamine tree' which stands in the way of your victory. You are the only one who can select and plant better 'mind seeds' which align with Faith. No one else can do this for you. Mental Freedom is your gift to yourself.

If we know that we are the divine sons of God as the Bible says we are, then we will make room in the soil of our mind for divine 'son of God' thoughts to be planted. When we plant Ideas we will manifest Actions. We all have spent years planting 'Sinner Ideas', and we all produced 'Sinner Actions'. Whenever we plant 'Son of God Ideas', we will produce 'Son of God Actions'.

So, how do we get rid of the sycamine tree? How do we make room in our mind for the mustard tree? How do we get rid of 'sinner ideas' and start having 'son of God ideas'? We find the answer right there in the parable. Where does the sycamine tree grow? It grows in our own mind. The parable says: *"If you had faith as a grain of mustard seed, you might **SAY** to this sycamine tree, 'Be plucked up by the root and be planted in the sea', and it should obey you."* So, as strange as it may sound, we **talk** to the negative mind-tree when we decide to uproot it. The 'sycamine tree' is within us, in our own mind. When we want to talk to it, we simply talk to ourselves.

We all carry on conversations with ourselves and with others in our mind. These are our *Inner Conversations.* They are some of the most powerful tools in our spiritual and mental toolkit, and they are far more significant than the conversations which we carry on outwardly. We are free to make our inner conversations very positive or very negative. Our inner conversations will always reveal our mentality. They will reveal to us the boundaries which we have set for our State of Mind. When we know that we are divine sons of God, we will start to talk like one in our mind. Those inner conversations, which we carry on with ourselves and with others, will match our 'son of God' identity. Whatever ideal 'thing' we choose, whether it is a natural 'thing', a mental 'thing' or a spiritual 'thing', we will live victoriously when our inner conversations indicate that that 'thing' is already ours.

Always remember this: *Your inner conversations don't fall behind you into your past. Rather, they go before you and dictate your future. When you improve the quality of your inner conversations, the quality of your circumstances will improve.* This Technique may seem too simple to work; but it works, and it is extremely powerful. The words which mentally come out of your mouth during your inner conversations are like *messengers* whom you send ahead of you in life to prepare your circumstances and experiences until you get there.

This spiritual and mental principle is explained in the Bible in mystical language: *"My word which proceeds from my [mental] mouth will not return to me without doing **all that I have sent it to do**. Rather, **it will accomplish whatever I choose,** and it will succeed in achieving the purpose for which I sent it." (Isaiah 55:11)*; and again: *"Behold, I will send* *my messenger who will prepare the way before me. And the Lord whom you seek* (that's the Ideal Circumstance) *shall suddenly come to His temple* (shall suddenly show up in your life) *..." (Malachi 3:1)*

A man may try to pray opposite to his inner conversations. His inner conversations are laced with fear, frustration, doubt and anger but his spoken prayers are filled with words of faith. Such prayers will never work. Harmony precedes Victory. Your harmonious inner conversations are powerful tools in expanding the boundaries of your State of Mind.

So here are some suggestions: Talk within yourself as if you already are the man whom you desire to be. Hear, within your own mind, other people talking to you and confirming that you already are the man whom you desire to be. Continuously plant the mind-seeds of positive inner conversations into the soil of your mind. The Bible says: *"...The word is very near to you;* **it's in your heart [i.e. in your feelings] and in your [mental] mouth**, *so that you may* **obey** *it* (in your daily experiences). *See, today I have given you a choice between life and prosperity or death and disaster... So,* **choose life***... (Deuteronomy 30:14-15 & 19).*

In Church, you will sometimes hear this instruction: *"Keep repeating scripture verses out loud. Confess the Word! This is how you sow the 'seed' of the word of God into your mind."* This is good advice. However, if you never get to the place where you can **feel** the reality of those scripture verses that you are reciting and confessing, then these 'seeds' have not germinated. They have not sprouted. They have not come to life in you. You will be reciting and confessing them, but they won't produce anything in your life. Those scripture verses are in your head, but they will have no effect in your life until they get into the feelings of your heart.

▣ So, here's a Technique to get more out of the scriptures. Whenever you come across a verse or a passage from the Bible: (1) which catches and holds your attention; (2) which really resonates with you and touches your *feelings;* (3) which teaches you a better way to act, think or feel which is different and not 'normal' to you; and (4) which makes you feel like you need it in order to make progress; don't read any other scripture for the next thirty days. Pretend that this is the only verse or the only passage in the entire Bible. Stick to that verse or that passage for at least thirty days and keep reading it and thinking about it more and more with *feeling.* Read it more than once each day, and start using that verse or passage in your inner conversations. First proclaim these scriptures in your mind; then, later on, say them out loud. Say them until you *feel* a connection in your spirit. You will find that whatever good 'thing' is promised by that verse or passage of scripture will then show up in your experience.

If you are serious about permanent transformation, and being renewed in the spirit of your mind, and having the mind of Christ, and living on this Earth as a beloved son of The Infinite, and being free to be like Christ, and breaking free from world system thinking, and permanently improving your circumstances and experiences, please work on your inner conversations.

Here's something else to remember: Always speak positively whenever you speak to yourself. Always speak to other people positively in your mind. *Never, ever argue with anyone in your mind.* Even if a person is your sworn enemy or just 'rubs you the wrong way', always see and hear them talking with you in a cordial manner during your inner conversations. See and hear everybody genuinely saying ideal things to you. Send this positive 'messenger' ahead of you.

Your inner conversations carry more weight in the spiritual realm than the words you speak aloud. This is why there is an Affirmation at the end of each Lesson in this book. When you practice repeating these Affirmations in your inner conversations, they bring about an upgrade in your State of Mind. They are good seeds which when planted in the soil of your mind, and when tended to maturity, will produce good things. Remember that whatever you desire to become, your inner conversations must indicate that you are already such a person.

Here are some more suggestions: Whenever you speak to yourself in your mind or whenever you speak to others in your mind, always speak as a victorious son of God. Even if the outer circumstances of your life may appear to be dire or disappointing at present, speak inwardly as someone who already has power; speak inwardly as someone who already has great faith; speak inwardly as someone who is already successful and living victoriously. Plant those good mind-seeds and give them time to grow and produce fruit. *"We walk by faith, not by sight" (2nd Corinthians 5:7)*; so practice ignoring outward appearances.

Don't waste precious energy in trying to 'fix' the outer circumstances of your life by your own human wisdom. Your inner conversations act as the steering wheel of your life. Turn them in whatever direction you want your life to go. Don't try to fight your old feelings. You give attention to anything which you fight, and you give power to anything which holds your attention. So, focus on the positive, and you will automatically eliminate the negative.

Even if it seems like the whole world is against you, change your inner conversations by saying internally statements such as: *"I am always victorious"; "I am The Infinite's favorite child"; "I am wonderful, and everybody loves me"; "I am healthy, happy and whole"; "I feel fabulous";* and *"Everything is going my way".* These simple decrees are the New Ideas which will pull up that old sycamine tree by the root. To strengthen these decrees, hold conversations in your mind where you hear other people confirming what you say. At first these may seem like empty words, especially if they don't seem to match your present circumstances; but if you keep saying them until you can *feel* them, you will get remarkable results. As was said before, this Technique may seem too simple and may go against logic, but it is very powerful and effective.

You may wonder how it is that your inner visions and inner

conversations have so much power. The answer is: *They have power because, as a son of The Infinite, you have power.* Power is part of your spiritual birthright. However, divine power is always to be handled and used in Divine Right Order and only for good purposes. You will notice that the people who follow world system thinking are always involved in some type of grab for power. That's because they have unknowingly distanced themselves from their divine power, and so they feel powerless. So they are always looking for ways to have power over people and to be in control of everything.

The Parable of the Overworked Bondservant

Now you might be wondering on what basis the claim can be made that the sycamine tree in the parable represents the bondservant's mentality. Here is the basis for that understanding: There is another parable which immediately follows the Parable of the Sycamine and Mustard Trees and it is *The Parable of the Overworked Bondservant.* Let's look again at the passage of scripture in Luke chapter 17 starting at verse 5, but this time we will go through to verse 10.

"And the apostles said to the Lord, 'Increase our faith'. And the Lord said, 'If you had faith as a grain of mustard seed, you might say to this sycamine tree, 'Be plucked up by the root and be planted in the sea', and it should obey you.

*But would any of you who has a **bondservant** plowing or feeding cattle, say to him when he returns from the field after a long day of work, 'Bondservant, come, sit down and relax, and have something to eat'? Instead, you would say to him, 'Prepare my meal! Put on your apron and serve me! Wait on me while I eat and drink! After I am finished, then you can eat and drink'!*

The master won't thank the bondservant because he did what the master commanded, will he?

So likewise, when you have done all that you have been commanded to do, say [to yourselves], *'We are worthless bondservants: we have only done what is our duty to do'."* (Please read this passage of scripture a second time before moving on. Let it sink in.)

Looking at these two parables of the trees and the overworked bondservant, you would wonder why Jesus would connect the two. On the surface, these parables seem to have no connection between them, but that is until you understand that in both parables Jesus was speaking of the need to break free of the bondservant's mentality.

The *Parable of the Two Trees* illustrates the need to remove the old bondservant's mentality, that Mental Captivity, and to replace it with a higher State of Mind which produces better things. All of this is done by changing our inner conversations. The *Parable of the Overworked Bondservant* then gives us a glimpse into how roughly a master treats his bondservants, and how that treatment gets ingrained into the mind of the bondservant to such an extent that it is reflected in the bondservant's inner conversations. This parable illustrates the state in which a man will live if he refuses to remove the 'sycamine tree' of negative expectation from his mind. It also reveals how a master will treat his bondservant, even if that 'master' is 'God'.

The *Parable of the Overworked Bondservant* also clearly reveals the inner conversations of a mentally captive Christian. After obeying all the 'commandments', and working himself half to death, he says to himself: "I am a worthless (unworthy) bondservant. I have only done what is my duty to do. Living in suffering and hardship is my duty to my Master. Carrying heavy, oppressive mental burdens is my duty to my Master. It is my duty to be in servitude to others even when I am too tired to even stand on my feet. It is my duty to suffer hunger while others feast. When I have done double-duty and gone the extra mile, I will not be appreciated or thanked or celebrated. It is my duty to toil, struggle, sacrifice and labor for my Master without reward. Obeying commandments is my duty." Do these inner conversations sound familiar to you?

Here's a thought to ponder. You will recall that when the Israelites were led by Moses out of slavery in Egypt, they were given an extensive list of commandments, many of which were extremely severe and carried harsh punishments for disobedience, including death. Why was this so? When the Israelites lived as slaves in Egypt, the Egyptians were the masters and overlords of the Israelites. The Egyptians harshly commanded them and brutally punished them for the slightest disobedience. This caused them to live in fear. When the Israelites became physically free and left Egypt, they didn't give up the mentality of captivity. They were travelling towards the promised land of Canaan, a land of freedom and abundance, but they still saw themselves as bondservants. In the minds of the masses of freed Israelites, there was a *need* for another master to take the place of the Egyptian slave-masters. So they just switched masters. The new 'master' they chose was 'God'.

The Israelites were physically free but they were still functioning with a slave mentality. Their minds could not process how to live in freedom. So, even though they were physically free, they had to be harshly commanded and brutally punished in order to be kept in line. This was the very same treatment which had been meted out to them by their Egyptian slave-masters. Identity determines treatment.

Sons of God are born free. (We will study this principle in detail at Level 2.) Sons of God don't need to be threatened, harshly commanded, punished and kept in line. That is the treatment meted out to those still living under the yokes of Mental Captivity. So, Jesus said to His disciples in John 13:34: *"I give you a new commandment, that you love one another. Love each other as I have loved you."* To expand this principle, 1st John 5:2-3 says: *"This is how we know that we love the children of God, when we love God and keep His commandments. For when we love God, we will keep His commandments, and **His commandments are not burdensome.**"*

Therefore, when God is dealing with believers living under mental bondage, His commandments are brutal and severe. However, when He is dealing with the sons of God, His commandments "are not burdensome". The Divine Father just needs to gently instruct His son, and the son will obey, because he deeply loves his Divine Father. When a man is a son of God living with the conscious awareness of his freedom, he will obey the Divine Father's instructions. (We will study this when we get to Level 3).

So, have you been talking to yourself like the overworked bondservant? Do your inner conversations indicate that you see yourself as worthless or not good enough? Do you obey God because it is your duty? Do you see God as your Master? Do you believe that you must suffer in order to please your Master? Does God have to harshly command you, threaten you and punish you to get your obedience? Do you live in fear of your Master's punishment?

The parable of the overworked bondservant teaches us that there is no gratitude shown by the master to his bondservant. The only form of gratitude, which the bondservant was shown, was more toil and hardship being heaped upon him. Even when the bondservant did double-duty, the master did not acknowledge his service. Have you been feeling as if God has overlooked you, that your work for Him is not recognized, that you are always giving but never receiving, and that you are overworked and underappreciated in the family of God? If so, now you know why. It is because you have assigned to yourself the identity of a bondservant, and your inner conversations have called forth certain negative experiences in your life.

The good news is that right now, at this very moment, you can change your identity from 'bondservant' to 'son'. As you saw in Lesson 1, your identity determines your treatment. If you see yourself as a bondservant, you will be treated as a bondservant; but if you see yourself as a son, you will be treated as a son. With this understanding, we see why Jesus connected the two parables.

Now, we have seen how the bondservant was treated in the parable we just read. Jesus also illustrated in another parable how *sons* are treated. The parable which illustrates the treatment given to sons is *The Parable of the Prodigal Son* found in Luke 15:11-32. The prodigal son was given the best robe, new shoes and the father's signet ring of authority. The father showered him with love, forgiveness, affection, attention and promotion. He was the father's Number One Priority, the father's Favorite Son. The prodigal son's mistakes and misdeeds were dismissed by the father. The servants in the house were commanded to dress him and to serve him. He was feasting on fattened calf. The father 'rolled out the red carpet' for the prodigal son; and this was a son who had made terrible mistakes, had gone as low as a man can go, and had disgraced himself, his father and his family! (See Luke 15:22-24)

Can you imagine any beloved son being treated by his father in the way this bondservant was treated by his master? Can you imagine any beloved son not being thanked and praised by his father for doing well? Can you imagine any such son calling himself worthless and obeying his father out of a sense of duty? No way! Identity determines treatment.

If you have been living in Mental Captivity, now is the time to start thinking differently. Now is the time to use your inner conversations to uproot that sycamine tree. Let's say it together: *"I am a divine, free-born, spirit-son of God giving service in my Father's house. I am not in servitude. I am in divine service, and I deserve to be treated as God's son."*

The disciples started their conversation with Jesus by making a request. They said to Jesus: "Increase our faith". By using these parables, Jesus illustrated to them that they didn't need their Faith to be increased. What they really needed was to upgrade their State of Mind. They needed to uproot the old sycamine tree and stop thinking like mental captives. Once we get Mental Captivity out of the way, we will realize that the Faith which we have is enough.

Every good 'thing' is already in the mustard seed which is already within us. Every good 'thing' is already in the good words which we select for our inner conversations. Every good 'thing' can be found in the positive mind-seeds which we will choose from now on. If we don't like our present circumstances, it's time to choose better mind-seeds.

So it's not about increasing our Faith. It's about creating the proper mental conditions where the good seed within us can manifest all the good which is already within it. When we start seeing God as our Divine Spirit-Father and start seeing ourselves as His divine, free-born, spirit-sons, our State of Mind will command our Faith to produce wonderful things. Our mentality grows out of how we truly see and feel about ourselves.

God will always deal with you at the level of your mentality

Infinite God will never force you to change your State of Mind. The Infinite will always deal with you at the level of your present mentality. This principle is very, very, very, very significant. Its significance cannot be overemphasized. We will examine this principle in depth at Level 2, when we will dig deeply into the subject of 'Spiritual Laws'. Always remember this principle, especially when you see Christians believing in and accepting 'hardship and suffering' as their lot in life. It's one thing to experience challenges here and there in life. It's quite another thing to believe in and expect hardship and suffering and punishment as your normal experience in life. Faith produces whatever you expect, whatever it *sees* in your State of Mind.

We were just examining the episode in the Old Testament where severe treatment was meted out to the Israelites in the wilderness after they left Egypt. What was happening? It is an illustration of the principle that God deals with people according to the level of their mentality. The collective mentality of the freed Israelites was unfortunately still stuck in captivity. If their mentality had been different they would have been treated differently.

Changing your mind is your job, not God's. Free will is a gift from God, and it includes freedom to choose your ideas and your identity. God is not going to interfere with that freedom. If you see yourself as His bondservant, He will treat you as His bondservant. If you see yourself as His son, He will treat you as His son. Identity determines treatment; and it's up to you to choose your identity.

Great Faith but a Low Mentality

Now, let's look at three examples in the New Testament of how God will deal with a person at the level of his or her mentality. As we study this, we will also see how a low mentality will give us terrible experiences even if we have great faith.

Acts 10:34 states that: *"God is no respecter of persons..."* This means that Infinite God does not relate to people based on their status in the world system. However, God does respect two things: *Faith* and a *High Mentality*. When these two things combine, God does great things. Christians in general have great faith in God, but unfortunately many devoted Christians have been mentally conditioned to believe in an inferior definition of themselves. This creates a Low Mentality, and blocks the manifestation of the goodness of God in a powerful way.

To see the first example of the effects of a person's mentality, let's look at another well-known passage of scripture.

Matthew 15:22-28: "A Canaanite woman from that region came, and kept crying to Him, 'Have mercy on me, O Lord, son of David. My daughter is grievously tormented by a demon'. But He did not say a word to her.

And His disciples came and urged Him, 'Send her away, for she keeps shouting at us.' He answered [the woman] *and said, 'I am only sent to the lost sheep of Israel.' Then she came and worshipped Him, and she said, 'Lord, help me.'*

But He answered her, 'It is not right to take the children's food and throw it to the dogs'. *And she said, 'That is true, Lord. But **the dogs eat the scraps which fall from their masters' table.'** Jesus answered her,* **'O woman, your faith is great***! Your request is granted.' And her daughter was healed instantly."* (Please read this passage of scripture a second time before moving on. Let it sink in.)

Why did Jesus ignore the Canaanite woman at first? Why did Jesus say to her, "I am only sent to the lost sheep of Israel"? Why did He tell her, "It is not right to take the children's food and give it to dogs"? Was He testing her faith? *No.* Was He saying she was a 'dog'? *No.* Was He trying to embarrass her? *No.* Was He trying to get her to give up and go away? *No.* So what was Jesus doing? *He was dealing with the Canaanite woman at the level of her mentality.* Jesus perceived her habits of thought; and when He spoke to her, He was declaring the inner workings of her thinking. Jesus remarked that she had great faith. She also had tremendous persistence. However, her faith and her persistence were not enough to shield her from the effects of her low mentality.

The State of Mind of the Canaanite woman

In her mind, the Canaanite woman saw herself as an unworthy, 'Gentile dog'. The word 'Gentile' is a word used by Jews to describe people who are not Jews. The word 'dog' was a derogatory word used by Jews to describe 'Gentiles'. The woman was keenly aware that she was not a Jew, and so she saw herself as someone who was less than the Jewish people. The woman had heard herself described as a 'dog' so often that she came to accept it as true. So, she told Jesus that as a 'dog' she would settle for the scraps which fall from her masters' table. Her mentality had trained and prepared her to expect sub-standard treatment, and so it was done. Faith is the substance of things expected by a person's State of Mind.

The Canaanite woman had selected her ideal 'thing'; and it was *the healing of her daughter'*. The Canaanite woman expected her daughter to be healed, and her daughter was eventually healed according to the faith of the woman; because Faith always says 'Yes!' to State of Mind. However, Faith does not work selectively. Faith supports in totality whatever it sees within the boundaries of a person's State of Mind, whether it is positive or negative.

So, the Canaanite woman expected the healing, but she also felt inferior and she expected to be treated as inferior because she was not a Jew. The daughter of the Canaanite woman was healed. The Canaanite woman received her 'thing'. However, she went through trauma, denial, embarrassment, humiliation, disdain and became a public spectacle before she got the 'thing'. Her State of Mind determined the negative circumstances under which she would receive her 'thing'; and her Faith said 'Yes!' to the negative as well as the positive. Jesus wasn't testing her. He was treating her according to her low mentality.

Remember, the land of Canaan was the land of plenty and abundance; but someone had taught this woman that she was unworthy. So here she was, a citizen of Canaan, expecting and settling for scraps. What do we know about this woman? She made the effort to seek after Jesus. She was reverent, persistent, a fervent intercessor and she had great faith. However, none of these things were enough to overcome the effects of her low mentality.

On one level of meaning this is a story of a healing. On a different level of meaning it shows us that even when God is willing, and even where there is great faith, a low mentality will cause us to have a hard time in getting God's best. The Canaanite woman made the mistake of mentally conforming to what people called her: i.e. 'unworthy Gentile dog'.

So, here are some suggestions: Never allow your self-identity to be shaped by people's negativity toward you. Never let people's opinion of you or society's opinion of you cause you to see yourself as 'less than' anyone, no matter what may have happened in your past. The Bible says: *"...God is no respecter of persons* (i.e. The Infinite does not relate to people based on their status in the world system)*; He welcomes and accepts **from every nation any person** who respects Him and works righteousness* (i.e. anyone who puts right-thinking to work).*" (Acts 10:34-35)* This tells us that Infinite God does not have any special people. Therefore, let no one deceive you into seeing yourself as inferior in any way. Keep your head, your faith and your mentality high.

The State of Mind of the Roman centurion

Now let's compare the Canaanite woman with another 'Gentile'. Let's look at the story of the Roman centurion, captain of 100 soldiers. The centurion was not a Jew. As a matter of fact, he represented the Roman Empire; the idol-worshipping oppressors of the Jews. Just like the Canaanite woman, the centurion needed a miracle on behalf of someone else, but his mentality was far different than that of the woman. Let's look at the similarities and the differences between their stories.

Matthew 8:5-10, 13 says: *"When Jesus entered [the town of] Capernaum, a certain centurion approached him and pleaded with him, saying, 'My servant is lying at home paralyzed and in terrible pain.'*

Jesus said to him, 'I will come and heal him.'

*The centurion replied, 'Lord, **I am not worthy** for you to visit my home. Just speak the word and my servant will be healed. I am a man under the authority of my superiors in the army, and I have soldiers whom I command. **I say to this man, 'Go!' and he goes, and I say to another man, 'Come!' and he comes, and I say to my servant, 'Do this!', and he does it.***

When Jesus heard this, He was amazed, and said to the people who were following Him: **'I have not found a faith as great as this anywhere in Israel.'...***And Jesus said to the centurion,* **'Go!'** **Let it be done for you exactly as you have believed.'** *And his servant was healed at that very moment."* (Please read this passage of scripture a second time before moving on. Let it sink in.)

The Canaanite woman stayed at a distance and cried to Jesus, begging for help over and over. The centurion approached Jesus and spoke once. The Canaanite woman's repeated request was ignored, but as soon as the centurion made his request, Jesus was ready to help. Jesus immediately said: "I will come and heal him". Why is this so? Do you notice that in the same manner that the Roman centurion gave commands to his soldiers and was obeyed, Jesus commanded the healing and it was done? Do you see it?

The centurion's identity, the way in which he perceived himself, caused him to expect to have certain experiences. He expected to be treated in a positive way. His experiences as a commander of soldiers had conditioned his mind to expect immediate cooperation, obedience and respect. *"Centurions don't beg";* this was his mentality and how he truly felt about himself. This high State of Mind was supported by his Faith. Jesus responded to the centurion's mentality, and treated him accordingly. By contrast, the Canaanite woman was used to being disdained, ignored and belittled. Those experiences defined her identity in her own mind, and set the boundaries of her mentality. That was how she expected to be treated, and so Jesus treated her according to her mentality. Jesus said that both the Canaanite woman and the Roman centurion had great faith. However, their difference in mentality determined how each was treated. Here's something to remember: No matter how strong your faith in God may be, you will never rise above the level of your mentality. Faith is the substance of things expected. Expectations are birthed out of your State of Mind. Even if you have been through demeaning experiences, don't let those experiences define you. Don't let them create your identity. Don't let them tell you who you are. Don't let them set the boundaries of your State of Mind. Don't let them dictate how you *feel* about yourself. Use the Mind Renewal Technique to rise above past experiences. Take back control of your mind and reclaim your true Divine Identity. The sons of The Infinite don't beg.

You are worthy because God says you are

Now let's look at this. Jesus was ready to go to the centurion's house to heal the servant, but then He hit upon the boundary set up by the centurion's State of Mind. The centurion uttered the dreaded words: *"I am not worthy..."* Those words stopped Jesus in his tracks. We will never know what other great blessings could have rested on the centurion's house, and what other mighty miracles would have been done there. The centurion received this much and no more, according to the limits of his mentality. His feelings of unworthiness restrained the move of God in his life. The centurion had exceptional faith, but his mentality limited the scope of the work of Jesus on his behalf.

As was said before, God will never try to change your State of Mind. He will deal with you at the level of your current mentality. Your State of Mind sets the boundaries within which your Faith will work. Wherever your mentality stops, God stops. You are worthy of *All Good* because The Infinite is your Father. It's not about your 'good works'. *All Good* is The Infinite's gift to you. You are the beneficiary of the favor of God which you can never earn and you never needed to earn. That *unearned favor* is called '*Grace*'. No son ever needs to earn his father's love and favor. So, never again think or say or sing: *"I am not worthy..."* It is an insult to your Divine Father.

The State of Mind of Zaccheus

Now let's look at the State of Mind of another man who didn't have any of the mental hang-ups which the Canaanite woman and the Roman centurion had. This was a man who was willing to allow Jesus full access to his life. This was a man who by his actions said to Jesus: *"Since You say I am worthy, then I am worthy"*. This man was Zaccheus.

Jesus was visiting the city of Jericho where Zaccheus lived. The Bible tells us that Zaccheus was an extremely wealthy man who earned his living by collecting taxes for the Roman Empire, and he was chief among the tax collectors. Tax collectors at that time were notorious for overtaxing the people and keeping the excess for themselves. Zaccheus had a bad reputation and he was disliked. People in the city classified him as a 'notorious sinner'. When he saw Jesus surrounded by multitudes of people walking through Jericho, Zaccheus wanted to get a good view, but he was short in stature. So he came up with a plan. He figured out where Jesus was headed, ran ahead of Him, climbed a tree by the side of the road and waited.

Let's pick up the story: *"And when Jesus came to the place, he looked up, and saw him (Zaccheus), and said to him: 'Zaccheus, hurry and climb down: **for today I must stay at your house.**' And he hurried and climbed down and **received Him into his house joyfully and with great excitement.** And when the people standing by saw it, they all grumbled, saying: 'He (Jesus) is gone to be the guest of a man who is a **notorious sinner.'***

*And Zaccheus stood, and said unto the Lord: 'See, Lord, I have decided to give a half of my possessions to the poor; and if I have taken anything from any man by cheating them, I will give them back four times as much.' And Jesus said to him, 'This day **salvation is come to this house** for he (Zaccheus) is also a **son of Abraham'.'"** (Luke 19:5-9)* (Please read this passage of scripture a second time before moving on. Let it sink in.)

Despite his reputation and his bad character, Zaccheus was willing to grasp an opportunity to receive mercy and favor from Jesus. Zaccheus had many faults, but false modesty was not one of them. Zaccheus could have walked around in inferiority like the Canaanite woman; but he didn't. Zaccheus could have said to Jesus, *'I am not worthy for you to come to my house',* like the centurion did; but Zaccheus didn't.

Instead Zaccheus willingly accepted the gift of *Grace.* Zaccheus had done nothing and could do nothing to earn the presence of Jesus in his house, but he was wise enough to accept Jesus' offer of fellowship. He 'rolled out the red carpet' and received Jesus into his house with great excitement and joy. He made the Son of God welcome in his house. No doubt he spread a lavish feast before Him. While the crowd was outside his house grumbling and describing Zaccheus as a "notorious sinner", Jesus was inside his house smiling and calling Zaccheus "a son of Abraham". Don't let people's opinions of you block your blessings. Feelings of worthiness elevated Zaccheus from 'sinner' to 'son'.

Today, the living Christ offers fellowship to every man. He says: *"Behold, I stand at the door and knock. If **any man** hears my voice and opens the door, **I will come in** to him, and dine with him, and he shall dine with Me." (Revelation 3:20)* Has anyone convinced you that you are a sinner and that you are somehow unworthy of God's goodness or God's fellowship? Now you can follow the example of Zaccheus and reject their definition of who you are. Be the son of The Infinite that you were created to be. Never settle for the scraps which fall from the master's table. Instead, feel free to take your seat at the table as a son in the Divine Family.

Why did Jesus call Zaccheus "a son of Abraham"? It was because this "notorious sinner" had faith enough to believe in Jesus and to believe in himself. God had told the patriarch Abraham that because of his faith, Abraham would be the 'father of many nations'. Abraham is also known as 'the father of faith'. God also told Abraham that he would be blessed; that he would be a blessing to others; and that, through Abraham, all families of the earth would be blessed. *(See Genesis 17:5 & Genesis 12:2).* That blessing of Abraham which is given to every 'son of Abraham' is *'Faith' (See Galatians 3:7-9).* Zaccheus had faith that he was worthy. So, he welcomed Jesus into his house. In return, he and his family got a blessing by being in the presence of Jesus, and he shared that blessing with all the inhabitants of Jericho.

Zaccheus experienced true repentance that day. His mind transformed. His outlook transformed. His character transformed. His reputation transformed. His life transformed. This rich man gave a half of all his possessions to the poor. So he transformed the lives of all the poor people in Jericho. Also, the people, whom Zaccheus had robbed, got a repayment of 400% of what had been taken from them. Can you imagine the burden of guilt that lifted from Zaccheus' heart? Can you imagine the elation in Jericho? An entire city was blessed because one man was willing to step out of mental servitude and say: "I am worthy since Jesus says I am worthy." Great things will happen when we stop feeling: "I am unworthy" and start feeling: "I am worthy because of The Infinite's gift of *Grace*". How will we fulfil our purpose of being a blessing to others if we cannot say and feel: "I am worthy to be blessed and to be a blessing"?

Here's a suggestion: Give up every thought, every idea and every memory which would cause you to say: "I am not worthy." Let no one deceive you by any means. It is <u>not</u> an indication of humility when a son of God says, "I am not worthy". Rather, it is an indication of the bondservant's mentality and a lack of knowledge of his divine rights as a son of The Infinite. It is the voice of False Humility, and it is just as dangerous as False Pride. True Humility always says: "Our Divine Father says we are worthy! Who are we to disagree with Him? Who are we to reject God's Grace? We will not insult our Divine Father by rejecting His gifts. We humbly receive and accept all of goodness of The Infinite with thanksgiving! We are worthy because our Divine Father says we are. We are worthy because we are divine sons of God in the Divine Family. We are worthy because of who our Divine Father is." That is the voice of True Humility.

Jesus clearly thought that the Roman centurion was worthy, but the Roman centurion thought otherwise. Zaccheus did not make that mistake. You are worthy of God's best because you are a son of God. You are in the Divine Family forever. Your Divine Father says you are worthy. Are you humbly agreeing with Him?

Rising above the crowd

Now let's look a little deeper into the mystical meaning of this story of Zaccheus. We notice that Zaccheus realized that, despite all of his advantages in many areas of his life, he had one disadvantage: he was short in stature; he was below the level of the crowd. However Zaccheus was willing to do something unusual so that he could get a better view of Jesus. First, he ran ahead of the crowd which was walking with Jesus. Next, he climbed a tree and set himself above the level of the crowd. Consequently, Jesus singled him out for fellowship.

This unusual act of Zaccheus has a spiritual truth hidden within it. It teaches us that whatever 'disadvantage' we may face in our lives, can have deeper fellowship with The Divine as long as we are willing to 'run ahead of the crowd' and then 'rise above the level of the crowd'. How do we do this? First, we expand our mind and allow our thinking to *advance* beyond what is popularly accepted as truth. By doing so, we advance beyond world system thinking. Next, we *elevate* our thinking above the level of the thinking of the multitudes of people who are walking with Jesus today. We make the effort to do whatever it takes, even unusual things, in order to have a higher mentality. We do unusual things, such as practicing our Mind Renewal Technique and consciously using our Inner Conversations.

Every person who walked with Jesus in that crowd had a need that Jesus could meet and a house in which Jesus could dine. However, the only house the Son of God chose to enter was the house of the man who ran ahead of the crowd and rose above the level of the crowd. The word **'house'** in this story and throughout the Bible symbolically represents **'the mind'.** The man who is: (1) willing to advance in his understanding; (2) willing to climb up mentally above the mental conditioning of the masses who are following Jesus; and (3) willing to have a high mentality, will have the son of God mentality come into his mental 'house'. Just like Zaccheus, the presence of 'son of God thinking' in his mental 'house' will elevate him from 'sinner' to 'son'. Do you see it?

Just as it was in the city of Jericho so long ago, multitudes of people are walking with Jesus today. Are you willing to run ahead of the crowd mentally, and advance in your understanding? Is your thinking below, at, or above the level of the crowd? Are you willing to make the effort to rise above the mentality of the crowd? Are you mentally positioned to attract divine fellowship? The stories of Zaccheus, the Roman centurion and the Canaanite woman prove that God will treat you according to the level of your mentality. God loves you and is willing to help you, but He won't change your State of Mind for you. You are always free to choose your State of Mind, and free to change your State of Mind at any time.

'Knowing' is higher than 'Believing'

In order to have the mentality of a son of Infinite God, let's know who we are in the Divine Family. Let's know that we are sons and not bondservants. Let's know that we are divine spirit-sons in the Divine Family. When we *know* we are sons of God, we have taken our first step on the path of Truth. It is not enough to hear it, to understand it or even to believe it. When we have a Knowing of this truth, we live in victory over world system thinking.

Now let's circle back to the topic of this Lesson: *You don't need to believe what you know.* 'Knowing' is a higher level of understanding than just 'Believing'. You may be wondering: *What is the difference between 'believing' something and 'knowing' something?*

Let's look at a practical example. Let's suppose that you meet someone for the first time, and you ask him: "What is your name?" and he replies: "I believe my name is John." What does that reply suggest? It suggests that he is not 100% sure of his name. He may have seen that name on his birth certificate, he may have been called by that name for years and he may actually believe it to be his name. However, he is not sure; that's why he has to believe it. His having to believe, that his name is 'John', suggests that he might be suffering from amnesia. If he were sure of his name, he would have replied: "I am John."

When you know something, you don't have to believe it. 'Knowing' is a higher level of understanding than 'Believing'. Now, let's personalize this principle. You no doubt have heard and read scriptures which tell you that you are a son of God. You may even understand and sincerely believe these scriptures. However, until you get to a point in your understanding where you know this to be the absolute truth of who you are to the exclusion of all else, you will not be truly free to be like Christ. If you are a committed Christian, no doubt you remember the day on which you started to follow Christ, and you may call yourself 'a child of God', but until you let go of every thought which tells you that God is your Master, you are still shackled by a bondservant's mentality.

If a man says, "I *believe* that I am a son of God", it is a sign that he is suffering from spiritual amnesia. He doesn't yet fully remember his original spiritual identity. Until he *knows* that he is a divine, free-born, spirit-son of God and until he *knows* that God is his Divine Spirit-Father, he will not have the Mind of Christ. Jesus knew that He was the beloved Son of God. He didn't have to believe it.

As soon as you get that Knowing in your spirit (that conscious awareness) that you are a beloved, divine, free-born, spirit-son of God, and as soon as it rings true within you to the point where you *feel* it, you will know the truth of who you are. The only truth that will set you free is the truth that you know, not at an intellectual level, but at a spiritual level. It's the truth that you know in your 'gut feelings' which will set you free; not the truth that you believe in your head. Once you know something, you no longer need to believe it.

Belief and Doubt live together

Wherever there is a belief, there is a doubt. Belief and Doubt go hand in hand; they are like heads and tails on a coin. However, when you go one level higher than just having a belief about something, when you get to the level where you know something to be the absolute truth, and when that knowing is so real that you can *feel* it, there is no room for belief and no room for doubt. At that point of *knowing*, it becomes a settled truth. It's a done deal.

Having a Belief is different from having Faith. Belief generally works at an intellectual level, but Faith works at a spiritual level. Belief is an intellectual exercise and it's based on what we think in our head. By contrast, Faith is a spiritual force; and it's a 'knowing' that we can *feel* deep in our spirit. So we can have a sincere Belief in God without really having Faith in God. We don't want to live at the level of Belief. We want to live at the level of Faith. When we get to the level of 'Knowing' and 'Feeling', we are living at the level of Faith.

Now that we have a clearer understanding, let's examine our opening text, our WORD FOR TODAY from the Apostle Paul. The Apostle Paul had to get to that stage of spiritual development where he graduated from 'believing' to 'knowing'. Only then was he able to say, *"I* **know** *the One in whom I have* **believed***, and I am* **certain** *that He is able..."* *(2nd Timothy 1:12)* 'Knowing' happens when the thing that you know becomes a part of you. When the man becomes fully persuaded of his name, he will say: 'I am John'. That name is a part of who he is. He fully identifies with it and feels it. It is as real as he is. It is who he is **now**. There's no need for reasoning or arguing or proving. When you know you are a divine spirit-son of God, it becomes an instinct, a reflex, and an identity. It is who you are. You don't have to think about it or try to prove it. It's *You*. It's not knowledge somewhere in your head. It is a knowing which is settled in your spirit. So, if you say, "I believe I am a son of God", you don't know it yet.

Know your own worthiness

The Canaanite woman clearly trusted Jesus, but she did not trust her own worthiness. She trusted that Jesus was able to help her, but she did not trust that she was worthy of His help. No doubt she said to herself: "Jesus is going to ignore me, but maybe if I pray enough, if I praise Him enough, if I beg enough, if I am persistent enough, if I am loud enough, if I humiliate myself enough, then He will help me". Have you ever taken the same approach?

Faith starts with knowing God, but Worthiness comes from knowing yourself, knowing your relationship to Him as His beloved divine, free-born, spirit-son and knowing your status as part of the Divine Family forever. Worthiness is a product of the Ideas which you hold in your State of Mind. You know you have accepted your worthiness when the thought of being a son of God, and the thought of the privileges which go with that status, fill you with feelings of excitement and joy.

So ask yourself this question: Do I believe that I am a son of God or do I know it? If there is any shadow of a doubt in your mind that you are a beloved, divine, free-born, spirit-son of God, you are still at the level of belief. You don't need to wait for anyone else to recognize that you are a son of God and to give you validation. All that is necessary is that you make the decision today to cast out of your mind the mentality of a bondservant, along with everything it produces.

Now you may say, *"I have heard people preach and teach that God is both my Master and my Father. I have even read where some writers of the epistles in the New Testament refer to themselves as 'slaves' or 'bondservants' as well as 'sons of God'. Can't I be both God's bondservant and God's son at the same time?"* The answer is *'No'*, but that is the focus of our next Lesson.

Have you ever wondered why some scriptures in the Bible seem to contradict each other? Have you ever wondered why there are so many contradictory interpretations of the Bible, and whether it is possible for you to know the truth? All of this will be explained in our next Lesson, in which we will investigate one of the deep secrets of the Bible: *The Mirror Secret*. See you then. Please read the Supporting Scriptures, Affirmation and the Review which follow this Lesson.

Supporting Scriptures

Hosea 6:3: "Then we shall know if we press on to know the Lord..."

*Matthew 7:9-11: "Parents, if your **son** asks you for bread, would you give him a stone? Or if your **son** asks you for a fish, would you give him a snake instead? So if you, who can be so hurtful, know how to give good gifts unto your **children**, how much more shall **your heavenly Father** give **good things** to them (to His sons) who ask Him?"*

*1st John 3:1: "Behold! What great love the Father has bestowed on us, that we should be called the sons of God: therefore **the world [system] does not recognize that this is who we are**, just as it does not recognize who He is."*

Affirmation

When challenges rise and confront me, when the road I am traveling gets rough,
I rest in my 'knowing' which tells me: "The Faith that you have is enough!"
My State of Mind makes its selection of the ideal 'thing' which I request,
My Faith looks within me and sees it; and my Faith's only answer is 'Yes'!
The 'thing' I have chosen is certain, for my State of Mind says, "It is done!",
And although I don't have all the answers, the victory is already won.
For my 'Now Faith' has sprung into action, to materialize all my ideals;
I now live it in my inner vision, till it transforms the way that I feel.
I'm a son at God's rich banquet table;
My good mind-seeds now flourish and grow;
And ALL GOOD is mine in the Family Divine;
I don't have to believe it. I KNOW!

Review

Q. How do my State of Mind and my Faith work together?
A. Your State of Mind determines the things that you receive, the *quality and the quantity* of the things you receive and the *circumstances* under which you receive those things. Your Faith determines *when* you are ready to receive them. Your State of Mind is the boss and your Faith is the employee. Your State of Mind sets the boundaries within which your faith will operate. God will always deal with you at the level of your mentality. Your State of Mind only holds Ideas.

Q. Will God change my State of Mind for me?
A. No. God gives you freedom to choose your Ideas, and by doing so you choose your State of Mind. Your State of Mind is your responsibility, yours alone. You can change it from negative to positive at any time, no matter how long you have been thinking negatively. God will always deal with you at the level of your mentality.

Q. What is 'NOW FAITH'?
A. 'Now Faith' is Active Faith which produces and materializes whatever a man's State of Mind can see, feel, enjoy and mentally accept right now.

Q. How do I get my Now Faith to produce more for me?
A. You do so by expanding the boundaries of your State of Mind to include whatever 'thing' you desire with such clarity and intensity that you can feel it, touch it, taste it, smell it, hear it, experience it and enjoy it mentally right now. Your Now Faith can only produce what it finds within the boundaries of your Now State of Mind.

Q. In the principle of Now Faith, what is the meaning of 'transplanting trees' and why does this practice hinder my victory?
A. Now Faith works by expanding our State of Mind wide enough to comfortably include the 'thing' which we desire. This is how we 'purchase the orchard', and by doing so, everything within it becomes

'ours'. By contrast, we 'transplant trees' when we do not expand our State of Mind, but rather we try to force desired 'things' to fit into our current state of mind. We try to get more faith, get more love, get more peace etc. when there is no room in our state of mind to comfortably receive and accommodate these new 'things'. This practice of 'transplanting trees' will never give us the victory, for there will be no room in our minds for these new 'things' until our State of Mind expands to accommodate them. Now Faith will only 'support' what it can find fitting *comfortably* within our State of Mind.

Q. By what means can I expand the boundaries of my State of Mind?
A. You can use the Mind Renewal Technique to create a clear, inner vision and experience your desired 'thing' as being real right now. You can also use your Inner Conversations as messengers which you send ahead of you to create better mental experiences which will materialize in your future.

Q. What is mental money?
A. Your thoughts, feelings and inner vision act as mental money which you use to mentally 'purchase' whatever 'thing' you desire and bring it within the boundaries of your State of Mind. The thing is then received mentally as being *'yours'*.

Q. In the parable of the sycamine tree and the mustard tree, what do these trees represent?
 A. The sycamine tree grows first and represents the old State of Mind of the mentally enslaved man who does not know the truth of his Divine Identity. This 'sycamine tree' of the old mentality is uprooted from your mind so that the mustard seed of Faith can be planted in your mind, take root there and produce good things for you. The son of God mentality grows out of Faith in your Divine Identity.

Q. How do I uproot the sycamine tree of the bondservant's mentality?
A. The sycamine tree of the bondservant's mentality is in your mind. The

Bible says that in order to uproot it, you speak to it. This means you speak within yourself in a positive way. Simply put: Change your inner conversations.

Q. Why did Jesus treat the Canaanite woman so harshly?
A. He treated her according to the level of her mentality. The Roman centurion was also treated according to the level of his mentality, as was Zaccheus. The requests of the woman and of the centurion were similar, but the circumstances under which Jesus met their needs were determined by their respective mentalities.

Q. What words will restrict how much God will do for me?
A. The words are: 'I am not worthy...' or 'I don't deserve...'

Q. What is 'False Humility'?
A. False Humility is the rejection of your Divine Identity and the assignment to yourself of an identity which is inferior to your Divine Identity. False Humility will cause you to say, think and sing such things as: "I am not worthy of God's goodness. I am not good enough. God has no reason to love me. I am not worthy to be called a son of God. I am not worthy of the least of God's mercies. I am not worthy to receive God's blessings." This is done in the misguided belief that you are being humble when you do so.

Q. Which is the higher level of understanding? Is it Believing or is it Knowing?
A. Knowing is higher than Believing. You do not have to believe what you know. Wherever there is a belief, there is room for a doubt. 'Knowing' happens when what you believe becomes so much part of who you are until you can *feel* it settled in your spirit.

Lesson 3: Get out of my house!

WORD FOR TODAY: "Can two walk together unless they are in agreement?"   (Amos 3:3)

You can't have it both ways

In the previous Lesson, we saw how our State of Mind and our Faith work together to produce results in our life. We saw from the scriptures that when we have Faith, we will have our desires fulfilled, but if our mentality is not high enough, the circumstances under which we receive what we desire will be unpleasant. We saw this principle play out in the experience of the Canaanite woman. Her story is a case study of how Faith, even great Faith, is restricted by a low mentality.

In the previous Lesson, we also saw the importance of progressing from 'believing' to 'knowing' that we are the sons of God. We understood that we need to choose whether we will have the State of Mind of 'God's bondservant' or the State of Mind of 'God's son'. We can't have it both ways. Now, let's see why making this choice is so crucial.

Conflict in Abraham's house

The Bible is written at several different levels of meaning. This means that there is a natural meaning to the stories recorded in the Bible, which any man who reads the Bible can understand. However, Bible stories also have deep spiritual principles and timeless truths hidden within them. Let's now look at one example in a well-known episode in the life of the ancient patriarch Abraham. When we start to dig deeply into his story, we will have a clearer understanding as to why it is so crucial for us to completely give up the mentality of God's human bondservant and accept the mentality of a spirit-son of God.

The Bible tells us, in the Book of Genesis, that God called Abraham from his homeland, and directed him to travel to a distant land which God promised to give to him as his own possession and as an inheritance for his descendants. Abraham obeyed and travelled with his wife and other relatives to the 'Promised Land'. He and his wife Sarah stayed in the Promised Land, but after a while they left and travelled to the land of Egypt. While in Egypt, Abraham had some negative experiences, and so he and Sarah his wife decided to return to the Promised Land. However, when they returned, they took with them an Egyptian slave-woman named Hagar whom the Egyptian king had given to Abraham as a gift. *(See Genesis 12:10-20)*

Besides all of this, Abraham and Sarah had a problem. They were both advanced in age and they had no child. How could Abraham ever give the Promised Land to his descendants if he remained childless?

Now let's pick up the story in Genesis 15:2-4, 6:

"And Abram (i.e. Abraham) *said, 'Lord God, what will You give me, seeing I am childless, and the one who is set to inherit my estate is this Eliezer of Damascus* (Abraham's chief bondservant)*?' And Abram said, See, You have given me no children: and so,* **this bondservant is going to be my heir.'**

And the Lord said to him: 'This man shall not be your heir; but **your own son shall be your heir.'**

...And he (Abraham) **believed** *the Lord; and He counted it to him for righteousness."* (Please read this passage of scripture a second time before moving on. Let it sink in.)

So God promised Abraham that he and his wife Sarah would have a son *(See Genesis 18:10-11)*. Abraham believed it to be true. Nevertheless, despite this belief, the Bible tells us that Abraham tried to work things out another way by conceiving a child with Hagar his Egyptian female slave (also known as 'the bondwoman'), all because he doubted that Sarah could bear a child at her advanced age. The Bible tells us that Abraham believed the promise of God. Nevertheless, Abraham also doubted that Sarah could bear the promised son at her advanced age. As we shared with you before, wherever there is a belief there is also a doubt. That doubt made Abraham decide to have a baby with Hagar the Egyptian slave-woman. He had strong belief, but his state of mind was not yet at a level to receive God's promise in the way in which God had purposed to make it happen. In Abraham's mind, the thought of Sarah giving birth to a child did not fall within the boundaries of what was possible. He couldn't see **how** it could ever happen **now**. Over the years, Abraham's circumstances had conditioned his state of mind to become restricted and narrow concerning what was possible in his life. His mentality was not expanded enough to receive the child that he had been promised. He would later receive the promised son. However, the circumstances under which he would have this son in his life would become unpleasant as a result of the choices he made while living under the control of his low mentality.

So Hagar the Egyptian bondwoman conceived, and gave birth to a male child named *Ishmael.* When Hagar saw that she had a child but Sarah was still barren, Hagar became haughty, and despised and disdained Sarah, even though Sarah was the 'lady of the house'. *(See Genesis 16:4-5)* Several years later, when Abraham's state of mind was at the right level of development, his wife Sarah gave birth to the promised son named *Isaac,* despite her advanced age. Now this was the dilemma: there were two children living in Abraham's house; one was Ishmael the child of Hagar the bondwoman and the other was Isaac the child of Sarah the freewoman. The question was: 'Which child should get the promised inheritance?' Consequently, there was conflict between the children and conflict between the mothers.

Then one day something remarkable happened. Sarah, Abraham's wife, saw the bondwoman's child Ishmael mocking the promised son Isaac. For Sarah, that was the final straw, and it became the turning point in Abraham's house. This is what happened next:

"So she (Sarah) *said to Abraham, 'Throw out this bondwoman and her son: for the son of the bondwoman shall not be heir with my son, even with Isaac.' And the request was very grievous to Abraham because of his son* (Ishmael).

And God said to Abraham, 'Do not be grieved because of the boy, and because of your bondwoman; in everything that Sarah has said, do as she has asked; for in Isaac (the promised son) *your lineage shall be'. "* *(Genesis 21:10-12)* (Please read this passage of scripture a second time before moving on. Let it sink in.)

The Bible goes on to tell us that early the next morning Abraham threw Hagar the slave-woman and her son Ishmael out of his house. His wife Sarah and Isaac the promised son remained with Abraham permanently. This outcome calls to mind the words of Jesus which we studied in Lesson 1: *"A slave has no permanent place in the family, but a son belongs to the family forever."*

A slave can't get the family inheritance

Now that we have the basic facts of this episode in the life of Abraham, it may seem as if an injustice was done to Hagar and Ishmael, and that the injustice was condoned by God. Many times, in the stories recorded in the Bible, you will see people acting in ways which may seem unjust, and yet they receive no correction from God but rather support and commendation. You may even see God portrayed as acting harshly and without compassion. This may seem puzzling at first. However, once you understand that the stories of the Bible are in fact *parables* illustrating higher truth, and once you dig deeper into each story and discover the higher truth, then the reason for the seeming injustice or lack of compassion will become crystal clear.

A *parable* is a story in which ordinary, natural people, objects and events are used as symbols to illustrate high spiritual truth. Therefore, as you read the Bible, resist the temptation to pass judgment on the action of the characters in the Bible, including God. These actions, even the ones which seem to be unjust or to lack compassion, are necessary to illustrate the truth which the story is designed to convey. The obvious, literal meaning of any passage of scripture will never tell you the truth hidden in the story.

So let's look at the spiritual parallels hidden in this story, and examine the higher truth which the story illustrates. First, let's see who in this story was qualified to be given the family inheritance:

◙ ELIEZER OF DAMASCUS: We see that Abraham desired to pass the family inheritance to a son of his, and not to his chief bondservant Eliezer of Damascus. He was worried that since he had no son, this bondservant would end up with the inheritance. God calmed those fears and promised Abraham that his own son would receive the inheritance.

You will recall that, in Lesson 1, we learned that the Divine Family is designed for sons and not for bondservants; and that only divine sons are qualified to receive the divine family inheritance. This story illustrates this spiritual principle: *The inheritance of the Divine Father is reserved for his children, not His bondservants.* Eliezer of Damascus was Abraham's chief bondservant. No doubt he was dutiful, trustworthy and hardworking. Nevertheless, his identity caused him to be disqualified from inheriting the family blessing.

So it's not enough to be religious or devoted or faithful or dutiful or hardworking in Church. It's not enough to be a good worker. We've got to have the right identity. We've got to be a 'free-born son' and not a 'bondservant' in our mind. If you find that you are living under the cloud of mental bondage, and seeing God as your Master and not as your Divine Father, you have excluded yourself from the spiritual inheritance which the Divine Father has reserved for His sons. Identity determines treatment.

◙ ISHMAEL, THE SON OF THE BONDWOMAN: Now Ishmael, the son of the bondwoman, was in a curious position in Abraham's house.

His position was somewhat different from that of the chief bondservant Eliezer of Damascus.

To Eliezer of Damascus, Abraham was only *'master'*; but to Ishmael, Abraham was both *'master and father'*. Ishmael was in a position of being both a bondservant and a son. Since the bondwoman was Ishmael's mother, Ishmael was a bondservant; but since Abraham was Ishmael's father, Ishmael could be considered as a son. So Ishmael's identity was mixed; *part bondservant and part son.* As a result of this, he too was excluded from the family inheritance.

Ishmael's position illustrates the state of mind of a man who tries to see God as his Master while at the same time seeing God as his Father. As was said before, these two states of mind cannot coexist. Ishmael was also disqualified from receiving the family inheritance, just like Eliezer of Damascus. If you have the mentality of God's bondservant mixed in with the mentality of God's son, then you are like Ishmael. You don't know whether God is 'Master' or 'Father' to you. In your mind, He is a bit of both. This inner conflict will block you from receiving the natural and spiritual inheritance reserved for the sons of the Divine Family.

▣ ISAAC, THE SON OF THE FREEWOMAN: Now Isaac, the son of Sarah the freewoman, had no inner conflict. He had no connection to Egypt or to slavery or to the bondwoman. Abraham was in no way his master. Abraham was his loving, doting father and nothing else. Isaac did not have a mixed identity in Abraham's house. Isaac had a single identity: **The Son of the Father.** As a result, Isaac was the only one qualified to be Abraham's heir. This reminds us of a verse we read in Lesson 1: *"And because you are sons, God has sent forth the Spirit of His Son into your hearts, crying, 'Father, our Father'. Wherefore you are no longer a slave, but a son. And since you are a son, you are an heir of God through Christ."* *(Galatians 4:6-7)*

This story therefore illustrates the truth that in order for us to receive our Divine Family inheritance of "all things" (which we will study at Level 2), it is essential to be in a *'Father-son'* relationship with God. This is to be our only relationship with Infinite God. Our sole identity in the Divine Family is to be *'the son of the Divine Father'*. When we have this single identity, it will be our Father's good pleasure to give us the Kingdom. (Luke 12:32)

Eliezer, Ishmael and Isaac were all in a relationship with Abraham, but only Isaac was in right relationship with Abraham where the inheritance was concerned. Similarly, it's not enough for us to be in a relationship with God. Rather, we ensure that we are in right relationship, in a Father-son relationship, with God.

The Parable of Abraham, the Bondwoman and the Freewoman

Now let's dig a little deeper. At a basic level of meaning, this episode in the life of Abraham is an ancient story of family drama. However within this story there are more hidden spiritual principles. As was said before, this story of Abraham and the people in his house is actually a parable. A parable is a story in which ordinary, natural people, objects and events are used as symbols to illustrate high spiritual truth.

Now here's one of the deep secrets of the Bible which every seeker of truth should always remember: From the Book of Genesis to the Book of Revelation, the entire Bible is written in the language of parables. Every story in the Bible is in fact a parable illustrating spiritual truth. Also, every person in every story in the Bible is a symbol which represents you, or some aspect or facet of you. Even the landscape in these stories, (the hills, mountains, valleys, rivers); all represent you or some aspect of you. *You are in every story in the Bible.* So the Bible isn't just telling you about some ancient people and faraway places; it's actually revealing to you the truth about you. So, let's examine this episode in Abraham's life from that level of meaning.

▣ THE HIGHER MEANING OF ABRAHAM & ABRAHAM'S HOUSE: *'Abraham'* in this story is a symbol which represents *you*. The *'Promised*

Land' represents all the mental territory which is given to you by The Infinite and is yours for the taking. Abraham's 'house' represents *your mind*. Ultimately, Abraham was in control of his house just as you are in control of your mind. Abraham had the right to choose who could or could not stay in his house. Similarly, you have the right to choose what ideas can or cannot stay in your mind. The people in Abraham's house represent different facets of your mind. Let's examine them.

◙ THE HIGHER MEANING OF ELIEZER OF DAMASCUS: Eliezer of Damascus, the chief bondservant in Abraham's house, represents *your natural mind* (your intellect). This is the area of your mind which you use to conduct your mundane tasks which are necessary for everyday life. This area of your mind is useful and necessary, and it serves you well. Over time, you have learned to rely on it and trust it to do your bidding. However, this 'Eliezer mind' is natural, and it cannot inherit the divine promises of God which operate in the spiritual. This is why the Bible tells us: *"The **natural man** (i.e. the natural mind, the intellect) **cannot receive** the **things** of the **Spirit of God** for they seem foolish to him: neither can he **know** them because they are **spiritually discerned."** (1st Corinthians 2:14).* So even though your natural mind (your intellect) is necessary and helpful, you cannot allow it to dominate your life. It is a servant to you, and must never rule you.

◙ THE HIGHER MEANING OF THE TWO WOMEN IN ABRAHAM'S HOUSE: The two women in Abraham's house, Hagar his Egyptian bondwoman and Sarah his wife, the freewoman, represent *two opposite mentalities in your mind;* two opposite ways of thinking. Hagar represents *Mental Captivity,* and Sarah represents *Mental Freedom.* Let's analyze each individually.

◙ THE HIGHER MEANING OF HAGAR: Hagar the Egyptian slave-woman represents *the state of mind of Mental Captivity to world system thinking* which you acquired. Abraham acquired the bondwoman Hagar in Egypt. Throughout the Bible, 'Egypt' is used as a symbol to represent 'the world system'.

Notice that Hagar the slave-woman was *not* the original lady in Abraham's house. Sarah the freewoman was living with him first. Abraham later *acquired* Hagar during his bad experiences in Egypt and took her into his house. This indicates that the state of mind of Mental Captivity is *not* our original state of mind. We *acquired* that negative state of mind from the programing which we received in the world system. By conforming to the world system, Mental Captivity moved into our 'house'. It took up residence in our mind. Abraham allowed Hagar the bondwoman to take up residence in his 'house'. Similarly, we allowed Mental Captivity to world system thinking to take up residence in our minds. Even if we are now mentally free, we all allowed the bondservant's mentality to take up residence in our minds. At some point, we let 'Hagar' move in to our 'house'.

◙ THE HIGHER MEANING OF SARAH: Now let's look at Sarah the freewoman, Abraham's wife. What does she represent? Sarah represents *the state of mind of Mental Freedom from world system thinking.* This state of mind was with Abraham (i.e. with you) from the very beginning. It has no links or ties to being a slave to sin. It did not originate in 'Egypt', (the world system). It is not under any form of bondage. It is therefore free from the bondservant's mentality.

Notice that Sarah, who represents Mental Freedom, was the original lady in Abraham's house; for Sarah was living in Abraham's house long before Hagar moved in. This indicates that *the state of mind of Mental Freedom is our original state of mind.* We came to Earth in a state of Mental Freedom. Afterwards, we acquired the mentality of the world system, and Mental Captivity then moved into our mental 'house'. This is why the Bible teaches the **'renewing** of our mind' which means *'making our mind as new as it was originally'*. To renew the mind is to bring the mind back to its original state of Mental Freedom.

◙ THE HIGHER MEANING OF THE TWO BOYS: *Both the bondwoman and the freewoman produced sons for Abraham; both gave birth.* This indicates that both the state of mind of Mental Captivity and the state of mind of Mental Freedom will produce or give birth to experiences in your life. Both states of mind will produce 'sons' (i.e. manifestations). Both states of mind will manifest themselves, first in your thinking and then in your experiences. *Both women produced sons when Abraham entertained them.* Any state of mind that you entertain, that you link your life force with, that you take pleasure in will produce 'sons' in your life (i.e. will produce the outward manifestations of your inner thoughts and feelings).

Trouble began in Abraham's house when both the bondwoman and the freewoman produced sons. Similarly, serious trouble begins for a Christian when both 'the bondservant sinner mentality' and 'the mentality of being free from sin' are manifesting at the same time. These are two opposite states of mind which are, at the same time, manifesting two opposite ways of thinking, acting and being. That's a recipe for inner conflict.

Now, notice that the bondwoman Hagar moved into Abraham's house *last,* long after he married and was living with Sarah, the original lady in his house. Nevertheless, the bondwoman birthed her child *first,* but it was not the child of God's choosing. Similarly, Mental Freedom is the State of Mind which you brought with you when you were born on Earth. Mental Freedom is your *original state of mind*; it is your 'Sarah', the original lady in your mental house. Mental Captivity to world system thinking is an acquired state of mind. It is your 'Hagar' which moved into your mind *last.*

Mental Captivity to world system thinking is *not* your original State of Mind. Nevertheless, just like Hagar, Mental Captivity became productive in your life *first,* while Mental Freedom, your 'Sarah', was still barren and unproductive. The experiences which your 'Hagar' produced in your life were not God's promise for you. Nevertheless, just like Hagar in the parable, your mentally captive state of mind became haughty, because it was productive in your life while your divine, spiritual aspect (your 'Sarah') was not productive. The mentally captive state of mind will always disdain and despise spiritual things and will try to exalt itself over the divine state of mind. This is why some men who are complete captives of world system thinking will despise spiritual things as being 'silly' or 'foolish' or 'not producing anything worthwhile'. It is 'Hagar' exalting herself and despising barren 'Sarah'.

The freewoman Sarah birthed her child **last,** *but this was the child of God's promise, the child with no links to slavery, the child to whom the inheritance belonged.* Similarly, Mental Freedom (which is your original State of Mind) becomes productive in you last; long after Mental Captivity produced its misguided manifestation. However, Mental Freedom produces in you "the Mind of Christ" which then manifests outwardly in your experiences. The Mind of Christ is the divine way of thinking which Mental Freedom produces. Mental Freedom produces New Ideal Ideas. Old things are passed away and all things become new. Even though the Mind of Christ is manifested *last* after your years of living with what Mental Captivity produced, it is the Mind of Christ in you which will inherit and enjoy the best that God has promised for you. Do you see the parallel?

As soon as these two sons started living together in Abraham's house, conflict ensued. Similarly, inner conflict will begin in the mind of any man who tries to have Mental Freedom working within him while still clinging to Mental Captivity and to all that it has produced in his life.

Now, when the time came that both Sarah and God demanded that Abraham throw the bondwoman and her son out of his house, Abraham was distressed and grieved. He didn't want to do it. It felt like a loss to him. Similarly, as you read this book and come to the realization that you are required to give up every trace of the bondservant's mentality, and give up seeing God as your Master, and give up every thought of seeing yourself as some type of a 'sinner', you may feel distressed and grieved. It may feel like a loss to you initially. However, the only things you are losing are the mental restraints which are holding you back from fully expressing the divine image.

You once lived completely by the dictates of world system thinking and the desires which it produced. You missed the mark of God's ideal for you. You were giving attention to and entertaining 'sin', entertaining your 'Hagar'. You were attached to your 'Ishmael', attached to all that 'sin' manifested in you. Meanwhile, your free, divine, original State of Mind, your 'Sarah', remained dormant and unproductive. It was in the background and you paid no attention to it. However, once you started to give attention to and consciously entertain your spiritual aspect, then that Mental Freedom, the 'Sarah' in you, became productive. A new life was manifested. After years of doting on 'Ishmael', 'Isaac' was born in your 'house'. After years of spiritual barrenness, the promised manifestation of Mental Freedom is born in your life experience.

This parable is telling us that once Mental Freedom becomes productive and we begin to gravitate towards spirituality, we are required to give up completely the old State of Mind which was enslaved to 'sin', the old State of Mind which is a captive to world system thinking, the old State of Mind which is used to having a master, the old State of Mind which is opposite to the divine mind in us and which is locked into the bondservant's mentality. We are also required to give up all the outward expressions which this captive State of Mind has produced in our life. The bondwoman and her son must go.

Trouble starts when we don't get rid of that old way of thinking, that old identity which tells us that God is our Master and that we are some kind of a 'sinner'. We will have internal conflicts when we refuse to evict from our mind everything which opposes the divine in us. We will have wars within. It will be 'hell' in our 'house'.

You can be a man with a bondservant's mentality and still be in a relationship with God. (After all, there is a relationship between master and bondservant). However, you cannot be a man with a bondservant's mentality and be in right relationship with God.

Make a choice

Now, for a time Abraham allowed both women and both boys to live in his house. He was hoping that in time they would all get along. However, the more time passed the worse things got. Abraham was resistant to change. He refused to choose between Ishmael and Isaac. Things came to a head when the bondwoman's child started to mock the promised child. Sarah then insisted that Abraham cast out the bondwoman and her son, and God agreed with Sarah.

Similarly, when Mental Freedom produces the Mind of Christ in you, it is born out of your higher awareness that you are a divine son of God. The Mind of Christ proclaims that you are free from world system thinking just as Jesus Christ was free from world system thinking. If at that stage you do not evict from your mind the negative, world system thinking and the attitudes and behavior which it has produced, then those attitudes and behavior will rise up and mock the truth that you are a divine, free-born, spirit-son of God.

Have you ever wondered why a man who is a devoted, committed Christian, and who sincerely believes that he is a born again, saved, sanctified child of God, will still be calling himself unworthy, a sinner, a wretch, a worm, or a beggar? Clearly, there is a conflict in the mind. What is happening here? The thinking and attitudes which are produced by the bondservant's mentality are mocking and belittling the divine identity which Mental Freedom has produced in him. It's the very same thing that Ishmael did to Isaac. At some point in time, the 'Sarah' in his mind, (the State of Mind of Mental Freedom), has to rise up in him and say: *"Enough is enough. Get this bondservant's mentality and what it has produced completely out of your mind. Cast them out of your mental house!"* You see, over the years he has developed an attachment to seeing God as his Master. It feels like he is being humble when he sees himself this way; but it is a 'false humility', and he is required to evict it from his mind since he wants to be free to truly **be** like Christ.

Sarah was grieved when she saw Isaac being mocked by the bondwoman's son. So she told Abraham: "Throw out this bondwoman and her child, because the son of the bondwoman cannot share the family inheritance with the free-born son". And God agreed with Sarah. Sarah represents Mental Freedom calling to you to throw out of your mind the Mental Captivity to world system thinking and every idea it has produced in your life.

Remember, 'Abraham' in the parable represents you and 'Sarah' represents 'Mental Freedom from world system thinking'. Just as God promised Abraham and Sarah that they would have a son who would inherit the 'Promised Land', God has promised that you and Mental Freedom would produce a 'son', *i.e. a 'manifestation of divine sonship'.* That 'son', that manifestation of divine sonship, will inherit the promises of God. God has given you vast mental territory, but the bondservant's mentality and its manifestation can't receive it. Your Father wants to give you the Kingdom, but He's waiting on you to set your 'house' in order. This is your hour of decision. Reading this book and even agreeing with the principles in it will be of no help to you unless you decide, once and for all, to let go of the old way of seeing yourself, and unless you actually do it.

Now at this point someone may say: *"Wasn't Sarah the one who urged Abraham to have a child with the bondwoman? What is the meaning of that in the parable?"* The Bible records that Sarah, feeling frustrated that she and Abraham were childless, *urged* Abraham to have a child with Hagar, the bondwoman. *(Genesis 16:1-4)* This tells us that the true nature of every man is to be creative in some way, for our divine Father is a Creator and we are created in the divine image. God's plan for every man is that he should create in harmony with the divine nature and in accordance with Divine Right Order. However, if our divine, spiritual nature (our 'Sarah') is barren and is not in productive mode, that 'freewoman' (that freedom to create), will still urge us to express our creativity somehow. Unfortunately, whatever we create at that time is not going to come from our divine nature. So, we will tend to create in ways which are contrary to God's best for us. For example, a man with an exceptional singing voice or a gift for music may feel the urge to create music which glorifies the world system; or a man with high intelligence and exceptional leadership ability may feel the urge to create a gang and become a gang leader. Without an active and productive divine nature, their God-given creative abilities will harmonize with world system thinking. This parable of Abraham's life teaches us that our freedom to create must always be exercised in harmony with the divine nature and in accordance with Divine Right Order, or else trouble will follow.

Being single-minded

Whatever the Mental Captivity produces in your life, it will mock and belittle and scorn what the mentality of Mental Freedom produces in you. It will mock the divine in you just as Ishmael mocked Isaac. This is why the Bible warns us that it is dangerous to be double-minded. What does this mean? A double-minded man is someone who has two opposite states of mind (one of freedom and one of captivity) residing within him, in a fight for supremacy and in a battle to control his life. One minute he says, *"I am a son of God"* and the next minute he says, *"I am unworthy of the least of God's mercies".*

What does the Bible say about such a man? It says: *"...Any man who wavers is like a wave of the sea driven with the wind and tossed. **Such a man should not expect to receive anything** [i.e. any 'thing'] **from the Lord**. A double-minded man is unstable in all his ways."* (James 1:6-8) Faith is the substance of 'things' expected. However, we have just read that the double-minded man should not expect to receive any 'thing' from the Lord. Why is this so? It's because his State of Mind is unstable. He cannot form a solid expectation of any good 'thing'. Faith can see nothing fixed and positive in him to support.

What is the solution? The double-minded man has to become single-minded. He has to choose once and for all the mentality of a divine son of God. He has to get rid of the mentality of being God's bondservant, and all the thoughts that this mentality has produced in him. He has to stop seeing God as his Master and stop believing that he is some kind of a sinner. He has to cut ties with world system thinking. Just like Abraham threw out the bondwoman and her son, every man has to throw out the Mental Captivity and all the ideas and attitudes it has produced. The two opposite mentalities of freedom and captivity will never harmonize. They will never agree. Our WORD FOR TODAY asks us a serious question: *"Can two walk together except they are in agreement?"* The answer is *'No'*.

Cast out the mocker

The bondwoman's boy was seen 'mocking' the promised son. As we know, the Old Testament in the Bible was translated from the Hebrew language to the English language centuries ago. In the Hebrew language, that word which is translated as *'mocking'* literally means *'laughing out loud in scorn and derision'*. Thoughts born out of mental captivity to world system thinking, thoughts born out of the mentality which you picked up during your sojourn in the world system, will mock the divine in you. These thoughts will create disharmony, instability and conflict in your mind. They will tell you that you are a fool to trust Infinite God, and that you would be smarter to follow the ways of the world.

However, Proverbs 22:10 gives the solution. It says: *"Throw out the mocker, and discord will leave; yes, strife and insults will end."* Whenever thoughts born out of mental bondage arise in your mind, (thoughts of inferiority and insecurity; thoughts of you being any type of sinner; thoughts of unworthiness; thoughts of being 'not good enough'; thoughts of self-condemnation, thoughts of self-criticism; thoughts of separation from God), you have the absolute right to use your inner conversation and tell them in no uncertain terms: *"Get out of my house! Get out of my mind! Get out of my life!"*

You can never be higher than 'son of God'

When Abraham's house was in chaos and conflict, there arose a rivalry for privileged positions among the people in the house. No doubt for many years Eliezer was sure he would get the inheritance. Then Hagar and Ishmael believed the inheritance would be theirs. Next, Sarah believed that the inheritance would be shared by her and Isaac.

In liberating our mind to the point where we feel free to live as a son of the true and living God, there is one thing to watch out for in the Church, and that is *rivalry for religious positions.* This rivalry will show up wherever the bondservant's mentality is present.

If you are a Christian, feel free to check yourself. Are you anxious about being promoted in your church group? Do you take glory in wearing special garments as a sign of your religious status? Do you crave lofty religious titles? Do you look down upon Christians who do not have such titles? Are you envious when other people are promoted or celebrated in your church? Do you feel offended if people do not address you by your correct religious title? Do you feel offended if you are not given a prominent seat in the church building? If you answered *'Yes'* to any of these questions, the bondwoman and her son are still relaxing on a comfortable sofa somewhere in your mind. It's time to throw them out. It's time to tell them: 'Get out of my house!'

Sons of God know that wherever and in whatever capacity they serve in the family of God, they are the sons of God giving service in their Father's house. The welfare of the Divine Family is their highest priority. True Humility is the hallmark of the sons of God. They are interested in promoting God's agenda, not their own. They are focused on promoting the interests of the Divine Family and not their own personal position. Always remember this: *There is no title or position which is higher than* ***'son of God'.*** When you are fully conscious and aware that you are a beloved, divine, free-born, spirit-son of God, you have truly arrived. There is no promotion which can place you higher than this. There is no recognition more awesome than being recognized by your Divine Father as His beloved son. There is no greater honor than to know your Spirit-Father and to be known by Him. Therefore, if you have a religious title or position, or if you are assigned one in future, always be mindful to keep it in proper perspective.

All debts are paid

While Hagar the bondwoman and her son were living in Abraham's house, Sarah was in discomfort. The bondwoman was a constant reminder of Egypt and of the negative experiences that occurred there. The bondwoman's son was a reminder of Sarah's years of barrenness. Make sure that Mental Freedom, your 'Sarah', is comfortable in your mind. You do that by letting go every trace of the memory of 'Egypt', every memory of 'sin' and what happened in the past. Resist the temptation to rehash the negatives of the past. The Bible says: *"If any man is **in Christ** (i.e. in the Divine, Ideal Self), he is a new creation. Old things are passed away. Look! All things are become new." (2nd Corinthians 5:17)*

You are an original son of God with an original state of Mental Freedom. Then you got mixed up with the world system. In your thinking, you became a captive servant to the world system because you had no idea of your true identity. You became something that originally you were not; you became a slave to 'sin'. You 'missed the mark' of your true ideal self. However, 'sin' could only control your actions temporarily; but it could not change your identity as a son of God. 'Sin' blocked your *fellowship* with God but it could not change your *eternal family relationship* with God. You have always been God's son. (We will study this truth deeply from the Bible at Level 2 of this Men's Bible Study.) 'Sin' could only dominate while the divine image of God in you was temporarily dormant, unproductive and in the background. However, 'sin' did not and could not remove the divine image of God from you. Your 'Hagar' could not throw your 'Sarah' out of your 'house'.

We all toiled and labored in the world system as servants to 'sin', and 'sin' paid us slave wages. The Bible says: *"The wages paid by sin is 'death'* (i.e. separation from our fellowship with God), *but the gift of God is 'eternal life'* (i.e. eternal oneness with God), *[and that gift was given to us] through Jesus Christ our Lord" (Romans 6:23).* How did He do it? When He was crucified on the cross of Calvary, Jesus Christ paid the full price to buy all of us back from the world system. All debts are paid. *"He was wounded for our transgressions. He was crushed for our sins. The punishment that brought us peace fell upon Him, and by His scourging we were healed." (Isaiah 53:5)* You may be wondering: 'Why would Jesus do this for me?' The answer is: *Because you are family to Him.* You may also be wondering: 'Jesus died more than two thousand years ago. How could his death have any effect on my life?' The answer is: *His death was physical but it had spiritual implications which are timeless.* (We will study this at Level 2).

The mental conditioning of the world system had blinded your mind to your true spiritual identity and had held you captive in your understanding of yourself. The knowledge of your true identity, which you instinctively had at birth, was gradually stripped from you in the world system. Its mental programing had impoverished you spiritually by robbing you of your spiritual birthright. It had oppressed you with heavy mental burdens which you had no need to carry. Jesus Christ came to reveal to you your true identity so you could be free to be like Him. He started His earthly ministry by announcing His Mission Statement. He said: *"The Spirit of the Lord is upon Me, because He has anointed Me to preach the Good News to the poor. He has sent me to proclaim freedom to the captives, and the recovery of sight to the blind; to set free those who are oppressed..." (Luke 4:18)*

Once you know the truth that you are a divine, free-born, spirit-son of God, that the divine inheritance is yours by divine right, and that you are in the Divine Family forever, you will feel free. You will no longer be a bondservant to sin or to God. That old way of thinking which has kept you restricted in your fellowship with God will be gone forever, and truth will take its place. Your spiritual amnesia will disappear. You will remember who you truly you are and who you have always been: *a son of Infinite God.*

Freedom is a State of Mind

Now, here's the key to victory. As strange as this may sound, you don't need to be free from anything and you don't need to fight anything and conquer anything in order to be free. You don't need to fight and conquer 'sin', or your past, or any weakness, situation, habit or enemy. As long as you see yourself as needing to be free from something, you will be bound, trapped, restricted and controlled by it. You are not free unless your mind is free. As long as you are fighting against and trying to conquer something, you are giving your attention, your focus, your strength, your mental energy and your power to it, and making it stronger. The only power your so-called enemy has over you is the power that you choose to give to it.

When you fight against something because you are *trying* to be free, it's like you are fiercely pushing with all your might, trying to open a door which is clearly marked "PULL". The harder you push, the more resistance you feel. The door to freedom, which is actually unlocked, will remain closed to you. Until you stop pushing, you will never open the door, and until you stop fighting, you will never realize that you are already free. *You can't win by fighting.* If you have ever watched a wrestling match, you have noticed how tightly locked together the wrestlers' bodies are. This tells you that you can't get free from something by wrestling with it.

Here's something to remember: As long as you are mentally in 'fighting mode', your life will be a battleground; and you will feel as if you are always under attack. When you are in fighting mode, you are telling Life: *"Give me someone or something to fight"*; and without a doubt, your request will be granted. Therefore, if you have a fighting, warrior mentality, it is like a magnet drawing toward you adverse circumstances, opposition, hostility, enemies and attacks. When natural enemies are not enough of a challenge, you will be given mental and spiritual enemies to fight.

Freedom is a state of mind. You don't have to fight against anything in order to be free. There is nothing for you to conquer. On the cross, Jesus did all the 'conquering' which was necessary. So, if you have been fighting or wrestling with anything, please know that these are self-defeating activities. Rather, relax, let go and use the Mind Renewal Technique to totally focus your mind on *Good* only. What is the highest Ideal that you can imagine for yourself? Focus on that Ideal and give no thought to anything else. Tune your mind to a higher frequency of thought and expectation, and keep your thoughts on that higher height by expecting only the best. Just as an aircraft soars high enough that it flies above all turbulence, similarly allow your thoughts to rise and remain above all ideas of opposition.

Notice that when Abraham cleared from his house the bondwoman and the son she had produced, all opposition ended and there was peace in the house. The persons left in Abraham's house were Eliezer, Sarah and Isaac. Similarly, when you clear from your mind the Mental Captivity to world system thinking and ideas which that mentality has produced, all opposition will cease and there will be peace in your mind. The only things which will remain with you are your Intellect (Eliezer), Mental Freedom (Sarah) and the promised Mind of Christ which Mental Freedom produces (Isaac). Do you see it?

You will not be truly free until your mind is free. Your mind is *not* free if you are fighting. Once you know the truth of your Divine Identity as 'The son of the Father', you will be free. You will walk in victory. You will never again see yourself as a bondservant to anyone or to anything.

Freedom is your original position. You need only be conscious and aware that you are a son in the Divine Family. Freedom was there all along, you just needed to be more aware of it. (We will study more about this at Level 2.) A man will sit in the mental prison created by his own ideas and his own self-image, until he becomes consciously aware that the prison doors are open and that he is free to leave at any time. He was always free to walk out of that prison; he just wasn't aware of his freedom. So you don't have to earn or buy or seek or find or fight for freedom. Just become consciously aware of the truth of your Divine Identity, and never again accept an inferior definition of yourself.

The Mirror Secret of the Bible

Now, since you have read as far as this, it demonstrates that you are serious about transforming rather than conforming. So let's now investigate one of the very deep secrets of the Bible. It is guaranteed that when you understand this secret, you will never again ask these questions: "Why do some scriptures in the Bible seem to contradict other Biblical scriptures?" or "Why are there so many different interpretations of the scriptures?" or "Why are there so many disputes among Christians about what the Bible says and means?"

Here is the explanation of *The Mirror Secret of the Bible*. Please pay close attention to it because we will be referring to it in the Lessons which follow:

The Bible is like a mirror. The state of mind of the man who is reading the Bible will always be reflected back to him through his understanding and interpretation of the scriptures he reads. Whatever scriptures you gravitate towards whenever you read the Bible, and the way in which you interpret those scriptures, these things will reveal to you who you are and what your state of mind is. When you look into the 'mirror' of the Bible, your state of mind will be reflected back at you. (Please read these statements a second time before moving on. Let them sink in.)

What does this mean? It means that whenever you read the Bible, the scriptures which represent, support and reflect your current state of mind will 'jump out' at you. They will catch and hold your attention. You will be 'blind' to all scriptures which do not support your current state of mind. Even if you read them, they will slip from your memory. Also, whatever scripture you read in the Bible, you will interpret it in such a way that it will match and reinforce your current state of mind.

Every man who looks into a mirror sees himself. The Bible is like a mirror. It reflects the state of mind of the reader back to himself. Millions of people, some with positive states of mind and some with negative states of mind, are reading and interpreting the Bible. Therefore, of necessity, there are verses in the Bible to represent, support and *reflect* every state of mind, whether positive or negative; for the Bible is a *'mirror'*. This is why there are so many different interpretations of scriptures. This is why all 'Bible-believing' Christians do not see eye-to-eye. This is why there are so many conflicting beliefs in religion, all claiming to be based on the Bible.

For example, there are Bible verses which can be used to promote *love,* and others which can be used to justify *hatred.* If your state of mind holds a belief in *war* or a belief in *peace*; a belief in *compassion* or a belief in *condemnation*; a belief in *mercy* or a belief in *punishment*; a belief in *forgiveness* or a belief in *revenge*; a belief in *respect for life* or a belief in *disregard for life*; a belief in *freedom* or a belief in *captivity*; *prosperity* or *poverty*; *ease* or *hardship*; *robust health* or *physical suffering*; *racial equality* or *racial prejudice*; the *equality of women with men* or the *inferiority of women*; your *oneness with God* or your *separation from God*; the *'son of God' Identity* or the *'sinner' Identity*; whatever beliefs your state of mind holds, you will find them reflected in the Bible when you read it. These are *not* contradictions in scripture. There is something in the Bible to reflect every state of mind whether positive or negative. That's how the 'mirror' works.

If you choose high-frequency thoughts of love, joy, peace, power, health, faith and oneness with God as a divine son of God, and if you accept these as your absolute truth, then this is what you will see reflected back at you when you read the Bible. By contrast, if you choose low-frequency thoughts of fear, hatred, suffering, stress, helplessness, punishment, anger, sickness, guilt, shame, unworthiness, condemnation, separation from God and servitude to God as God's bondservant, and if you accept these as your absolute truth, then this is what you will see reflected back at you when you read the Bible. It can be heaven in your mind or it can be hell in your mind. You can live with heaven in you or you can live with hell in you. It's all up to you.

There is something in the Bible to reflect every state of mind. This explains why the writers of some of the Epistles in the New Testament refer to themselves as 'slaves' or 'bondservants' (depending on what the version of the Bible you are reading), and why these same writers refer to themselves as the 'sons' or the 'children' of God. Readers of the Bible who have the bondservant's mentality will gravitate towards the verses which reflect the bondservant's mentality; but readers of the Bible who have the son of God mentality will gravitate towards the verses which reflect the son of God mentality. The mirror of the Bible always reflects back to us whatever is our predominant state of mind.

Therefore, as soon as we upgrade our state of mind, we will start to see truth in the Bible which we have never seen before. It's the same Bible which we have been reading for years; it's the same 'mirror' into which we are looking. However, it is now giving us a different reflection of who we are because we have changed. In our thinking, we have been transformed from 'bondservant' to 'son of God' by the renewing of our mind. So the 'mirror' starts showing us a different reflection. When we get to Level 3, we will investigate this truth further.

Looking into the Mirror

Let's look at what the Bible itself says about this 'mirror' in James 1:23-25: *"Any man who just listens to the Word and does not do what it* *says, is like a man **staring at his natural face in a mirror. He looks at himself** and walks away and immediately forgets **what type of man he is.***

*But if you **look intently** into THE PERFECT LAW WHICH SETS YOU FREE, and you **keep on looking**, not being a man who just hears and then forgets, but **being a man who does the work required**, you will be blessed in all the work that you do."* (Please read this passage of scripture a second time before moving on. Let it sink in.)

So, within the scriptures recorded in the Bible you will find verses which reflect every state of mind, both positive and negative. Whatever you gravitate towards when you read the Bible, and the way in which you interpret what you read, will reveal to you who you are and what your state of mind is. When you look into the 'mirror' of the Bible, your current state of mind will be reflected back at you. You will be *"looking at yourself"*.

If you are seeing a negative state of mind reflected back at you in the passages which you select from the Bible and in your interpretation of them, and if you forget the negativity in yourself which the 'mirror' has shown you, and you walk away, make no changes in yourself and refuse to renew your mind, you will never be free to be like Christ. That's the bad news.

The good news is that if, at present, you have a negative state of mind, you don't have to be held prisoner by it. Freedom is possible. That's because even though the Bible contains something to reflect every state of mind, it also contains something called *"The Perfect Law Which Sets You Free"* also known as *"The Perfect Law of Liberty"*. This law is a law of mind; it is a law of consciousness; it is a way of thinking which will liberate you from world system thinking. This law is also known as *The Mind of Christ*. This is the *divine mind;* the ideal state of mind which every son of God is empowered to express. It is the ultimate state of mind which elevates our thinking above world system thinking. The passage, which we have just read from the Book of James, tells us that in order to get the benefit of this perfect law of freedom of the mind, we must focus on this state of mind intently. Then we are required to do the work to renew our state of mind until it harmonizes with the state of mind of Mental Freedom. If we are willing to do the work, we will be blessed in the work that we do.

The word *"perfect"* in the verses which we have just read, is translated from a Greek word which means *'completeness of moral and mental character derived from work'*. It refers to *'maturity which comes after discipline and training'*. So this law of mind is actually the *Perfecting* Law of Liberty. Like fruit ripened to perfection, it will allow us to be spiritually mature, whole and complete in our moral and mental character if we put in the work required to discipline and train ourselves to think with the Divine Mind which is already in us. This is what the mirror is all about. God is not going to do the work for us.

Jesus Christ is described in Ephesians 4:13 as "the perfect man" meaning 'a man who perfectly embodies spiritual maturity and Self-Mastery and who lives in the fullness of the Ideal Self'. This is the true meaning of 'expressing the Divine Image'. The teaching of Jesus Christ was designed to bring His disciples to that same state of spiritual maturity, that same level of consciousness, that same Mind which He so perfectly embodied, that same level of divine wholeness and completeness. That is why His disciples called Him "Master".

People preach and teach from their State of Mind

Now that we have seen how the 'mirror' works, we understand that when any preacher or religious teacher reads the Bible, he will be drawn to passages and interpretations of those passages which reflect his current state of mind. Therefore every preacher will preach from *his state of mind* only. Every Bible teacher will teach what he sees in the Bible, looking through the lens of his own state of mind. Therefore, when listening to any preacher or religious teacher, remember to humbly depend on the Holy Spirit to show you what information to accept and what to reject.

Whenever you hear a preacher or a religious teacher, the first thing to do is to identify the State of Mind behind his or her words. Ask yourself as you listen: *'Is this speaker seeing God as 'Father' or as 'Master' or as a mixture of both? Does this speaker believe in fighting or fearing or fixing the world system? Am I listening to a Threat Promoter? Are these words taking me to the level of a son of God or are they making me comfortable with living at the level of God's human bondservant? Are these words promoting my oneness with God or my separation from 'God in the sky'? Are these the words of the Mind of Christ? Do these words feel right to my spirit? Can I detect the 'super Christian' mentality or the 'not good enough' mentality? Is love being served at this table?'* Then be sensitive to the answer you hear in your spirit.

This is not about criticizing, judging or condemning any preacher or religious teacher. It's about being selective as to what information you will and will not receive into your spirit. No son of God is required to indiscriminately accept *everything* spoken from behind a pulpit. You have the absolute freedom to get up from any table whenever love and truth are not being served there. So, don't be distracted by the speaker's popularity, or by his or her strong personal conviction or emotion, or by the large congregation, or by a flashy presentation. Rather, listen with the 'ears' of your divine spirit. *Your State of Mind is up to you regardless of what others do.* Your State of Mind is your responsibility, yours alone. If you don't deliberately select your thoughts and align your State of Mind with the Divine Mind, well-meaning people will be only too happy to mold you into their own image.

Transforming into God's image

If our State of Mind is not fully harmonized with the Mind of Christ, we will have a distorted image. In some ways we will be like

Christ, but in other ways we will not be like Him at all. We cannot truly walk with Christ unless our mind harmonizes with His Mind. *Two cannot walk together unless they are in agreement.* Let's feel free to throw out of our minds everything and anything which is not in harmony with the State of Mind of the Son of God.

Now, you may be wondering what you can do to ensure that you are molded into the image of Christ, and nobody else's. You may also be wondering how you will find *The Perfect Law Which Sets You Free* when you read the Bible.

The answer can be found in 2nd Corinthians 3:17-18. It says: *"Now the Lord is that Spirit: and **where the Spirit of the Lord is, there is freedom.** But we all, **with uncovered faces**, are seeing the glory of the Lord as if we are looking in a **mirror**, and we are **transformed into the same image** from one level of glory to a higher level of glory, even as by the Spirit of the Lord."* (Please read this passage of scripture a second time before moving on. Let it sink in.)

What is this passage of scripture telling us? It is telling us what will happen when we use the 'mirror' of the Bible correctly. Here's the process:

▣ SELECT YOUR IDENTITY: First and foremost, we upgrade our state of mind to the point where we see ourselves as a beloved, divine, free-born, spirit-son of God right now. We continue to make mental adjustments until we completely free ourselves from a bondservant's identity.

▣ LOOK IN THE 'MIRROR': Once our sole identity is 'beloved, divine, free-born spirit-son of God', then the matching state of mind will catch and hold our attention when we read the Bible. This high state of mind is what the 'mirror' of the Bible will reflect back to us, for the mirror will always reflect our chosen identity. We will be blind to everything else which does not match that identity.

▣ LET THE HOLY SPIRIT GUIDE YOU: Once our identity is 'beloved, divine, free-born, spirit-son of God', we become sensitive to anything which is opposite to the 'son of God' state of mind. The Holy Spirit will guide us as we sift through all the available states of mind in the Bible until we locate the Mind of Christ. If a character in the Bible is on track with the Mind of Christ, we will know; if they are off-track, we will know. We will become more and more discerning. We will also become more and more attracted to the passages in the Bible which clearly reflect the thinking of Christ. We will become focused, intently focused, on His way of thinking.

▣ RECLAIM YOUR ORIGINAL STATE OF MIND: We will adapt to this new way of thinking: The Perfect Law of Liberty. It will become the standard to which every thought in our mind is subject. The more we adapt to this law of mind, the more free we feel; and the more free we feel, the easier it is to be like Christ. This new way of thinking is not really new. It is the original state of mind which we brought with us when we were born on Earth. We will gravitate toward thoughts which are in harmony with our freedom to be like Christ, and we will drift away from world system thinking. When opposing thoughts arise in our mind, we will disown them and distance ourselves from them. The more we identify divine thinking and change our thoughts to match it, the more we will be transformed to be just like Christ from within. Our Character will follow our divine Identity. We will go through this process in detail at Level 2 of this Men's Bible Study.

▣ KEEP WALKING THE SPIRITUAL PATH: As we gradually conform to His image by the renewing of our mind, we will express one level of glory, and then a greater level of glory in our daily lives. Therefore, God has designed us for constant improvement, fruitfulness and increase as we live powerfully, masterfully and victoriously in this present world. This is not just in spiritual matters, but in all areas of our life. More and more of the Light of God in us will shine forth in all of our actions and activities.

▣ SEE YOURSELF AS GOD SEES YOU: The scripture says that we will begin to reflect the glory of the Son of God because *'our faces are uncovered'*. What does this mean? It means that by seeing ourselves as sons of God, we have removed from our faces the 'veil' and the 'mask' of the old inferior identity, that old state of mind. We are seeing ourselves clearly for the very first time. We do not see ourselves as 'sinners'. Rather, we see ourselves as what we are: beloved, divine, free-born spirit-sons of God, who at one time had sold ourselves out to become slaves to sin, but who are now reconciled to God. We once again have the fellowship with God which matches our eternal family relationship with God. We see ourselves as God sees us. We look beyond our natural bodies, beyond the earthly image, beyond the old identity shaped by our earthly past. We understand that we are more than physical, more than human, more than mere mortals. We recognize our true divine, spiritual identity. And when we see ourselves clearly, all we can see is the magnificence of the radiant glory of the divine image of the son of God.

The Eastern sage Rumi got a glimpse of this truth in his search for the Divine. He said: *When your heart is free from its ego and all its limitations then you will perceive the eternal Beloved One. It is not possible to see yourself without a mirror; so gaze at the Beloved One, for He is your brightest mirror.*

The Mind of Christ will speak in you

When men try to study the Bible without first seeing themselves as sons of God, they are confronted with all the available states of mind, both positive and negative, mixed together. Then they try to figure it all out, but some verses seem to contradict each other, and other verses are mysterious and make little sense. Then they get frustrated and say: 'Well, maybe this preacher or that Bible teacher can help me.' Then they gravitate to preachers and teachers who reinforce their current state of mind, and they are back to square one. Has this ever been your experience? However, when a man starts out by seeing himself as a beloved, divine, free-born spirit-son of God, he has indicated that he is interested in freedom. He has chosen to live as a divine son and not as a human bondservant in the Divine Family. He has chosen 'divine fellowship and service' over 'servitude'. Once he shows an interest in freedom, he immediately gets access to that Perfect Law of Freedom when he reads the Bible. Anyone who is content to remain in Mental Captivity is denied access to this Law when he reads the Bible.

When you connect with the thinking of Christ in His words, the Spirit of the Lord which gives you freedom to be like Him becomes activated. The passages in the Bible which reveal the Mind of the Son of God come alive. They jump out at you; they catch and hold your attention. They remain in your memory. Every other state of mind fades away. First, the words of freedom will begin to speak to you. Then as you continue to focus on them, you will hear them speaking in you, within your heart. Once divine truth finds a resting place within your heart, they transform your thinking so you can be free to be like Christ.

Now in case you are wondering: *'How will I understand what I read in the Bible? How will I know how to study the Bible effectively? How will I know that I am on the right track in my study? How will I get a clear understanding of the perfect Law which sets me free?'* These questions and many more will be answered in our next Lesson. See you then. Please read the Supporting Scriptures, the Affirmation and the Review which follow this Lesson.

Supporting Scriptures

1st Corinthians 15:45-49: "The first man Adam was made a living soul; the last Adam (i.e. Jesus Christ) *is a quickening Spirit* (i.e. a Spirit who brings someone back to life). *The spiritual man did not come first. The natural man was first, and afterwards came the spiritual man.*

The first man was of the earth, and so he was earthy. The second man is the Lord from heaven. Anyone who is merely earthy is just like that first earthly man. But those who are heavenly are just like the man from heaven. *And just as we have borne the image of the earthly man, we shall also bear the image of the heavenly man."*

2nd Corinthians 5:16-17: *"So from now on, we do not know anyone from a human point of view. And even though we used to think of Christ in that way, we do not know Him that way anymore. Therefore, anyone who is in Christ is a new creation. The former things have vanished. Look at this! All things are become new."*

Philippians 4:6: *"...The things that are true, the things that are worthy of respect, the things that are fair and just, the things that are pure, the things that are lovely and commendable, if something is excellent and praiseworthy, meditate on these things."*

Affirmation

My mind is a 'house' where my thoughts reside; a house which I control,
And I do not allow conflicting thoughts to harass and disturb my soul;
I refuse to be mocked and ridiculed by thoughts which are unkind,
I'm supposed to be free, because freedom is my original state of mind.

I refuse to be a double-minded man, with thoughts tossing to and fro;
So any thought, opposing my Father's plan, is a thought which has to go.
I've thrown out of my 'house' forevermore the bondservant's mentality,
I've thrown out every trace of servitude and mental captivity,
I've evicted all thoughts of self-abuse and insecurity,
And I've emptied out all the past mistakes which were stored in my memory.

I'm aligning my mind with the Mind of Christ, that Law of Liberty,
And the scriptures now mirror the glory of my Divine Identity.
I walk in the Light of the truth I know, this truth which has set me free:
I'm 'THE SON OF THE FATHER'; that's ALL I AM, a son in God's Family.

Review

Q. In this Lesson, what does Abraham represent and what does Abraham's

house represent?
A. Abraham represents 'you' and Abraham's house represents 'your mind'.

Q. In this Lesson, what do the freewoman Sarah and her son Isaac represent?
A. Sarah the freewoman produced Isaac. Sarah represents your original state of mind: *the state of mind of Mental Freedom.* Isaac represents everything which this state of mind produces.

Q. In this Lesson, what do the bondwoman Hagar and her son Ishmael represent?
A. Hagar the bondwoman produced Ishmael. Hagar represents *the state of mind of Mental Captivity.* This is *not* your original state of mind. It was acquired later, when you mentally conformed to the thinking of the world system. Ishmael represents everything that this state of mind produces.

Q. God promised that Abraham and Sarah that they would have a son, even though they were childless and advanced in years. He also promised that this son would inherit the Promised Land. What does that teach us?
A. It teaches that you (Abraham) and Mental Freedom from world system thinking (Sarah) will be able to produce a Manifestation of a new life (a son) which will inherit the promises of God. You will take all the mental territory which is freely given to you by God to enjoy. This promise will be fulfilled, even though for many years of your life the state of mind of Mental Freedom was dormant and unproductive in you.

Q. The bondwoman and her son could not live peacefully with the freewoman and her son in Abraham's house. There was conflict. What does this teach us?
A. It teaches us that Mental Captivity and Mental Freedom are opposite to each other. They will never agree. These opposite states of mind and all they produce cannot coexist peacefully in your mind.

Q. Abraham tried to get the boys and their mothers to coexist peacefully in his house. Can't I try to have these two states of mind coexist peacefully in my mind?

A. No. The same thing which happened in Abraham's house will happen in your mind. There will be conflict between freedom and captivity. So, choose one and reject the other. Do what Abraham did. Throw out the bondservant's state of mind and everything it has produced in your life and forever keep Mental Freedom and all it has produced. Only the 'son of God' mentality can inherit the promises of God, just as Isaac was the only child who could get the family inheritance. Be single-minded, not double-minded.

Q. After Abraham cast the bondwoman and her son out of his house, who were the people who remained in his house and what do they represent spiritually?

A. The only people who were left in his house were:

- Eliezer of Damascus his chief bondservant who represents *the natural mind* of a man (the intellect);

- Sarah his wife who represents *Mental Freedom*; and

- Isaac the promised son whom Sarah bore. Isaac represents everything which Mental Freedom produces. This is the part of us which will receive the divine inheritance which is reserved for the sons of God. This is 'the Mind of Christ'.

Q. Do I have to be free from anything and do I have to fight against anything in order to be free in my mind?

A. Freedom is your true state, your original state. It is your birthright as a divine being. Freedom is a state of mind. All you need to do is to become *consciously aware* that you are already free. Allow yourself to *feel* freedom in your mind and you will experience it in the physical world. *As long as you believe that you were born as a slave to sin, you will never experience freedom. Rather, come to know the truth that you were born free.* This may sound strange to you, but we will study this truth from the Bible at Level 2. You are a free-born son of God. When you wake up from spiritual amnesia, you will clearly remember who you are. As soon as you remember who you are, you will return to freedom, your original position.

Q. What is the highest title I can have?
A. The highest title is 'son of God'.

Q. What is the Mirror Secret of the Bible?
A. The Bible is like a mirror. The state of mind of the man reading the Bible will be reflected back to him through his understanding and interpretation of the scriptures.

Q. Why do I sometimes see verses in the Bible which seem to contradict other verses in the Bible?
A. The Bible works like a mirror reflecting the state of mind of anyone who reads it. Therefore there are verses in the Bible to reflect every state of mind, whether positive or negative.

Q. How will I know what is the truth?
A. Jesus said, 'I am...the truth' (John 14:6). Among all the states of mind in the Bible there is also to be found "the Mind of Christ". This is a "law of mind". It is a way of thinking also known as the *"perfect law which sets you free"* or *"the perfect law of liberty".* To find truth, endeavor to find the Mind of Christ in the Bible.

Q. How do I find the mind of Christ in the Bible?
A. First, you recognize Jesus Christ as the Son of God who came to teach us who we are by showing us who He is. Recognize that you are also a son of God. When you become *consciously aware* that you are a son of God, you develop 'the son of God state of mind'. This is the state of mind which will be reflected back to you when you read the Bible, and that state of mind is the Truth.

Q. What should I look out for when I listen to preachers or Bible teachers?
A. Always seek to discover the speaker's state of mind. Every person will preach or teach from his or her own state of mind, and that state of mind can be positive, negative or a mixture of both. Depend totally upon the Holy Spirit to guide you as to what to accept and what to reject. As you listen with the 'ears' of your divine spirit, ask yourself continually: Are these words helping me to live more fully as a son of God or are they keeping me shackled to a bondservant's mentality? Is my spirit comfortable listening to this? Does this feel right to my spirit? Do I hear the 'super Christian' mentality or the 'not good enough' mentality? Are love and truth being served here?

Lesson 4: Seeing with the eyes of an eagle

WORD FOR TODAY: "Then He opened their understanding that they might understand the scriptures."   (Luke 24:45)

The courage to transform

Let's recap a bit. In the previous Lesson, we saw that just as Abraham had to throw out the slave-woman and her child from his house, we are required to be rid of Mental Captivity and everything which it produces. We are free to cast out of our mind unceremoniously and without apology any thought which is opposite to the thinking of a son of God. This takes courage, but it can be done. The mentality of a beloved, divine, free-born son of God will never harmonize with the mentality of a bondservant. Two cannot walk together unless they are in agreement. A choice has to be made. Therefore, since we desire to be free to be like Christ, we are required to choose Mental Freedom and everything it produces. We are also required to dismiss from our thinking all traces of Mental Captivity and everything it produces.

We also examined together one of the deep secrets of the Bible: *the Bible is like a mirror reflecting back to the reader his own state of mind.* Therefore, every state of mind both positive and negative can be found in the Bible. The scriptures towards which we gravitate, and our understanding and interpretation of them, will reveal our current state of mind.

Within the Bible, mixed in with all the many and varied states of mind, there is also the Mind of Christ. The Mind of Christ is a way of thinking. It will lift us above world system thinking. The Bible teaches that if we focus intently on this Mind, and do the work which is required to change our thinking to match this way of thinking, we will be blessed in all the work we do. This also takes courage, but it can be done. Now let's continue from this point.

Looking with fresh eyes

Jesus Christ was not in favor of Mental Captivity to world system thinking. He was in favor of Mental Freedom. He taught us that when we know the Truth, the Truth would set us free from mental bondage. Nevertheless, many sincere men cling to mental bondage without ever being aware of what they are doing to themselves. One way in which they cling to mental bondage is the way in which they read, study and understand the scriptures recorded in the Bible. There is a way to read the Bible which will open and expand our mind; and there is a way to read the Bible which will close, lock and shackle our mind. So it is not enough to read or even to study the Bible. We are required to know how to *"rightly divide the word of truth" (2nd Timothy 2:15);* i.e. be able and willing to differentiate between the positive and negative states of mind reflected in the Bible.

Infinite God is a big God. We all have to expand our thinking since we want to think like The Infinite. Mind Expansion is the aim of the game. So, let's be willing to understand what we read in the Bible in a very broad sense. Let's be willing to see the big picture. We run into trouble when, as the saying goes, we get so focused on the individual threads that we can't see the tapestry. In this Lesson, we will understand how to see the scriptures with fresh eyes. We will be allowing ourselves a panoramic view of the scriptures, rather than confining ourselves to a narrow view.

The two openings

Jesus spent a lot of time teaching His disciples. In our WORD FOR TODAY, we read that Jesus *'opened their understanding'* so that they might understand the scriptures. Now this seems strange. The disciples of Jesus were Jews. They had been rigorously taught the scriptures from childhood and they had a good knowledge of the scriptures. Why then would Jesus need to open their understanding so they could understand the scriptures?

In order to answer this question, let's examine an event in the childhood of Jesus. The Bible tells us that when Jesus was twelve years old, He was having a discussion with the learned religious teachers in the Jewish temple at Jerusalem, concerning the meaning of the Old Testament scriptures. The Bible also tells us that He was listening to these teachers and asking them questions which they could not properly answer. He then answered those questions, *"...and all who heard Him were astonished at His **understanding** and answers." (Luke 2:47)* This story illustrates that even though the great teachers in the temple were versed in their *knowledge* of the scriptures, yet Jesus possessed a level of *understanding* of the scriptures which was broader and higher than theirs. A man can be very knowledgeable of the scriptures and be well-schooled in the Bible and still lack understanding. So this is why Jesus had to open the understanding of His disciples. He had to expand their thinking. Remember, Mind Expansion is the aim of the mental game.

As modern students of the scriptures, we all are required to allow our understanding to be opened (i.e. expanded); but then there's more. *We also allow the scriptures to be 'opened' to us,* so that we can see the higher meanings and patterns which are hidden within them. This is what Jesus did for the two men on the road to the village of Emmaus. Jesus opened the scriptures to them, and they were amazed. *(See Luke 24:27-32)*

This opening of our understanding and opening of the scriptures are performed by the Holy Spirit, the Great Spirit of Truth. Let us humbly ask the Holy Spirit for help; and let us be willing to accept and receive such 'openings'.

Going deeper; going higher

As was said before, the Holy Spirit is 'Spirit-God in action and in communication'. The Bible says that the Holy Spirit is the *"Spirit of Truth"* who will *"**guide** you into **all truth**" (John 16:13)*. There is truth; and then there is a higher dimension of spiritual understanding, known as 'All Truth', into which we are to be guided. If it were easy for anybody to find and to navigate the dimension of All Truth, no Guide would be required.

The Spirit of Truth will guide us into the dimension of All Truth, but only if we are first willing to admit that we are *completely ignorant* as to what the scriptures truly mean. Many people find this extremely difficult to do, especially if they have been reading and studying the Bible extensively for many years, and consider themselves to be well-versed in the scriptures. When we bear in mind that Truth is always unfolding and there is always more Truth to be known, we realize that there is *always* a higher level of Truth, of which we are now ignorant.

If you are willing to admit that you are completely and totally ignorant as to the true meaning of the scriptures, and you are willing to see more in the Bible than you have previously seen, then more will be revealed to you. However, if your Intellect says: *'I don't need to hear anything else on this scripture because I know what it means'*, or *'I've never heard this before and so it must be wrong'* or *'They don't teach it this way in my church so I'm going to reject it'*, then your understanding locks down, the Bible locks down, and you can understand no more than you already understand. Your study of the Bible is then limited to a rehearsal of past learning.

In order to advance spiritually, be willing to go beyond what your Intellect already understands. So, as we progress together in this Bible Study, there may be concepts presented which are new to you. All that is necessary is that you keep an open mind. Here's a tip: *Every time you read the Bible, read it as if you are reading it for the first time in your life.* Here's another tip: *Every time you read a passage or a verse from the Bible, even one with which you are very familiar, humbly ask the Holy Spirit: "What does this mean?"* Higher Truth will be revealed to you when you are ready to receive it. As the Eastern proverb says: *"When the student is ready, the teacher appears."*

Watching with eagle eyes

In this Lesson and the Lessons following, we will rise to a level of understanding which is higher than 'believing' and higher than 'knowing'. In these Lessons we will be *'Watching'*.

'Believing' is the lowest level of spiritual understanding. Your Beliefs can make you blind to the Truth. *'Knowing'* is a higher level of spiritual understanding than just 'Believing', as we have seen in a previous Lesson. *'Watching'* is an even higher level of understanding, where you get a panoramic view of the scriptures. *Watching* is how you navigate the dimension of All Truth.

In *Watching,* your mind expands and becomes clear and open as the sky: without form, without boundaries, without preconceived notions and without any emotional attachments to what you already believe. In *Watching*, you are *not* trying to prove or validate the beliefs which you already have. You simply desire to know the whole truth, whatever the whole truth may be.

If a man's mind has room to receive new information then more will be given to him. The more his mind expands, the more information will be given to him by the Holy Spirit. This is one reason why Mind Expansion is the aim of the mental game. However, if a man is convinced that whatever he already believes, about any subject in the scriptures, is *all* the truth that is available on that subject, how can more ever be given to him? If he rejects information because he thinks that he already knows what the scripture means, then he is someone whose mind is full. There is no room in his mind to receive more information. All that he will be able to receive is a duplicate of his current level of understanding.

So here are some suggestions: In studying the Bible at the level of Watching, be willing to detach yourself and stand at a distance from whatever you are seeking to understand. If you are too close to it emotionally, you won't see it clearly. So, when you start to see more truth in the scriptures, if at that moment you begin to feel fear, or uncertainty, or anxiety, or anger because your beliefs are being challenged, it is a signal that you are too emotionally invested. Since you desire to watch, develop a willingness to examine all information dispassionately. You are required to be calm and clear-minded in order to see All Truth.

When you relax and allow your understanding to expand, you begin to feel a sense of lightness and openness. You begin to soar above narrow interpretations of the scriptures. You rise above mental conditioning, above religious conflicts, above rigid, traditional interpretations, and most importantly, you rise above what you already believe. You begin to see into that dimension of understanding which Jesus referred to as 'All Truth'. Then you begin to realize that All Truth is far more expansive than what you presently hold as 'truth'. In Watching, your awareness opens. There is no new truth; there is just new awareness of the truth that was there all along. Light is shed on the scriptures.

So, Watching gives us a panoramic view of the scriptures. We are seeing as it were through the eyes of a soaring eagle, but at the same time we are still able to perceive minute distinctions. We begin to see patterns, templates and connections in the scriptures which we had never seen before. We gain increased awareness of the infinite nature of God and how vast and powerful The Infinite is. We stop seeing God and life merely from an earthly, human perspective or from a narrow religious perspective. When we begin to watch, we begin to see everything from the perspective of eternity.

The Bible is a mystical Book

Many people regard the Bible primarily as a religious book. Religious interpretations of the Bible are many and varied and tend to contradict each other. This is why there are so many different religious groups and Christian denominations. However, for seekers of Truth, the Bible is more than a religious book. The Bible is a mystical book which is full of symbolic language which only the Holy Spirit, the Great Spirit of Truth, can decipher.

The Bible is a book of mysteries and secrets. In the symbolic language of the Bible, words have both a natural and a spiritual meaning. Many natural events recorded in the Bible are used to portray spiritual principles. We saw an example of this in Lesson 3 when we analyzed a particular episode in the life of Abraham. On one level of meaning it is just a story, but at a different level it is also a parable illustrating spiritual principles. As it has been said before, the entire Bible is written in the language of parables. This is why, as seekers of Truth, we look beyond the literal interpretations of the scriptures, and we don't allow such interpretations to limit our understanding of the Bible.

Jesus taught in parables; then He explained the meaning hidden within them. The meaning behind each parable in the Bible has to be revealed to us by the Holy Spirit. The fact that you are studying along with us indicates that you are ready and willing to see more in the Bible than you have previously seen. You are walking the path of a seeker of Truth being guided by the Holy Spirit into the dimension of All Truth.

Love the Truth

Jesus Christ had a higher level of understanding of the scriptures and of the dimension of All Truth. He desired to take His disciples to a higher, mystical level of meaning. He had a method of doing this. First, He would teach the curious multitudes of people who gathered to hear Him, but He would teach those multitudes in parables only. Afterwards,

He would explain the secret meaning of those parables to His truth-seeking disciples in private. In Luke 8:9-10 we read: *"His disciples asked Him* [in private]*: 'What is the meaning of this parable?' He replied: 'You have been allowed to **understand the secrets** of the kingdom of God, but I speak to others in **parables;** so that even though they look they will not really see, and even though they hear they will not **understand'.* "

The secrets of the Kingdom of God were imparted to the disciples, to those who were committed to know the truth and were committed to be like Christ. These secrets were not imparted to the multitudes who gathered to hear Him just out of curiosity; and it's just the same today. Therefore, personal, private study of the Bible, with the Holy Spirit as your Guide, is crucial for your spiritual development.

Truth is hidden in the Bible, hidden in plain sight. It is possible for a man to read the Bible from beginning to end many times and yet not see the truth hidden in it. To be a true disciple of Christ you are required to love spiritual Truth above all else. You are required to have a deep, insatiable hunger and thirst for the *continuous revelation* of Truth to you. *Deuteronomy 29:29* says: *"The secret things belong to the Lord our God, but the things which are **revealed** belong to us..."* When you are humble enough to admit that you are completely ignorant of spiritual Truth, and when you love and are hungry for spiritual Truth, you are qualified for spiritual Truth to be revealed to you by the Holy Spirit. Your understanding will be opened and the 'parables' in the Bible will open to you one at a time.

As was said before, the Bible is written at several different levels of meaning. If we consider the way an onion looks when it is sliced in two; there is a circle, within a circle, within a circle and so on. The Bible is written in the same way. Each passage of scripture has a meaning within a meaning within a meaning. So, our study of the Bible has to progress from one level of meaning to the next. We can confine ourselves to the obvious, literal meaning of the scripture. However, this 'surface meaning' will take us only so far and no further. Seekers of Truth have a desire to move on to different levels of understanding, and are willing to dig deeper to find more truth in each passage of scripture.

It's not about being 'right'

Nowadays, there is an expression which has become fashionable among many Christian believers, and that expression is *'Bible-believing Christian'*. Be careful with this expression; not because there is anything wrong with being a 'Bible-believing Christian', but because there are certain attitudes which have become associated with this expression; attitudes which can block you from receiving more truth. As was said before, your beliefs can blind you to the Truth.

You can become so fascinated with your beliefs and your interpretations of the scriptures, and so determined to prove that your views are right, that these distractions end up blinding you to the Truth in the very scriptures which you read. This fascination can lead you down the path of trying to change the world system to match with your beliefs, and being in a state of turmoil and uncertainty because you see the world going in a direction which is in opposition to your beliefs. Then, before you know it, you are caught in the trap of arguing, being on the defensive, being confrontational, frustrated, disillusioned, disgusted and angry with the world.

In the world system during the time of Jesus Christ, there was brutality, rampant sensuality, slavery, oppression through heavy taxation and occupation of the land of Israel by the idol-worshipping, pagan, Jew-hating Roman Empire. Jesus Christ was the embodiment of Truth, and He left the world system as He found it. It was *not* His mission to 'fix the world system', and it is not the mission of any son of God to do so. His mission and our mission is the expression of the Kingdom of heaven, first internally and then externally.

May we tell you that the world system is exactly what it is supposed to be? The world system has been granted a specific length of time during which to dominate the Earth, and its dominance will not continue one day longer than the appointed time. Therefore, no matter how dire the condition of the world looks, Infinite God is still in control. God's divine purpose will win out in the end. It's a done deal. Whenever the world system rebels against God, it is playing right into His hands. It's all part of the master plan.

The plans which The Infinite has for the Earth will work out perfectly and on schedule. Nothing or no one can stop it. Once you know this to be true, you will be amused when you see Christians trying to manipulate the political system in order to 'help God out'. The Infinite has already triumphed. Good has already prevailed. It's a foregone conclusion. With this level of consciousness, whenever you watch current events on the news or whenever you see turmoil throughout the world system, it will be like watching a scary movie when you already know that the good guys triumph in the end. Nothing you see or hear will perplex you. When you see life from the perspective of eternity, it makes all the difference. We will study this in future Lessons. Infinite God defends us; we don't have to defend Infinite God. If we somehow feel that we have to defend God, our concept of God is too small. The Infinite cannot be attacked or threatened by anyone or anything.

What does the Bible tell us should be our approach to the world system? It says: *"Do all things without complaining and arguing so that you may become blameless and pure, and **be the unblemished sons of God**, above reproach, living in the midst of a crooked and twisted generation, among whom you shine as lights in the world." (Philippians 2:14-15)*

When Jesus Christ was on Earth fulfilling His divine mission, He had nothing to prove to His detractors. He did not spend any time or energy trying to convince anyone that He was right. He left the political system as it was, and He refused to take sides in political disputes. *(See Mark 12:13-17)* Sons of God take their pattern from Jesus Christ. Sons of God have nothing to prove. We are in the world but we are not of the world. We know our Father and we are known of Him.

Always remember that the masses of people, who are captives of the world system, are in darkness. They are ignorant of the Truth and blind to the reality of The Infinite. You wouldn't criticize a blind man if he made a mistake, or if he stumbled and fell while walking, or if he lost his way. You wouldn't be angry with him. Rather, you would have compassion for him. So, if you are a devout Christian, please don't be angry because people in the world system are not 'Bible-believing'. Don't be offended because their ways are not your ways. They are just as spiritually blind as you once were, so feel compassion for them. Say like Christ: *'Father, forgive them, for they know not what they do.'* Be a light in a dark place, and keep your mind free from anger and criticism. The more you walk in divine awareness, the more you will rise above an 'us versus them' mentality. The more you become aware of the higher universal Truth and the more you see the big picture, the more peace you will have in your soul even in the midst of changing times.

New garments, new wineskins

Now this question arises: *"How does a seeker of Truth find Truth?"* The first step is to know your divine spiritual identity. The second step is clearly shown in two well-known parables of Jesus Christ recorded in Luke 5:36-39.

▣ Here is the first parable; THE PARABLE OF THE GARMENTS: *"He told them this parable: No one tears a strip of cloth from a new garment and uses it to patch an old, worn-out garment. If he does, the new cloth will tear the old garment, and the patch from the new garment will not match the old." (Luke 5:36)* (Please read this verse a second time before moving on. Let it sink in.)

▣ THE MEANING OF THE GARMENTS: What does this Parable of the Garments mean? In this parable, the *'garment'* represents *'spiritual understanding'.* The one wearing the garment is *your mind.* Your *old way of thinking* and your *traditional way of understanding* constitute the *'old garment'* which your mind is wearing. When your mind encounters a different level of spiritual understanding, it is like being offered a new garment in exchange for the old.

Now, some people don't want to give up their old understanding and their traditional way of thinking. They just want to patch the worn out places in the old garment by using fragments cut from the new garment to fill in the missing bits. They just want a little bit of the new understanding to tack on to their usual way of thinking. Jesus said that this cannot work. Sometimes they even try to pretend that they have accepted the new understanding while still secretly holding on to the old, traditional understanding deep in their minds. That's like trying to fit into a new garment while still wearing the old garment underneath the new. It makes no sense to try to use pieces from a new garment to patch an old one, and then put the patched-up old garment back on. Also it makes no sense to try to put on a new garment while still wearing an old, worn-out garment underneath.

So what's the process of change? For a man to exchange an old garment which he is wearing and replace it with a new garment, he must take off the old garment, become *naked* and then put on the new garment.

▣ THE MEANING OF NAKEDNESS: Now in understanding this parable, *'nakedness'* is a symbol which represents *'spiritual ignorance'*. This symbol is used throughout the Bible. Before the Spirit of Truth can teach us, it is necessary for us to admit that we are spiritually ignorant. When we admit that we are completely ignorant of spiritual Truth, and when we approach the study of the Bible with humility, we will be granted access to higher spiritual Truth.

So, as a seeker of Truth, you are required to strip off from your mind 'the old garment', (that old, traditional understanding), and allow your mind to become *'completely naked'* (i.e. completely spiritually ignorant). Then you put on 'the new garment' which is the new understanding of Truth which is offered to you by the Holy Spirit. Be willing to have a *naked mind*, a mind which is not wrapped up and clothed in your old understanding. Be willing to strip from your mind 'the old garment', that old understanding in which it has been wrapped all these years. Once your mind has become completely naked, you are in a position where the Spirit of Truth can clothe your mind with 'the new garment', that new understanding which originates in the dimension of All Truth.

⊡ THE MEANING OF THE PARABLE OF THE GARMENTS: This parable was told by Jesus when He was speaking directly to the scribes and Pharisees. They were the religious leaders, the devoted students of the scriptures and the upholders of Jewish religious traditions. He used this parable to explain to them that people develop a type of traditional, religious understanding which they have lived by for years. That is the 'old garment'. When such people encounter a higher spiritual understanding (that's the 'new garment'), it makes no sense to try to incorporate the new teaching into the old.

The new understanding will never match up with the old understanding, just as a patch of the new cloth will never match the old. Also, the new, spiritual understanding is of a better quality than the old. The new understanding will put stress on the traditional understanding. Seekers of Truth come to realize that the old, traditional way of thinking and the new way of thinking cannot be combined. The old way of thinking has to be surrendered and replaced with the new. Old things must pass away in order for all things to become new.

When many people encounter a new understanding of spiritual Truth, they try to include it into their old way of thinking. It just can't work. This is why we have been encouraging you to give up thinking of God as your Master. That thinking is part of the 'old garment'. You can't mix it with your *knowing* that you are a beloved, divine son of God. That old understanding becomes threadbare with use. It develops gaps, holes and tears. The seeker of Truth knows that he needs something more. He needs *a new revelation* of spiritual Truth.

'Head Knowledge' is religious knowledge which comes from our own human intellect and effort. By contrast, 'Revealed Knowledge' is spiritual knowledge which is 'downloaded' into our spirit by the Holy Spirit. If we depend exclusively on theology and Head Knowledge, and if we disregard and reject the idea that higher Truth has to be *revealed* to us by the Holy Spirit, there will come a day when life will start asking us serious questions which our theology and our Head Knowledge cannot properly answer. Then the deficiency of the 'old garment' will be clearly seen. Theology, though instructive, will take us only so far and no further; but All Truth answers all questions. This principle is clearly illustrated in the episode when the child Jesus was asking questions of the intellectual teachers of the scriptures, questions which they could not properly answer. Jesus, being the embodiment of Truth, then answered those questions, and astounded those who heard Him.

It's a challenge to give up the 'old garment', that old way of thinking. It's old and threadbare but you're used to it. You look around and see others still proudly wearing their old garment, and you wonder what they will say when you show up wearing something new. What will they think when you start living your life fully as a beloved, divine, spirit-son of God? What will they say when you stop singing the songs of the mentally enslaved? Truly, their reaction to you is not the real issue. The only question is: *Are you willing to live according to the Truth that you know, and be free?* You can choose to keep the old garment or you can exchange it for the new. There is no pressure. The seeker of Truth will take up the offer of the new garment, for he has a love of Truth above all else.

▣ ARE YOU AWAKE OR ASLEEP? So, we can choose to keep wearing the old garment of our traditional understanding or we can surrender it, allow our minds to be *completely naked* by admitting that we are ignorant, and then put on the new garment of the revealed understanding of divine Truth. Truth is always available; it's up to us to be willing to become aware of Truth.

Now, in the mystical teachings, to be *'awake'* is to be 'consciously aware of and to understand divine Truth' but to be *'asleep'* is to be 'unconscious and unaware of divine Truth'. Please remember this as you read passages from the New Testament which contain these expressions. We can choose to live our lives *'awake'*, i.e. conscious and fully aware of divine Truth, or we can choose to be contented to live *'asleep'*, i.e. unconscious and unaware of the dimension of All Truth. Sadly, many devout Christians are 'sleepwalking' through their Christian life.

The Eastern sage Rumi got a glimpse of this choice. He said: *There are those who don't truly want to change; let them sleep. I am not depending on my brain or on my reasoning. I have torn that old garment to shreds and thrown it away. This Love,* [the Love of Truth], *goes beyond the study of theology. If you feel you can improve your mind just with theology, then go on sleeping. If your mind is not completely naked, wrap your beautiful garment of empty words around you, and sleep.*

Those are strong words, but they are accurate in describing the choice before us. So what will you do? Will you try to combine what you have been reading in this book and use it to 'fill in the blanks' in your old way of thinking? Are you willing to give up the old way altogether and to cast every trace of the bondservant mentality out of your mind once and for all? Will you try to go on with a double-mind? These are questions which only you can answer for yourself.

▣ Now, here is the second parable; THE PARABLE OF THE WINE AND THE WINESKINS: *"No one pours new wine into old wineskins. If he does, the new wine will burst the skins, the wine will be spilled and the skins will be ruined. New wine must be poured into new wineskins, and both are preserved." (Luke 5:37-38)* (Please read these verses a second time before moving on. Let them sink in.)

In the Middle East, wineskins were animal skins which were

used to make bag-like containers within which new wine would be poured and stored. As the wine fermented, and aged, and alcohol was created, the skins would expand to accommodate the process of fermentation. An old wineskin which had previously been used in the fermenting process would have already expanded to maximum capacity and become rigid. If new, unfermented wine was poured into it, no more expansion would be possible. The wineskin would burst and the wine would be spilled.

What does this Parable of the Wine and the Wineskins mean?

▣ THE MEANING OF THE 'WINE' AND THE 'WINSESKINS': In this parable *'wine'* represents *'spiritual understanding'*. The *'wineskins'* represent *'the consciousness of a man'*. The consciousness is where spiritual understanding is received and stored in any man. Even when you believe the truth, you will not enjoy its fullness until you become fully aware and fully *conscious* of the truth that you believe. This is what it means to 'know the truth'.

A man who has previously received a level of spiritual understanding has had that level of understanding 'fermenting' and aging in his consciousness for years. The understanding starts out new, but over time it becomes old. Just like an old wineskin, his consciousness has expanded to its maximum capacity to accommodate the 'fermenting' process, and has become rigid and inflexible. He has reached the limits of the old way of thinking. His consciousness can hold only that old level of understanding and no more. It gets to the stage of 'old wine being stored in old wineskins'. If a new level of spiritual understanding is introduced to such a man whose consciousness has not been made new, when the 'fermenting' of this new understanding begins to take place, his consciousness has no way to expand. He will have no choice but to reject the new level of understanding. He will cast it out of his mind. The *'wine'* will be *'spilled'*. So *'new wine must be poured into new wineskins'*.

▣ THE MEANING OF THE PARABLE OF THE WINE AND THE

WINESKINS: Jesus was explaining that before any man can receive and retain a new level of spiritual understanding, the man's consciousness and state of mind have to be made new. *The man's mind has to be renewed first.* This is done by consciously preparing the mind to receive and accommodate new ideas. This renewal of mind makes the man's consciousness flexible so that it can receive new revelation of truth. A flexible mind can expand wide enough to receive and retain that higher level of understanding. Remember, Mind Expansion is the aim of the mental game. An inflexible mind cannot expand. An inflexible mind boasts: *"I am already knowledgeable! I have been studying the scriptures extensively! I have a high degree of religious training!"* By contrast, a flexible mind says to the Holy Spirit: *"I am a child. I don't know anything by myself, and I don't want to know anything except the Truth. Please teach me and keep revealing more Truth to me."* It takes humility to have a flexible mind.

We invite newness of mind when we become conscious that we are ignorant of higher spiritual truth. Our minds are renewed when we are willing to release our mental grip on the information that we already have, and when we are open and receptive to a new level of understanding. The new consciousness will be flexible, and therefore able to expand to accommodate this new level of spiritual understanding, just as new wineskins are flexible enough to expand and accommodate the fermenting wine.

The new, higher truth which we receive will preserve our new level of consciousness and make it stronger. Also our new level of consciousness will preserve and retain the new higher truth so it can be poured out into the lives of other people. Both the consciousness and the spiritual understanding will be "preserved". Our old, inflexible mindset cannot receive and retain new spiritual understanding. Just like in the parable of the garments, the old and the new cannot be combined. So every seeker of Truth will ask and answer this question: *Do I have an open, flexible mind or a narrow, rigid mind?*

◙ OLD WINE OR NEW WINE? The last portion of this parable says: *"No one immediately desires new wine after he has been drinking old wine. He will say, 'The old wine is better'." (Luke 5:39)*

What does this mean? Wine stored for too long in an old wineskin becomes sour. It loses its flavor. New wine is fresh and sweet to the taste. People who have been drinking old, sour wine long enough get accustomed to the sour taste. When they taste new wine, they will reject it and say that the old, sour wine tastes better. The 'old wine' represents the old, traditional understanding. The 'new wine' represents fresh revelation of divine Truth.

◙ WHY DO THEY SAY "THE OLD WINE IS BETTER"?: Whenever people who are used to the old, traditional level of understanding taste a bit of the sweet, new revelation, their tendency is to desire to remain at their old level of understanding. They say: *"The old understanding, the old approach, the old belief system is better"*. People tend to want more of whatever they are used to. They become comfortable and satisfied with the old way of thinking. However, since you are reading this book, it indicates that you have a desire for the new, and that's a very good thing. Allow your mind and your thinking to be flexible and to accommodate things which you read which may be new to you. Be willing to think in new ways. This is how your consciousness is made new.

Be teachable rather than knowledgeable

So, with these parables in mind, how does a seeker of Truth find Truth? A seeker of Truth must be willing to think in new ways. He must be willing to grow beyond the boundaries of his old, traditional way of thinking. He must allow his mind, and his consciousness, to be made new and flexible. He must be open and receptive to different levels of understanding. He must be willing to understand familiar scriptures in new ways. He must not try to bend the new information to make it fit into his old way of thinking. He must allow his mind to expand and to accommodate new revelation of divine truth. He must be willing to exchange the old for the new.

Many Christians find this extremely challenging; especially if they have been reading and studying the scriptures in a traditional way for many years. The tendency is to hold rigidly and tightly to the old way of thinking, and to immediately dismiss anything that does not conform to and fit within it. The mind which is locked into traditional thinking will resist the revelation of divine Truth. That's the reason why the scribes and Pharisees rejected the teachings of Jesus Christ.

However, for those who desire to receive more understanding, remember that your mind is like a cup. If it is already full of information, ideas and opinions, there is no room for divine revelation of Truth. There is much more to the scriptures than we all have been taught traditionally. There is much that we have looked at in the Bible without really seeing it; and that's because we have been looking at it from the perspective of our old understanding.

When we all allow our understanding to be opened, we will begin to see what has been hidden in plain sight. As seekers of Truth, the cry of our heart to the Holy Spirit is: *"Teach me! Show me and tell me things which I have never seen or heard before!"* Truth is always unfolding. Therefore, our goal is to be *teachable* rather than *knowledgeable*, and that requires us to be humble and hungry for Truth.

The Keys of Understanding

Many people study the Bible in 'fragments'. They read various Biblical passages here and there, and they get an understanding of what a particular passage means, whether from their personal study or by listening to others. When people study the Bible in 'fragments', they try to put bits and pieces of Scriptural information together. They listen to a sermon here and a Bible Study lesson there, and then they do their best to apply what they have learned. They'll get a little bit of teaching on

Faith, a little bit on Forgiveness, a little bit on Love, a little bit on Grace and so on. Then they have the daunting task of remembering all these bits and pieces of information, and applying them correctly.

Now this approach to the study of the Bible has its benefits, but it is limited in its effect and very time-consuming. It's like trying to complete a giant jigsaw puzzle when many of the pieces are missing, and you don't have a picture of what the finished puzzle should look like. You'll be trying to put together these small, scattered bits of spiritual information in your mind, just as you would assemble puzzle pieces. However, there will be big gaps in your understanding, and you will not have an overall context to guide you.

If you study the Bible in 'fragments', there will always be information missing, and there will be areas in your life which you still can't figure out. If you persist in this method, you will run yourself ragged spiritually, and end up feeling overwhelmed and frustrated. Whenever you hear new instructions given in any sermon, your reaction will tend to be: *"Oh no, not again! Just when I thought I was making progress, here's one more thing that I'm not doing right!"*

The good news is that you don't have to learn spiritual Truth in 'fragments'. There is another option available to you. You can get the Keys of Understanding. These are key pieces of information which will unlock and open the dimension of All Truth to you. These Keys will give you access to All Truth, rather than fragments of Truth.

When you get these Keys of Understanding, it's as if you have been given the picture of what the completed jigsaw puzzle should look like plus all the puzzle pieces neatly grouped and organized plus the frame of the puzzle already assembled for you. You still have some bits of information to assemble, but now it's just a matter of time before you put it all together. With these Keys of Understanding, it's not a struggle, and it's not trial and error. Everything will fit into place. Jesus Christ gave us these Keys in His teaching, but many times we read them without recognizing their significance.

When you use these Keys of Understanding, it will be clear to you how and where each passage of scripture, to which you are attracted, fits into the overall context of spiritual Truth. You will have the big picture. These Keys will create the foundation of truth upon which the Holy Spirit can build and increase your understanding. One of the greatest Keys of Understanding is: **knowing that you are a beloved, divine, free-born, spirit-son of God.** This is why immersing yourself in this topic is vital for boosting your ability to live a victorious life.

Remember that, in your personal study of the Bible, you really don't need to know *everything* or study *everything* in minute detail; you just need to know what *you* need to know. The Holy Spirit knows you better than you know yourself. The Holy Spirit knows what *you* need to know; and the Holy Spirit will teach you what *you* need to know on a personal level, if you will only ask for wisdom. The Bible says: *"If any man lacks wisdom, let him ask God for it, and He will give it to him. For God gives generously to everyone and He will not reprimand you for asking." (James 1:5)* Be willing to admit to that you lack wisdom. Never let pride or ego tell you otherwise.

God is both a keeper of secrets and a revealer of secrets. There are certain secrets to your personal life; secrets which God knows but you don't, secrets that you will never figure out on your own, secrets that you need to know in order to experience and enjoy complete victory. These secrets will be revealed to you personally. So, let this prayer be the deep desire of your heart: *"Holy Spirit, give me your wisdom, and reveal to me the deep secrets to my life".* This is one of the greatest prayers a son of God can ever pray. You will be amazed as to what the Holy Spirit will personally reveal to you about you. Keep praying this prayer always, because no matter how much the Holy Spirit reveals to you, there is always more for you to know. Be just as hungry for Wisdom as you are for Truth.

Knowing the Heavenly Father

Another fundamental Key of Understanding is: *'knowing the Heavenly Father'.* Perhaps some readers may now be thinking: *"This one is easy. I know that the Heavenly Father is God, and He is an old man with a long, white beard up in heaven, beyond the skies above, sitting on a throne."* Is that the image that comes to mind when you hear the expression 'Heavenly Father'? For many Christians, it is. However, when you look with fresh eyes at what Jesus taught about the Father, you may re-think such traditional ideas. The Truth is hidden in plain sight, but it will be revealed to those who are hungry for Truth.

Now this is Level 1, so let's just lay a foundation for now. When we get to Level 2 of this Bible Study, we will delve into this topic in detail, and we will study additional Keys of Understanding. We cannot truly live as sons of God unless we know our Father. It's one thing to stop seeing God as our Master, but it's another thing to open our consciousness wide enough to receive what Jesus taught about the Divine Father.

In Matthew 11:25-27 we read: *"At that time Jesus answered and said, 'I thank You, Father, Lord of heaven and earth, because **You have hid these things from the wise and prudent,** and You have **revealed them to babies.** Even so, Father: for so it seemed good to You.*

*All things are delivered to Me by My Father: and **no man knows the Son, except the Father. The only ones who know the Father are the Son, and anyone to whom the Son reveals the Father."** (Please read this passage of scripture a second time before moving on. Let it sink in.)

This text tells us that the Truth about the Father will be revealed to us. It is a deep secret which is hidden from those who are wise in their own understanding, but it will be revealed to *'babies'*; (i.e. to those who are willing to confess that they are ignorant of spiritual Truth but who are also hungry for Truth and are willing to be fed). We all start out as spiritual babies, undeveloped in our understanding and needing spiritual food, which is the Living Truth. However, as spiritual babies, we are hungry for Truth. We love the Truth which is the spiritual food necessary for the nourishment of our souls and spirits. The Father will reveal hidden Truth to such 'babies'.

We start out as spiritual babies but we don't remain as babies. The more we feed on spiritual Truth, the more we grow in our spiritual understanding until we get to the stage where we mature and become as *'little children'* spiritually. When spiritual babies start to know the Truth which is hidden in the Bible, they start to grow and develop. So, 1st Peter 2:2 gives this instruction to all spiritual babies: *"..Desire* [i.e. intensely crave] *the sincere* [the unadulterated] *milk of the Word that you may grow by using it."*

When we grow spiritually from the 'baby' stage to the stage of being 'little children', we have positioned ourselves to get access to the secrets of the kingdom of heaven. We get to enter into the dimension of All Truth. This is why Jesus said: *"...Unless you are converted, and become as **little children**, you shall not **enter** into the **kingdom of heaven**. Whoever therefore shall **humble himself** as this little child, he is the greatest in the kingdom of heaven." (Matthew 18:3-4)*

We become spiritually childlike when we admit that we are completely ignorant of Spiritual Truth. We humble ourselves and ask the Holy Spirit lots of questions, so that the Great Spirit of Truth may teach us. Little children love to ask questions. They always want to know more.

▣ THE STAGES OF SPIRITUAL DEVELOPMENT: You may be wondering: *'How can a man know if he has progressed from being a spiritual 'baby' to being a 'little child' spiritually?'* The Bible gives us the answer. John, the beloved disciple of Jesus, teaches us the further stages of spiritual development in the *Book of 1st John.* These further stages are *'little children', 'young men'* and *'fathers'.* These are spiritual descriptions, and have nothing to do with physical gender.

The more your knowledge of the Divine Father grows, the more you grow and mature spiritually. This is why 1st John 2:13 says: *"...I write to you **little children, because you have known the Father.**"* You know that you have progressed from being a 'baby' to being a 'little child' when you know the Father. By being like Christ, the Son of God, and by knowing that right now you are a son of God, your consciousness expands to a level where you can know the Father. In the original Greek text, the word translated *'babies'* literally means *'children who are too young to speak.'* You know you are growing up spiritually when you begin to speak as a son of God both inwardly and outwardly. You speak as a son of God whenever you use your Inner Conversations correctly. You also stop calling yourself a sinner, a wretch, a worm or a beggar. You stop singing the songs of the mentally enslaved. You stop saying, 'I am not worthy'. Sons of God don't speak of themselves in such a manner.

Whenever you read the Four Gospels in the Bible (i.e. the Books of Matthew, Mark, Luke and John), you will notice that the teaching of Jesus was 'Father-centered'. The Divine Father was the focus of His message. Even the Lord's Prayer starts with the words *'Our Father' (Matthew 6:9)*. The Gospel of John gives much insight into the Divine Father. You can only know that you have a Heavenly Father when you fully know that you are His son. If you are a mere servant and not a son, you have no Father. All you have is a Master. Do you see it?

"The only ones who know the Father are the Son, and anyone to whom the Son reveals the Father" (Matthew 11:27).

Jesus Christ came to reveal the Father to us as one of the 'Keys of Understanding'. The first step in accessing this revelation is to know that you are a son of God. Once you take that first step, more and more of the Father will be revealed to you. We will study the Divine Father in detail when we get to Level 2 of this Men's Bible Study.

What would Jesus do?

Jesus Christ, the Son of God, is the great Pattern. He is that glorious template of what it means to be a son of God. It is He who reveals to us who and what the Father is. Hebrews 1:3 tells us that the man Jesus Christ was the 'express image' of the invisible God, the express image of Divinity. As was mentioned in a previous Lesson, that phrase 'express image' is a translation of the Greek word from which is derived the English word 'character'. It is an engraved stamp which produces an exact copy of the engraving. If a man tries to have the character of Christ the Son of God without first knowing that he himself is a son of God, he is trying to produce a copy of an image that he doesn't possess. He is trying to make the image without using the stamp.

When you know that you are a son of God and that you are part of the Divine Family forever, you think like a son of God. If you think like a son of God, you will act like a son of God. You will have the *Mind of Christ*. When you think like a son of God with the Mind of Christ, you don't have to wonder: *'What would Jesus do?'* The divine image of the Son of God, His 'character', is stamped in your consciousness; so you are like Him from the inside out.

A disciplined mind

In this Lesson, we have been studying the importance of Truth. For a disciple of Christ, Truth is paramount; because this entire world system in which we live is a complete deception. It is based on two things: *Lies and Fear*. If you buy into the system, you become a slave to the system. Remember that although you live in the world system, you are not of the world system.

You have a choice. You don't have to believe the lies and you don't have to be afraid. You can instead choose to live according to the principles on which the Kingdom of heaven is based. Those principles are: *Truth and Love*. In 2nd Thessalonians 2:10-12, the Bible teaches us that because people do not have a love for the truth, God will send them a powerful deception and they will believe a lie. This is a fact for all mankind throughout the ages. We all were born in this deceptive system, and we have been brought up to buy into its lies and its fears. The only way to transcend the world system is to have a love for the Truth, to know the Truth and to live in love. Then we will not be afraid.

In physical slavery, wherever practiced around the world throughout history and into modern times, fear is the main thing used to control the slaves. Fear ensures the slaves' obedience. Fear ensures that they won't rebel. Fear ensures that they won't leave the slave-master. Fear in the mind of a follower of Christ is a symptom of mental bondage. The more you become free to be like Christ, the less fear you will have.

One of the main fears that many Christians suffer from is the fear of 'hell'. Many Christians are in Church, not because they love God so much, but because they are afraid of hell. When you know the Truth, the claws of fear lose their grip on your mind. *"God has not given us the spirit of fear: but [He has given us the spirit] of power, of love and of a disciplined mind." (2nd Timothy 1:7)* So if your mind is harassed by fear, that fear doesn't come from God.

When you know the Truth, you come to understand that God is *not* suspending your soul over the flames of hell, ready to throw you in on a whim. He isn't adding up your faults, sins and transgressions. As a matter of fact, He does not even remember them. You will hear people say that God does not forget anything, but that's not true. In Isaiah 43:25, our Father says: *"I, yes, I am the One who blots out your transgressions for My own sake **and I will not remember your sins.**"* Jesus Christ has taken upon Himself *all* our sins when He was crucified and died on the cross, and in exchange He has given us *all* of His righteousness. As a son of God, you may remember and identify yourself with your sinful activities if you choose; but God doesn't remember them and He doesn't identify you with them. He has already eradicated from existence all of your sins. He forgets your sins because they no longer exist. All debts are paid.

You are the only one who can keep your past errors alive in your mind, through feelings of self-condemnation. However, you are always free to let it all go and remember that you are in the Divine Family forever. You are a son of God and you are forgiven. Your mind can break free from shame and guilt and condemnation and self-loathing and regret and fear. This calls for a renewing of the mind. This is why the Bible tells us: *"Don't be conformed to this world [system], but be transformed by the renewing of your mind..." (Romans 12:2).*

True Biblical repentance (which is far different from traditional repentance) will remove shame and guilt and self-condemnation and self-loathing and regret and fear from your mind. We will study True Repentance when we get to Level 2; and we guarantee you that when you get that truth, you will never feel condemned again. You will be free. Remember this: *"There is no fear in love, for perfect love casts out fear. Fear causes torment. Any man who is fearful is not made perfect in love."* (1st John 4:18)

This entire world system is based on Lies and Fear. The Kingdom of heaven is based on Truth and Love. Here is a very useful point and is worth remembering: *Anything that is 'fear-based' is part of the world system, no matter what label it bears.* You are a son of God and you have nothing to fear. If you believe that you should fear 'fear itself', you are still living in fear. *"Yea, though I walk through the valley of the shadow of death, I will fear no evil, for You are with me." (Psalm 23:4)* So, please feel free to give up any ideas and any ideologies (religious or otherwise) which are designed to feed your fears and anxieties.

There are people and entities in this world which profit financially from the fears of others. We call them 'fearmongers'. If someone or something is trying to terrify you for any reason at all, they are trying to manipulate you. Never allow your mind to be held prisoner by the fearmongers; and they are everywhere, even in Church. When you know the truth of your Divine Identity, you live from the consciousness of love, and not from the consciousness of fear.

If you have low self-esteem, it is not because anything is wrong with you. Low self-esteem occurs because you have not yet tuned in to the whole truth of your Divine Identity. You have not yet tuned in to your Divine Ideal Self. Your self-esteem does not come from your human identity; it comes from your Divine Identity. When you fully understand this, you will no longer be held captive by anything which happened in the past. As a seeker of Truth, you are required to know the truth of who you really are, not from the perspective of the world system but from the perspective of the Kingdom of heaven. The world system may have an opinion of you, but that is not what counts. What really matters is how you are perceived by The Infinite, because that's not an opinion. The Infinite knows the truth of who you are as a Divine Spirit-Being.

Now you may be saying to yourself: *"I want to know the truth of who I am as a divine being. I want to know what it means for me personally to be a son of God."* Those are topics for our next Lesson when we will be getting into some very deep Truth. See you then. Please read the Supporting Scriptures, Affirmation and the Review which follow this Lesson.

Supporting Scriptures

*Ephesians 4:14-15: "...From this time forward we will no longer be [spiritual] **infants,** tossed to and fro and blown about by every wind of doctrine, by the trickery of people and by their cunning schemes whereby they plot to deceive us; but by **speaking the truth in love**, we **grow up** in every aspect to become **the mature body of Christ** who is our Head."*

John 14:16-17: "And I will ask the Father, and He will send you another Helper who will be with you forever. He is the Spirit of Truth [the Holy Spirit] whom the world [those in the world system] cannot receive because it does not see Him and cannot recognize Him. But you know Him, because He lives with you and shall be in you."

1st John 1:6: "If we say that we have fellowship with Him, and yet we are walking in darkness [i.e. living in ignorance]*, we are lying, and we are not doing the truth."*

Affirmation

I am now soaring in heaven's skies, looking at life through my eagle eyes,
Seeing more clearly the Truth in me, feeling more deeply that I am free;
Trusting God's mercy and all He's said, I am convinced that all debts are paid;
Why should I fear when to me is given
God's full forgiveness and love from heaven?
So, away with fearmongering threats of hell!
I'm the son of the Father, and all is well!

My old, worn-out garment I've given up;
My mind is now open, an empty cup,
Emptied of all that I thought was truth,
but were lies I was told from my early youth.
Valley so dark with your lies and fear, I shall not tremble for God is here;
Terror in me you shall never find, but power and love and a disciplined mind;
World, you're contented to live earth-bound,
but my soul has ascended to higher ground;
I live on the heights of the realms above, with God's revelation of truth and love!

Review

Q. What two things need to happen before a seeker of Truth will be able to receive a higher understanding of the scriptures?
A. (1) The understanding of the seeker of Truth must be expanded by the renewing of his mind; and (2) the scriptures themselves must be 'opened' by the Holy Spirit to reveal the truth hidden in the Bible.

Q. If a man has been studying the Bible for years and has a level of understanding of the scriptures, what should he do to have more truth revealed to him?

A. He should:

1. be willing to admit that he is ignorant concerning what the scriptures recorded in the Bible truly mean;

2. acknowledge that there is much, much more in the Bible than he has been taught to believe;

3. realize that Truth is always unfolding;

4. be willing to see familiar passages of scripture in a new light;

5. be willing to expand his consciousness and be mentally flexible; and

6. be willing to empty himself of his own understanding and humbly learn from the Spirit of Truth.

Q. In studying the Bible, what are the three levels of understanding available to me?
A. The three levels of understanding are *Believing*, *Knowing* and *Watching*. *Believing* is the lowest level of understanding. *Believing* can blind you to the truth. *Knowing* is higher than *Believing*. *Knowing* happens when the truth that you know becomes a part of you. *Watching* is the level at which divine revelation is imparted to the seeker of truth. In *Watching*, you rise above your preconceived ideas and have a panoramic view of the scriptures.

Q. What will qualify me to be given a revelation of spiritual Truth?
A. You are qualified when you are humble enough to admit that you are ignorant and when you love spiritual Truth above all else. Then the Holy Spirit will guide you.

Q. Why is it necessary for me to be a seeker of Truth?
A. It is necessary because we live in a world of deception, and spiritual Truth is not easy to find. This is why you need the Holy Spirit, the Great

Spirit of Truth, to guide you into the dimension of All Truth. If the dimension of All Truth were easy to find and navigate, no Guide would be required.

Q. In the language of parables, 'garments', 'nakedness', 'wine' and 'wineskins' are symbols. What do these symbols represent?
A. *Garments* represent 'spiritual understanding' while *Nakedness* represents 'spiritual ignorance'. *Wine* represents 'spiritual understanding' and '*Wineskins*' represent 'the consciousness of the seeker of truth'.

Q. What is the lesson in the Parables of the Garments and the Wine and Wineskins?
A. The lesson of the Garments is that the seeker of truth must be willing to give up his old understanding and exchange it for the new. He must not try to mix the old and the new. The lesson of the wine and wineskins is that the consciousness of the seeker of truth must be made new before he can receive and retain a new understanding of spiritual truth. He must not cling to his old way of thinking.

Q. What are the two ways in which the Bible can be studied?
A. You can study the Bible either by picking from it fragments of understanding from individual passages of scripture, or you can get the Keys of Understanding, which are fundamental principles which will give you a comprehensive understanding.

Q. What are two of the Keys of Understanding?
A. (1) Knowing that you are a son of God; and (2) Knowing the Divine Father. There are more Keys which we will investigate at Level 2 of this Bible Study.

Q. What is the world system based on?
A. The world system is based on Lies and Fear.

Q. *What is the Kingdom of heaven based on?*
A. The Kingdom of heaven is based on Truth and Love.

Q. What is one of the most important prayers that a son of God can ever pray?
A. *"Holy Spirit, give me your wisdom, and reveal to me the deep secrets to my life."*

回 *You're doing great!* You've completed 4 Lessons. You have only 3 more Lessons to go. There is much more waiting to be shared with you, so keep going all the way through to the end.

回 To receive Jackie Goldsmith's free 30-day Devotional titled "Walk in the Light" in your email inbox, send your request to:

voiceoflightforchrist@gmail.com

回 *Let's hear from you:* You can give your feedback about this book by clicking on the Stars on Amazon.com. It's quick and easy. On your Amazon.com home page, click on *'Orders'*, then click on the *'Write a product review'* button, then click on the number of Stars. One Star is the lowest rating; Five Stars is the highest rating. After clicking on the Stars, you have the option to also share your thoughts about this book by writing your comments if you wish.

Your rating will also help others to find and benefit from this book.

Lesson 5: Come up higher!

WORD FOR TODAY: "We do not focus on the things which are seen, but rather on the things which are not seen. The things which are seen are temporary. The things which are not seen are eternal."   (2nd Corinthians 4:18)

Truth is the Mind of Christ

Let's recap a bit. In the previous Lesson we studied together the importance of being a seeker of Truth. Truth is hidden in the Bible; therefore we are required to seek for it with the Spirit of Truth as our Guide. The Holy Spirit is the Spirit of Truth. Truth characterizes the Mind of Christ; and this Mind is what we are searching for when we read or listen to the Bible. In order to receive higher Truth, we are required to allow our minds to be renewed, open, expanded and flexible.

In order to see the truth in the Bible, we are also required to get a panoramic view of the scriptures while still observing its minute details. To get this panoramic view, we humble ourselves and allow the Holy Spirit to take us up higher spiritually. Then we will study the Bible as if we are looking through the eyes of a soaring eagle. By understanding the Truth which is the Mind of Christ, we will come to understand the truth of who we are. This is one of the greatest levels of truth that a son of God can attain. When we understand who we are by looking through the eyes of God, it makes all the difference. Now let's continue from this point.

Finding the Truth of who you are

In order to really know the truth of your identity, there is a mental obstacle which you are required to rise above. That obstacle is

Opinion. You will become aware of the truth of who you are, but only after you have given yourself unconditional permission to rise above all opinions of who you are. The opinions of: the world system, the media, history, society, your teachers, your family, your friends, your enemies, the judge, the jury, the warden, the parole board, tradition, and even the opinions of religion; release all these things from your mind. Most importantly, release your own opinion of who you are. Your opinion of yourself has been created based on the programing which you received in the world system.

Truth is higher than anybody's opinions. Even if these opinions seem to be supported by facts, Truth is still higher than opinions. *Facts are different from Truth. Facts can change but Truth never changes.* Everything that will ever make you feel badly about yourself comes from the facts of your life. But, your facts are not your Truth. Opinions are not your Truth. Your past is not your Truth. Your circumstances are not your Truth. Your habits are not your Truth. Opinions, your past, your circumstances and your habits all dwell in the realm of facts, not in the realm of Truth. We will go into this in detail in our next Lesson. When you have tuned out all opinions and all facts, you are free to find out the Truth of who you are.

Man is Mind

Now before we get into more of the higher truth of what it really means to be a son of The Infinite, let's lay a foundation.

In previous Lessons, you will notice that great emphasis is placed on The Mind. There is a reason for this. Simply put: *Man is Mind.* Let's think about this. Whenever you interact with anyone, you are interacting with whatever is in the mind of that person. The body is just a means of expressing the mind. Similarly, whenever you interact with yourself, you are interacting with whatever is in your mind.

◙ YOUR TWO MINDS: As was said in the Introduction to this book, human beings are, at the same time both physical and non-physical. The physical, human body is the 'house' in which the non-physical (i.e. spiritual, divine) being lives. So, the physical, human aspect of a man has its own Natural Mind and its own way of thinking, which is known as 'The Intellect'. On the other hand, the non-physical, spiritual, divine aspect of a man has its own Divine Mind and its own way of thinking, which is referred to in the Bible as 'The Mind of Christ'. These two Minds are *not* the same.

Man is Mind. *The human aspect of Man is 'Natural Mind'; but the spiritual aspect of Man is 'Divine Mind'.* The Natural Man (i.e. the Natural Mind, The Intellect) gravitates towards world system thinking. By contrast, the Divine Man (i.e. the Divine Mind, The Mind of Christ) gravitates towards the Truth. So you have a choice of what type of Mind (what type of Man) you will be; for *"...as a man thinks (as a mind thinks),... so is he" (Proverbs 23:7)*

So let's look at what the Bible says about these two opposite types of Mind and two opposite types of Men, one Natural and the other Divine. As we studied in Lesson 3, *"**The natural Man** (i.e. the Natural Mind, The Intellect) cannot receive **the things of the Spirit of God, for they seem foolish to him:** neither can he **know** them because they are **spiritually discerned.**" (1st Corinthians 2:14).* This verse teaches us that Spiritual Truth can only be understood with the divine, spiritual mind in man, and not with the Intellect. So a man whose mind has not been renewed to be open to spiritual Truth will tend to reject and despise spiritual guidance. His natural mind has no capacity to receive such things.

The natural Mind (the Intellect) is a 'servant mind'. We need this Natural Mind to serve us in this natural world, just as Abraham needed his servant Eliezer of Damascus. However, this 'servant mind' must never be allowed to rule us. If we allow our Intellect to dominate our spiritual aspect, and if we confine ourselves to being just 'a Natural Man with an Intellect', we shut down our divine spiritual Mind and we block our God-connection to the divine spiritual power which we carry within us. This is how we live when we surrender to world system thinking, and when we allow the world system to define us as being 'only human'. We are being ruled by our 'servant'.

By contrast, we become free to be like Christ when we give recognition to our divine spiritual aspect. Then we come into agreement with our true identity of being 'a Divine Man with a Divine Mind'. We recognize that we are a spirit-son of Infinite God. Therefore, we are not limited to the Natural Mind because *"...we have the Mind of Christ" (1st Corinthians 2:16)*. This Divine Mind is the 'Master mind', the 'Teacher mind'. It is *the Mind of the Christ in you*; the Mind that is built into the divine image. It is designed to train the Natural Mind (i.e. the Intellect) how to think. The Intellect is a 'follower' by nature; so it is always looking for someone or something to follow. If the divine 'Teacher mind' is not activated in a man, the Intellect is never called to its true teacher. It is therefore schooled by and blindly follows world system thinking.

The Bible tells us that Jesus Christ walked around choosing disciples. He called men who were involved in their daily livelihoods to be his disciples. He said to them: "Follow Me." Whether they defined themselves as being 'fishermen' or 'tax collectors', they immediately gave up that occupation and that understanding of who they were, and followed Him as 'Disciples of Christ'. This episode of Jesus Christ calling disciples to follow Him has a deeper mystical meaning. It represents the Divine Mind in man calling the Natural Mind in man to follow it as its disciple. The Natural Mind (the Natural Man, the Intellect) is required to hear this call and to obey it by forsaking the natural understanding of who he is, and by following the Divine Truth of who he really is.

Since Man is Mind, the only way you can choose what kind of man you will be from now on is by consciously choosing what kind of thoughts you will think from now on. The world system is very skilled at projecting into our minds negative thoughts and feelings which did not originate from us. More and more, technology is being used to do this. We can also absorb other people's thoughts and feelings if we spend a lot of time with them. Therefore, always remember that you have the right to protect your Mental Freedom even from your friends. If any thoughts and feelings try to come into you which are opposite to the type of man you choose to be, you have the absolute divine right to challenge those thoughts and feelings. Challenge them with the same intensity as you would challenge a stranger who is trying to break into your house.

The little 'i' and the big 'I'

So, there is an aspect of you which is *natural and human* and there is an aspect of you which is *supernatural and divine*. You may still be wondering: *How can any aspect of me be divine?* There is an aspect of you which is divine because Divine Spirit-God is the Father, *the Source*, of your spirit. When the Bible says that you are a son of God, it's *not* a figurative expression. It is the absolute truth of who you are right now.

We repeat for emphasis: there is an aspect of you which is *human* and there is an aspect of you which is *divine*. The human side of you expresses itself through the natural tendencies of your human body, your human identity, your human mind and your human emotions. Those natural tendencies are referred to as *'human nature'*. Human nature is something which the human side of you learned in the world system; and the world system is devoted to mentally conditioning you to be a slave to human nature. Human nature is heavily promoted in world culture and in popular entertainment. This is why you never define yourself as being *'only human'*, because if you do, you put yourself under the domination of human nature, and you distance yourself from your divine, spiritual nature.

▣ THE HUMAN SIDE OF YOU: After we, the spirit-sons of God housed within human bodies, are born in this world system, our human aspect begins the process of developing *a human self (i.e. individuality).*

That human individuality includes all that we identify within ourselves as a human individual who is separate and distinct from all other human individuals. In the world system, we become fully aware of our human self. We learn how to take care of our human bodies. We go to educational institutions to train our human minds. We are made subject to a certain level of discipline which teaches us how to control our human emotions. However, the world system does not teach us or make us aware that we are, in truth, the divine spirit-sons of God. It does not teach us that we have a Divine spirit-Self.

Even in Church, we are traditionally taught that we are a human body plus a soul; but that the soul only becomes relevant after our body dies. Truthfully, your soul is just your individuality stripped of its human body; so your soul is *not* your Divine spirit-Self. If we are not mindful, we will go through earthly life without ever being taught about our own Divine spirit-Self and the power which it has; and our soul will pay the price for our lack of knowledge. So, let's now take the time to learn more about this truth.

We have *a human individuality,* which our human aspect refers to as "I" or as "me". This is the "I" and the "me" with which most persons are familiar. However, this human 'I', this human 'me' is *not* the truth of who we are. This is a false self, a false identity which the world system taught us to create; and it is inferior to our true divine identity. Therefore, our human individuality is *the little i* and *the little me*. It is physical, power-hungry, body obsessed, insecure, fearful, and needy. It always feels 'not good enough' in some way; and no matter how much it gets or achieves, it is never satisfied. Our little i is a sensation-seeker. It always feels that it is lacking something which it needs to feel whole and complete. So, it keeps searching for that 'something' somewhere out there; but can get no satisfaction no matter how it tries.

Our Natural Mind is always preoccupied with this false identity (this little i) which it has created; and so our Natural Mind (the Natural Man, the Intellect) will worry, manipulate, hate, rage, envy, lie, cheat, steal, plot, scheme, take revenge, attack and even kill, just in order to keep giving the little i whatever it demands. By analyzing our way of thinking, we can easily see whether our little i is controlling our life. Nevertheless, the little i must never be seen as an enemy. It's just a manifestation of our lack of awareness of our Divine Identity. The more we raise our awareness of our Divine Identity, the more we will understand the true purpose of our little i. (We will study this true purpose at Level 2 and Level 3 of this Men's Bible Study).

By contrast, our Divine Mind does not acknowledge our human individuality. Our Divine Mind is not preoccupied with the demands of the little i, the little me. Our Divine Mind gives no recognition to this false identity, because our Divine Mind only recognizes and gravitates towards Truth. Therefore, it is our *Divine Self, our Divine Identity,* which our Divine Mind refers to as "I" or as "ME". This is 'the big I' and 'the big ME'. This is the divine I, the divine ME. It's the real I and the real ME; and it's *not* the same as the human i or the human me. So, whenever we say the words "I" or "Me", we can be speaking from our human identity or we can be speaking from our Divine Identity; we can be referring to the little i or the big I, the little me or the big ME.

When Jesus Christ used the words "I" or "I AM" or "ME" in speaking of Himself, He rarely spoke from His human identity. Never once is it recorded in the Four Gospels that He said of Himself: 'I am Jesus'. Rather, He always said simply: "I AM". That expression 'I AM' speaks of being divine. His focus was on His divine I and His divine ME. Your Divine I knows the truth that it is *already* whole and complete. It is not searching for anything 'out there'. It is not a sensation-seeker. It knows that it lacks absolutely nothing; for it is conscious that it carries within itself the *Allness* of The Infinite. It knows that it is already full of divine power, so it has no need to be power-hungry. It knows that whatever it requires is already within The Infinite. Your Divine Identity, your big I, knows that since it is the image of The Infinite, it is not just good enough; rather, it is more than enough.

The Divine Master

▣ THE DIVINE SIDE OF YOU: In God's divine plan, it is the Divine Self in man (the big I; the big ME) which is to be in control of every aspect of man. This is why we were created in God's divine spiritual image. The Divine Self has the Divine Mind. However, in this earthly environment where our divine aspect is not recognized, our Divine Self remains dormant until we come to the conscious awareness that it exists.

When the Divine Self is dormant and unproductive, the Natural Mind takes over and tries to do the job of the Divine Mind which is housed within the Divine Self. *(Remember Sarah and Hagar)*. Therefore, for most of our lives, while we did not know the truth of our Divine Identity, our human mind has been in control of our body. Over the years, our human mind has guided our body, sometimes in a positive direction and sometimes in a negative direction. The good news is that, if at any time you don't like the direction in which your human mind has been leading your body, then *you*, (the real you, the divine you) have the power to intervene and change the thinking of your mind. This change comes about by the process of *Mind Renewal*, where the Intellect is brought into obedience to the Divine Mind. The truth for which you are seeking is not 'out there'. It is already within your own Divine Self.

Your Natural Mind will be truly renewed when it starts to follow your Divine Mind as its disciple. Once your Natural Mind is renewed, it starts going in a positive direction, and your physical body has no choice but to obey and change direction. Then your Divine Mind will be in control of both your Natural Mind and your physical body. The more your awareness of your Divine Self increases, the more your obedience to your Divine Mind increases.

So, you are human and divine. Since you are divine, you are more than just body, soul, mind and emotions. Your *Divine Self*, which is *pure spirit,* is your higher self. It is *not* your human ego. It is The Real You. It is the absolute truth of who you are. It is your Spirit Self, and it comes directly from Spirit-God. So, your Divine Self has never 'sinned' and can never 'sin'. It cannot miss the target of the divine image of God. Your Divine Self has its own Divine Mind; and it is not, nor has it ever been, subject to world system thinking or to human nature. You are a Divine Spirit-Being with a divine mind who has temporarily taken on a human aspect and a human appearance in order to have a human experience in this world.

Your Divine Self, *(that image of God)*, is the Master-Teacher within you. Your soul, your human mind, your human body, your human will and your human emotions are supposed to be Disciples of your Divine Self. They are to be trained by and follow your Divine Self. Your Divine Self is the part of you which has the 'God connection'. This is the part of you which is controlled by and in oneness with the Holy Spirit.

The Divine Self is sometimes referred to in the New Testament in mystical language simply as *"Christ" (e.g. 2nd Corinthians 5:17)* or as *"Christ in you". (Colossians 1:27).* The Divine Mind within you is therefore known as *"the Mind of Christ"* (i.e. the mind of the Christ in you.) Do you see it?

When a man is not consciously aware of and is not in conscious connection with his Divine Self, the only thing with which he is working is his human identity and Intellect. The Natural Mind (the Intellect) takes over and begins to direct the body to do anything it pleases. There is no divine awareness to control the Natural Mind and to protect it from world system thinking. This is how we lived when we were complete 'slaves to sin'.

Please remember this: When you *'commit your life to* **Christ***',* it is more than a commitment to follow the teachings of the man Jesus Christ who taught over two thousand years ago. Truthfully, it is also a commitment to awaking the Christ in you (i.e. your Divine Self), and bringing it out of dormancy. It is a commitment to allowing 'Christ in you' through the Holy Spirit to be the Master-Teacher of your soul, body, mind and emotions for the rest of your earthly life. When the divine aspect of you becomes activated and empowered by the Holy Spirit's action and communication, the Natural Mind can be trained. The Divine Self will train the Natural Mind to be in harmony with Divinity and to be obedient to the leading of the Holy Spirit.

You will recall this verse which we studied earlier where **Christ** says: *"If any **man serve Me, let him follow Me** [let him be My disciple; be what I am; think as I think; have the same mind that I have]; and where I am [in consciousness], **there shall also My servant be** [in consciousness]: if any **man serve Me**, My Father will honor him."* *(John 12:26)* From a mystical point of view, this is Christ (the Divine Self in you) speaking here. Christ in you is telling you that your human identity (i.e. man) is called to follow and serve your inner, divine identity (i.e. Christ) *as its disciple.*

As the spirit-sons of God, we don't conform to the opinions which others have of us; neither do we change our thinking just to conform to traditional, religious ideas of who we are 'supposed' to be as 'good Christians'. Instead, we seek for the eternal Truth about ourselves, and then we renew our minds and transform to the point that we express that Truth. The divine truth of who you are is an eternal Truth. It was true before you were born in human appearance, and it remains true no matter what has happened to you since then.

The first step in activating our Divine Self and bringing it out of dormancy is to become consciously aware that we have a divine aspect. Then we are free to renew our Natural Mind to be in harmony with the Divinity which is the truth of who we are. The more we are keenly aware of our divine aspect, the more power it wields in our life. The Bible says: *"Don't be conformed to this world [system], but **be transformed by the renewing of your mind...**"* *(Romans 12:2)* Therefore, if there is any area of our life that needs to be transformed, Mind Renewal is the way to go about it.

Mind Renewal releases the power of transformation in a man's life. Without it, there will be no permanent change in the man. This is why it is possible for a man to have a religious experience, and to pray the 'sinner's prayer' while weeping before an altar in church, and to be a religious devotee, and to be self-righteous, and yet inwardly be no different than before. How is this possible? It is possible because his Divine Spirit-Self has not been activated, and his Natural Mind has not been divinely renewed to be its Disciple. The Divine Mind is an inner guidance system which allows us to be divinely guided in Divine Right Order. Let's be conscious that this Mind exists, and let's be willing to set our Intellect aside and follow where the Divine Mind leads us.

Breaking free from the tyranny of your thoughts

So here's the process: First, we renew our Natural Mind, and then we rise above our Natural Mind. Why would we ever need to rise above our Natural Mind? We need to do this because the Natural Mind is Memory, and Memory is from the past.

If you are depending exclusively on your Natural Mind (i.e. your Intellect) you are controlled by the past and you are a captive of the past. Let's think about it for a moment. If you are using your Natural Mind to think about *the past*, then you are dealing with the past. If you are thinking about *the present*, you are still dealing with the past, because 'the present' is nothing more than the manifestation of your past habits, past thoughts, past feelings, past moods and past actions which have become present circumstances. If you are thinking about *the future*, you are still dealing with the past, because you are using information stored in your memory and information about the present to anticipate future events.

However, you don't have to be a captive of the past. There is another option available to you. You can think with the Divine Mind. For Divinity, there is no past, no present and no future. Past, present and future exist in man's concept of Time; not in the realm of Eternity. For Divinity, everything exists in the Eternal Now. You will recall this principle from Lesson 2 of this book. Memory is a product of Time. So if you have been traumatized in the past and are haunted by memories, there is a way to rise above all of that. You will ultimately get to the stage where you are free from being controlled and dominated by your Natural Mind. You will be free from the tyranny of memories. It is a process, and we will go through that process at Level 2 of this Bible Study. Your willingness to experience Mind Renewal is the first step. Just be willing.

The Natural Mind will terrorize you if you let it. It will chatter when you want to sleep. It will instruct you to do things against your better judgment. It will lock you into patterns of fear and anger. Your Natural Mind does the bidding of your little i, your human identity. The thoughts produced by the Natural Mind are power-hungry, needy and always crave something more. No matter how much you meet its demands, it always demands more. The Natural Mind always feels that it is lacking something which is 'out there'; and in going after that 'something out there', the Natural Mind leads the body into 'sinful' activities.

In the episode of Adam and Eve in the Book of Genesis, this feeling of lack, inadequacy and insufficiency led them into 'sin'. That is why true Holiness is Wholeness; where you come to the realization that, as a divine being, you lack nothing. Everything is within you, within your Divine Self. When you have that awareness, it separates you and sets you apart from world system thinking. The Divine Self is the 'seat' or 'throne' of the glory of God in you. You will find within your Divine Self those "riches in glory by Christ Jesus" from which your every need is already supplied. *(See Philippians 4:19)*

When we become conscious and aware of our Divine Self, the Divine Self can take control. It can subject our Natural Mind to the Mind of Christ which is the Divine Mind. So, if your Natural Mind has been pressuring and tormenting you with unwanted thoughts, and if you have had enough and you need release, just come quickly to the awareness that your Natural Mind is doing the bidding of your human identity, your little i. Become conscious and aware that the little i is not the real you. Your Divine Self, your higher self, is the Real You. Practice differentiating between the thoughts which originate in your Natural Mind and the thoughts which originate in your Divine Mind. Any thought which is not helping you to feel whole and complete is coming from your Natural Mind. *(See Galatians 5:16-26 & Philippians 4:8 for guidance on this point.)*

◙ THE PEACE OF MIND TECHNIQUE: Here's a Technique to mentally position yourself to be free from the tyranny of the thoughts of your Natural Mind. Set aside some quiet time for yourself. Close your eyes and relax. Be a calm, silent observer, and watch your thoughts pass through your mind as you would watch clouds float across the sky. Don't become emotionally attached to your thoughts. Distance yourself from your thoughts and simply observe them. Whatever thoughts arise in your mind during this quiet time, don't judge them, don't try to fight them, and don't try to block them. If you do, they become more intense. Just watch them float through your mind, and let them pass through unhindered as you observe them. See them as being powerless to influence how you feel. If unwanted thoughts speak to you, acknowledge them by saying: "Thank you for sharing. You're free to go." Then watch them float away. See yourself as the master and not the victim of your thoughts. Since you desire to be free from the tyranny of your thoughts, practice this Technique faithfully. It will give you greater mastery of your thinking.

Who is the one observing the thoughts? It is the real you, your Divine Spirit-Self, your higher self, your big I, your Divine Identity, which is untouched by the turmoil of the Natural Mind. The Divine Self is a 'seer', a 'watcher', an 'observer'. So, by using this Technique, you become more aligned with your Divine Mind and less attached to the thoughts and demands of your Natural Mind. When your Divine Self takes more and more control of your thoughts, your mind feels lighter, more open, more relaxed, more calm, more flexible, more buoyant, happy and free. The pressure lifts, fear goes away, uncertainty flees, and you no longer feel like a victim who is struggling to get the victory.

Some Christians fall into the trap of waiting for God to renew their minds. They mistakenly believe that if they are members of a church for a long enough period of time, then their minds will automatically change. Unfortunately, it doesn't happen that way. Many Christians are taught to fight against their unwanted thoughts. Therefore, their mind becomes a battleground, and they have no peace. So, in desperation, they go into denial. They stuff their unwanted thoughts down into a hidden place in their mind, and convince themselves that those thoughts are no longer there. However, those suppressed thoughts will stay hidden temporarily. They will gather power and resurface days, weeks, months and even years later; and they will come back with a vengeance. Those thoughts will be so strong at that point that they will manifest themselves outwardly; and that Christian will be powerless to prevent that manifestation.

There is mind renewal work which is to be done, and no one can do it for us. It's not difficult but it requires commitment. Do you remember what we read in James 1:25 about how the 'mirror' works? We read that"...*any man who looks into the perfect law which sets you free, not being a forgetful hearer but **a doer of the work, that man shall be blessed in the work which he does.**"* So the aim is to have a disciplined mind. It doesn't come by wishing and hoping. It comes by diligent practice. When we get to Level 2 of this Bible Study, we will go through more of this process.

Separated from God?

Now you may be wondering: *Since the Divine Self is the truth of who we are, how could we have been unaware of it for so long even though we believe in God?* One of the major barriers which prevents many believers in God from walking in full conscious awareness of their divine spirit-Self is their belief that there is a gap of separation between themselves and Infinite God. They believe that God is an old man sitting on a throne somewhere far away in a place called 'heaven' which is somewhere far above their heads. Therefore, when they pray, they project their thoughts away from Earth, and they try to 'reach out' to a God whom they believe is at a far distance or in outer space. They also believe that God's presence comes and goes. So, they sing religious songs begging this far-away, transient God: "Do not pass me by". Therefore, many Christians believe more strongly in God's absence than they do in God's presence.

However, when you become consciously aware of your inner Divine spirit-Self, you will know that within you there is that 'God connection', that oneness with your Divine Spirit-Father, which is permanent. When you hold this awareness long enough, you will get to a stage in consciousness where you will speak from your Divine "I" and say like Jesus Christ did: *"I and my Father are one" (John 10:30).* In that state of oneness, there can be no separation. 'God in you' cannot 'pass you by'. Therefore, there is no need to search for God 'out there'. God is infinite, but God is also personal. That's why you have the God-connection within you.

The Bible tells us that God's plan is that we should be like Him. Genesis 1:27 tells us that we are designed to express the image of God. As was said in an earlier Lesson, that image is not physical; it is mental and spiritual. The more we think like God, the more we become like God in character. In our human selves, we can't do it. That's where the Mind of Christ, (the Divine Mind in the Divine Self), comes in.

Here's something to remember: *'Christ' is not the surname of Jesus.* Rather, 'Christ' refers to the Divine Self which dwelled within the man called Jesus. Jesus so fully and completely expressed that inner Christ, (that perfect, inner Divine Self), that the name 'Christ' became forever connected to His birth name which was 'Jesus'. In Hebrews 1:3, the Bible tells us that Jesus Christ is the express image of God. As we study His ministry as recorded in The Four Gospels, we see that He was the living embodiment of what it means to be in God's image. He was the complete outward expression of the inner Christ. The more we think like the Son of the Divine Father, the more we will express that divine image, and the more we will be like Christ.

So, since we are created in the image of God, why is it that we have had such difficulty in expressing the image of God in our lives? It is because we have been separated from God in consciousness. We have been unconscious and unaware of our Divine Identity. We have been separated from God in our minds, because the world system has given us an identity which is opposite to God, and it has also trained us to think thoughts which are opposite to the thoughts of God. Over time, our thoughts and our understanding of who we are became *unlike God*: i.e. un-Godlike or ungodly. *Colossians 1:21* describes the mental state of men with an ungodly mind. It says: *"...you were separated from God. You were hostile to Him in your minds as expressed by your evil actions..."* These ungodly thoughts created a barrier which blocked us from the divinity which is in our spirit. These ungodly thoughts were manifested in actions which are opposite to the ways of God.

Now since the problem starts by being separated from God because of the un-Godlike thoughts in our minds, the solution is to allow ourselves to be one with God in our minds. The more we think with our Divine Mind, the more we think like God, and the more we become like God in character. The more we think Godlike thoughts, the less we feel separated from God. The more we think Godlike thoughts, the more we produce Godlike words and actions. When we think Godlike thoughts and express these thoughts in Godlike words and actions, there will be no more enslavement to 'sin'. We will no longer be 'missing the mark' of the divine image of God. So, since we desire to be free from world system thinking, let's be willing to give ourselves unconditional permission to think differently from now on.

Your thoughts are not My thoughts

Now, in order to think godly (i.e. Godlike) thoughts, we are required to understand more of the truth about God. We may have to re-examine some of our current ideas in order to completely align our minds with Truth.

If you ask many people: "Where is God?" they will tell you that God is in heaven. And if you ask them: "Where is heaven?" they will say that heaven is somewhere 'up there' or 'up above' or 'beyond the sky'. So many people believe in the idea that God is 'up there, far away in heaven somewhere'. They believe that God is 'the Man upstairs' and that 'God is watching us from a distance'. This is one of the greatest deceptions of world system thinking. Do you hold these ideas anywhere in your mind? Many people, even devout Christians, have mentally created distance, a gap, a divide between God and mankind. This idea promotes the feeling of separation from God. It blocks people from knowing that oneness with God is their true reality.

This idea, that 'God is far away up in heaven', has had the effect of pushing God off the Earth. You may have learned this idea in Church, but it is a major part of world system thinking. The more Christians hold this idea in their minds, the more they strengthen and empower the world system. This is exactly the environment which the world system wants to create on Earth: an environment where God is absent, and there is no power here higher than itself. If you hold this idea anywhere in your mind that God is 'up there far away in heaven somewhere', you will not think that you are truly one with God. This idea of distance between you and God will cause you to separate yourself from God mentally, which will have a negative effect on your thoughts and your actions.

There is a hidden meaning in these well-known verses: *"For My thoughts are not your thoughts, neither are your ways My ways, says the Lord."* (Why is this so?) ***"For as the heavens are higher than the earth,*** *so are My ways higher than your ways, and My thoughts than your thoughts."* (Isaiah 55:8-9) (Please read these verses a second time before moving on. Let them sink in.)

The hidden meaning is this: *As far away as you separate heaven from earth in your mind, that is how far out of reach God's thoughts and God's ways will be to you.* If you read the verses again with this understanding, you will clearly see this hidden meaning.

These verses are revealing to us one of the dangers of believing that God is to be found 'up in the sky'. If you think of God as being at a distance, far away, up there, in the sky, beyond the blue, above the clouds, in outer space, in some distant place called 'heaven' which is higher than the Earth; and if you see God as being 'up above' and separated from you who are living 'down here on Earth'; you have put a barrier of space and distance between God and you; between His thoughts and ways and your thoughts and ways.

So, in your mind, feel free to close the gap between yourself and God, and feel free to close the gap between Earth and Heaven. As far as your Divine Self is concerned, heaven and earth are one. There is no 'above and below'. The Bible tells us that *God is not far from every one of us. (Acts 17:27)* He is far from those who are separated from Him in their thinking. So, feel free to let go of this idea of separation and distance existing between you and God. Then speak from your divine "I", and say like Christ: *"I and my Father are one" (John 10:30).* And please know that you are not being presumptuous when you affirm this truth. In John 17:21, Jesus spoke from His Divine Spirit and prayed for all those who would believe on Him, and these were His words: *"...that they may be one; as you, Father, are in me and I am in you, that they also may be one in us..."* Our being aware that we are one with God is the main focus of the prayer of Jesus recorded in The Gospel of John chapter 17. You will find it beneficial to read this awesome prayer regularly as it gives deep insight into the mind of the Son of God.

Christ in you, the hope of glory

It is God's will that you become fully conscious and aware that you are one with God. That is what it means to "know the truth". Traditionally, we have been taught to focus on our human identity, and we are not consciously aware that we have a Divine Identity which is pure spirit; this is why many times we struggle spiritually. Let's say this next statement aloud so it will sink in. Use your fingers and tap your chest as you say this statement three times: "I have a human identity and I have a Divine Identity. The Divine Identity is the truth of who I am."

For many Christians, we have been ignoring our Divine Identity while trying to spiritualize our human identity, but that won't work. We have been trying to think spiritually with our Natural Mind, but that won't work either. The Bible says: *"All [humans] have sinned* (have missed the target of divinity) *and **fall short** of the **glory** of God" (Romans 3:23).* Nevertheless, many Christians have still been desperately trying to express the glory of God strictly from the human side of themselves. It's impossible, because the Bible tells us that: *"...**Christ in you** (i.e. the Divine Self) is the **hope of glory**" (Colossians 1:27).* What does this verse mean? The Christ in you, the God in you, the Divine Identity in you is your only hope of expressing the divine glory of God. There is no need to try to be spiritual once you know the truth that you are indeed spirit.

We repeat for emphasis: There is a human aspect to you and there is a divine aspect to you. You are not unique in this. Jesus Christ was the same way. On His human side the Bible calls Him "Son of man" *(e.g. Mark 14:21),* but on His divine side the Bible calls Him "Son of God" *(e.g. John 20:31).* When He was born they called His name 'Jesus' *(Matthew 1:21),* but when He began to fully express His inner divinity, He became known as 'Christ'. He became the complete outward expression of the inner Christ. This is why when He asked His disciples: *"Who do you say that I AM?"* Peter replied truthfully: *"You are the Christ, the Son of the living God" (Matthew 16:15-16).* So the Christ in you, the inner Christ, the Divine Self is the part of you which is the son of the living God. The divine spirit in you is your only hope of expressing the glory of God.

If we deny and reject the divinity which is within us, how will we ever outwardly express the glory of the Divine Father? How will we ever outwardly express God's divine image? The little i can't do it by itself. Now at this point you may be wondering: *"Won't the Holy Spirit help us to express the glory of God?"* Yes, that's true. However, the Holy Spirit (who is Spirit-God in action and in communication) will connect with our own, inner divine spirit only, not with our human aspect. The Holy Spirit wakes our divine spirit out of dormancy, and anoints it, activates it and communicates with it. The Holy Spirit and our divine spirit speak the same language. It's a Spirit-to-spirit connection.

We know that whenever we read the New Testament in the Bible, and we see the word 'Spirit' spelled with a capital 'S', this refers to the Holy Spirit. On the other hand, when we see the word 'spirit' spelled with a common 's', it is usually referring to our divine spirit. Spirit communicates with spirit. Spirit cooperates with spirit. Spirit understands spirit. The Holy Spirit communicates with, cooperates with and understands our divine spirit. Likewise, our divine spirit communicates with, cooperates with and understands the Holy Spirit. The Psalmist says: *"Deep calls to deep..." (Psalm 42:7).* It's a Spirit-to-spirit connection.

The Bible says: *"...No eye has seen, no ear has heard and no heart has imagined the things which God has prepared for those persons who love Him."* [This tells us that our Intellect, using our five senses or using our human thoughts from our Natural Mind, can't really get a revelation of the thoughts of God]. *"But God has **revealed** these things to us* [God has revealed these things to our divine spirit] *by His [Holy]Spirit; for the [Holy]Spirit searches all things, even **the deep things of God**...No one knows the thoughts of God except the [Holy] Spirit of God."* (1st Corinthians 2:9-11)

Then the scripture continues: *"We have not received the spirit of the world* [system], *but* [we have received] **the spirit which is of God** [that's our divine spirit]; *that we might* **know the things** [i.e. the 'things'] *which are* **freely given** *to us of God." (1st Corinthians 2:12 KJV)* (Please read these passages of scripture a second time before moving on. Let them sink in.)

Your divine aspect, your divine spirit, is the part of you which has the 'God connection'. Your divine spirit is the part of you which is one with God. That's the part of you with which the Holy Spirit will communicate. The Holy Spirit will 'download' information and revelation of divine Truth into your spirit. If you ignore your divine spirit, you will be unaware of the things which God has ordained for you, and you will struggle spiritually. You are a beloved, divine spirit-son of God living temporarily in a human body. *"Those who are led by the Spirit of God, they are the sons of God". (Romans 8:14)* The Holy Spirit leads; and our divine spirit follows the leading of the Holy Spirit.

Real Godliness, Real Righteousness

When a man decides to walk with God, Mind Renewal is a must. He has to be willing to think differently than before. Unfortunately, some Christians become very frustrated because they try to force themselves to live a godly life without first putting in the discipline to have a godly mind. Jesus taught us that wrongdoing originates from wrong thinking. He said: *"From the heart* (i.e. from the deeper mind) *proceed* **evil thoughts**...*these are the things which make a man unclean." (Matthew 15:19-20)* We will study "the heart" extensively at Level 2.

As was said before, the only way we can be like God in character is to have God-like thoughts, for *"...as a man thinks,... so is he" (Proverbs 23:7)*. This is what the Bible refers to as Godliness, that is, thinking like God so we can be like God in character. Just as 'Sin' is a way of thinking, Godliness is also a way of thinking. Godliness comes when we think with the Mind of Christ, that Divine Mind which is in our spirit. It is possible to have a self-righteous, 'holier than thou' attitude and still be ungodly (unlike God). We can obey every religious rule and still "miss the mark". We can be self-righteous and yet not have the righteousness of God. Such attitudes come from the Natural Mind, not from the Divine Mind.

Self-righteousness is external. It is trying to imitate somebody's version of Christ in our actions, in our speech and in our outward appearance. Self-righteousness is our attempt to comply with the rules, regulations, prejudices, biases, pet peeves and pet projects of a particular religious group or a particular religious leader. By contrast, the righteousness of God is internal, within our divine spirit. It is *not* an imitation. It is *being* like Christ on the inside and having His attitude, His point of view and His mentality. It is *thinking* like a son of God. This is real righteousness (right-thinking), when the Mind of Christ is fused with our Natural Mind, and we become fully conscious and fully aware that the little i has no righteousness of its own.

All of our true righteousness (right-thinking) comes from the divine. When we live with this conscious awareness, Christ becomes part of our identity. We are fully conscious and aware of the presence of the inner Christ, and we feel free to express that inner Christ in our outward actions. Once our mind is right, we no longer have to worry about controlling the actions of our body. Imitating Christ is not necessary. Acting like Christ is not necessary. Pretending to be like Christ is not necessary. Trying to figure out: *'What would Jesus do?'* is not necessary. When we follow our 'right mind' (that's the Divine Mind), our body will be right and do right.

Being a right-thinking Christian

If we habitually think right thoughts, we will automatically do what is right. Then and only then will we be renewed in the spirit of our mind. Many Christians aim to be 'Bible-believing Christians'. However, the true aim is to be Righteous Christians (i.e. Right-Thinking Christians). If we know the Bible but we don't know the Truth, we won't be thinking right. Right-thinking brings us into the true righteousness of God which is higher than religious self-righteousness. This is a level of thinking which originates in the Divine Mind and takes charge of a Natural Mind which is wide open to Truth.

Now, here is the problem which Jesus had with the *scribes and Pharisees,* who were religious leaders of His day. The scribes in Jesus' day were extremely well-versed in the traditional knowledge of scriptures, but their minds were closed to a higher revelation of divine Truth. The Pharisees would pray and thank God that they were "not as other people are". They had an external, religious righteousness. They kept all of their religious rules, they congregated in the temple, they carried out their religious services but their minds and their hearts were unlike God. Their religious hang-ups and prejudices were still intact.

Every modern-day seeker of Truth has to put in the work to find and eliminate the 'scribe and Pharisee' which live in his own mind. The 'scribe and Pharisee' in our mind will reject Truth, and will prefer and choose traditional thinking over fresh revelation. The 'scribe and Pharisee' in our mind will resist the truth of our Divine Self. Since we desire to be free to be like Christ, then that external righteousness, that human self-righteousness, that 'holier than thou' attitude, that 'I am already versed in the scriptures' attitude, will have to go. So, Jesus told His disciples: *"Except your righteousness shall exceed* [shall be of a higher quality than] *the righteousness of the scribes and Pharisees, you shall never enter into the kingdom of heaven* [i.e. you shall never experience oneness with God]*" (Matthew 5:20).*

If you want the Bible to open up to you on this subject of true righteousness, whenever you see the word 'righteous' as you read the Bible, substitute it with the phrase 'right-thinking'. Try it and see what happens.

Seeing the unseen

So we clearly understand that we have a human identity and a divine identity. It is the big I, the Divine Identity, the Christ in us, the inner Christ, the Divine Spirit-Self which gives us hope that we can express the glory of God. Many times we focus on our little i and are unaware of the power of our Divine Identity. We depend on our soul to do what our spirit is designed to do. We forget that the Divine Self is who we truly are.

Many Christians may doubt that they are truly the Divine Self because they have been mentally conditioned to see themselves as sinners, wretches and worms. However, since we are now in Lesson 5, such shackles would have been broken from our minds. The Natural Mind (the Intellect) will want to struggle with the truth that we have a Divine Identity with its own Divine Mind. That's because the Natural Mind does not want to give up its dominance over our lives which it has enjoyed all these years. However, this truth, that we are divine, is very easy to grasp. Just say 'Yes' to it, and come into agreement with it.

How is it that we have a Divine Identity? We have a Divine Identity because we are created in the image of God who is Divine Spirit. It's not a physical image; it's a spiritual and mental image. We are the beloved, divine, free-born, spirit-sons of God; and whatever our Father is, we are. We are divine spirits temporarily wearing physical bodies. We are spirits in disguise. When we get to Level 2, we will study this in depth.

Now you may be wondering: *"If our divine identity is so important, how is it that we are mostly unaware of it?"* We are unaware of it because it is unseen. When we look in a mirror, we see our human body only, and so we tend to focus exclusively on that side of ourselves. However, in order to be like Christ, we cannot be reluctant to walk in our Divine Identity. It was the Divine Identity which made Jesus Christ who He was. He was more than just a teacher. He was the Son of God. His 'Son of God' status came from His Divine Identity.

When Jesus referred to God as 'Father', He was claiming divinity, and the Pharisees hated Him for it. The Pharisees were focusing on His human identity. They could not see His Divine Identity. All they could see when they looked at Jesus Christ was just a man from the village of Nazareth claiming to be divine. So our Divine Identity is unseen; yet, spiritually, it is more significant than our visible human identity. Now, we have a choice. We can either focus on our visible human identity or on our invisible Divine Identity. Let's examine our opening text, our WORD FOR TODAY, and find out where our focus should be. Should it be on what is seen or on what is unseen? What does the scripture say?

"We do not focus on the things which are seen, but rather on the things which are not seen. The things which are seen are temporary. The things which are not seen are eternal." (2nd Corinthians 4:18) (Please read this verse a second time before moving on. Let it sink in.)

Let us examine this verse as it relates to our human identity and our Divine Identity. Jesus Christ did not focus on His human identity and He rarely spoke from His human self. When He did refer to His human identity, He spoke of it in the third person and called it "the Son of man" (e.g. See Luke 7:34). His focus was on His Divine Self. Never once is it recorded in the Bible that Jesus Christ said of Himself: 'I was born in Bethlehem', or 'I grew up in Nazareth' or 'I was born in a manger because there was no room in the inn.' Rather He focused completely on His Divine Identity. Speaking from His Divine "I", He said: *"I proceeded and came forth from God" (John 8:42)* and *"I and my Father are one" (John 10:30)* and *"Before Abraham existed, I AM" (John 8:58).*

The phrase "I AM" is the 'God phrase'. It speaks of being divine. Be very mindful as to what words you attach to the expression "I am" when you speak of yourself. There is creative power in those words. We will study this principle in depth at Level 2. In order to be like Christ, feel free to focus on your divine aspect, because it is the eternal truth of who you are. Focus on your Divine Identity, that thing which is not seen. Your body and all the circumstances which relate to it, though essential and clearly visible, are just temporary.

Looking beyond what we can see

Our WORD FOR TODAY tells us that *"...we do not focus on the things which are seen but rather **we focus on the things which are not seen**..."* Now this seems strange. How can we focus on something which is not seen? The word 'focus' is translated from a Greek word from which we get the English word 'scope'. It conveys the meaning of a sentry standing on a watchtower using binoculars to focus on an object at a distance, an object which people at ground level cannot see. It's like a soaring eagle using its telescopic vision to view the landscape from a great height, and seeing objects on the ground which would be invisible to other birds.

Mentally, we go up higher. This is how we 'focus'. This is how we are able to perceive the unseen, eternal things which the world system cannot see. We rise above our attachment to the world system and its thinking. We rise above and look beyond our traditional understanding. We rise above and look beyond our mental conditioning. We do not allow such things to distort our vision. Therefore, since we desire to perceive spiritual Truth, let's be willing to look far beyond the things which are familiar to us. When we read the Bible, let's allow ourselves to go beyond a surface understanding of the scriptures. Let's allow the Spirit of Truth to show us more than we have seen before.

Using your eye of faith

At one level of meaning, the expression 'focusing on unseen things' means that seekers of Truth look beyond the surface meaning of the scriptures. Seekers of Truth do not confine their study to Bible facts which any person can understand. Rather they look beyond to the things which are not seen, to the hidden truths which are the secrets of the Kingdom of heaven. They go after the mystical meaning of the scriptures, and so they don't take everything they read literally.

However, at a different level of meaning, we can in another way focus on things which are not seen. We can do this by using our eye of faith. You may be wondering whether you have an eye of faith. Yes, you do, and since you have been practicing the Mind Renewal Technique which was outlined in Lesson 2, you have been using that eye of faith without knowing it. How you see yourself in your mind is crucial to living a victorious life. You are not free unless your mind is free.

If you see yourself as some kind of a sinner, that is who you will be. If you see yourself as someone with a weakness, that is who you will be. If you see yourself as a victim of circumstances, that is who you will be. If you see yourself as victorious, then that is who you will be. When you see yourself clearly in your State of Mind living a victorious life, you have evidence of the coming change. It may not have materialized yet, but you can see it already. *"...Faith is... the evidence of things not [yet physically] seen." (Hebrews 11:1)* We can only walk by faith when we are looking through the eye of faith.

Faith works best when there is a clear inner vision; that's why the Mind Renewal Technique is so essential. How you see yourself through the eye of faith is more important than how you see yourself through your natural eyes. When you close your outer eyes and see things in your imagination, what is actually happening is your faith is looking into your mind and seeing what's there.

Remember, Faith is always searching your State of Mind for some 'thing' to support. So let's consciously create clear, positive mental images, hold them in our minds and create the *feeling* to match. This will give our faith something positive, something wonderful, some 'thing' exceptional to support. *What Faith sees is what you get.* That's how faith works. The more you are a right-thinking man, the more you will see the right images of yourself in your mind using your eye of faith, regardless of how the outer circumstances of your life may seem at present. This is how you live by divine faith.

Now let's examine the second part of today's text: *"The things which are seen are temporary. The things which are not seen are eternal."* What does this mean? It means that anything which can be perceived with our natural eyes is temporary. It had a beginning and it will end. The things which are not seen are eternal, having no beginning and no ending.

So with this understanding let's amplify today's text: *"We do not focus on the things which are seen* [with our natural eyes] *but rather we focus on the things which are not seen* [with our natural eyes but can be seen with our inner eye of faith]. *The things which are seen* [with our natural eyes] *are temporary* [they have a beginning and an ending]. *The things which are not seen* [with our natural eyes but can be seen with our inner eye of faith] *are eternal things* [having no beginning and no ending]*"* (2nd Corinthians 4:18). (Please read this passage of scripture a second time before moving on. Let it sink in.)

In order to be free to be like Christ, we are required to withdraw our focus from any temporary things which can cloud our perception of Truth. Our human aspect and all the circumstances which relate to it are important. We pay much attention to these things because they are seen. However the text encourages us to focus on the unseen, eternal things. Our Divine Self falls into this category.

Who is your God?

Even with the best of efforts, many men struggle spiritually because their *concept of God* is limited, and sometimes even negative. Here's something worth remembering: *No two people believe in the same God.* Even within Christianity, no two Christians believe in the same God. Every man's concept of God is created by a combination of what he is taught to believe, his own personal experiences and his own state of mind.

Your ideas about God will determine your experience with God; for as was said before, God will deal with you according to your own mentality. So a believer in God is always interacting with his own concept of who and what God is. That concept is based on his beliefs, experiences and mentality. This is why you cannot rest your faith on the expression that says: *"What God has done for others He will do for you"*. Many people have lost faith in God because of trusting this expression, only to find that it did not work. Then they feel as if somehow God loves them less than He loves other people, which is not true.

The spiritual path is your personal journey with your God. *Your* God, *(i.e. your concept of God)* is the only God with whom *you* are interacting. *Your* God will deal with *you* at the level of *your* mentality. *Your* Faith will only support the 'thing' which it can clearly see within the boundaries of *your* State of Mind. No two people believe in the same God, and no two people have identical States of Mind. You cannot base your faith on other people's experiences or other people's testimony. Their God is not your God; and their State of Mind is not your State of Mind. Make the decision to get to the truth of who *your* God is, and refine *your* concept of *your* God based on that truth. (We will go through this process in detail at Level 2.)

So let's get to a place mentally where we are not trying to believe in somebody's concept of God or in religion's concept of God. Let's get to a place spiritually where we are not dependent on any other Christian's experience or testimony. Let's get to a place in consciousness where we know The Infinite for ourselves and have our own personal, selected God-consciousness. Let's really get to know The One in whom we have believed.

If you wish to take your understanding of God to a higher level, you will find it helpful to read The Gospel of John from a Bible where the words of Jesus are printed in red ink. Better yet, listen to a recording of this Gospel. If you study from a Bible which is not the King James Version, please compare what your Bible says with what is written in the King James Version of the Bible.

Refining your concept of God

If you believe in a severe, warlike, angry, oppressive and vindictive God, please know that this is just one of many available concepts of God. You have been attracted to this concept because of your beliefs, your experiences and your state of mind. The little i is very attracted to this concept of God. Now, you may say: *"But that's the God I see when I read certain passages in the Old Testament in the Bible!"*

Do you remember the Mirror Secret of the Bible which we studied in Lesson 3? There is something in the Bible to reflect every state of mind. The ideas to which we are attracted in the Bible and our interpretation of them will reflect who we are and how we think. All else will fade from view.

God is portrayed in both positive and negative ways in the Bible because, at a basic level of meaning, there is something in the Bible to reflect every state of mind. This is why God in the Old Testament is portrayed in a different way than the Heavenly Father in the New Testament. God is *not* both good and evil. *The Infinite does not have a split personality.* There is something in the Bible to reflect every state of mind. (Another reason for this negative portrayal of God is that the stories in the Bible are in fact parables.)

In the famous Sermon on the Mount, Jesus Christ addressed this issue. He revised many of the Old Testament teachings. One such teaching to which He made reference was the idea that it is right to hate your enemies, and that being angry and oppressive to enemies was God's way of dealing with them. Jesus said the opposite. He said: *"You have heard that it was said by people in the ancient times, 'You shall love your* *neighbor and hate your enemy'. But I say to you, Love your enemies...**that** **you may be the children of your Father*** who is in heaven* [who is in the spiritual dimension]." (Matthew 5:43-45)*

Why is the concept of God in the Old Testament often portrayed as a severe, warlike, angry, oppressive and vindictive God? This portrayal of God as severe, warlike, angry, oppressive and vindictive is a reflection of the collective mentality of the ancient people who are the characters of the Old Testament. It is a reflection of the collective state of mind of the ancient people who inhabited that region which is now known as 'the Middle East'. God deals with people at the level of their mentality. You will always portray in your own attitudes the image of your concept of God. Your concept of God develops out of the qualities of character which you admire, enthrone and worship in your own mentality.

By contrast, the mentality of Jesus Christ was love, goodness, mercy, compassion, grace and forgiveness. As a result, the Heavenly Father whom Jesus portrayed had the same qualities. Your big I, your Divine I, is always attracted to this concept of God. As a divine son, it always gravitates towards the Heavenly Father whom Jesus Christ portrayed. Jesus Christ came from the 'bosom' of the Father. So, when He tells us of the beautiful qualities of the Divine Father, there is no doubt that we are getting the unadulterated truth.

So, if you have been holding a belief in a severe, warlike, angry, oppressive, unforgiving, vengeful God, you may wish to ask yourself: *"Why do I have the need to believe in harshness, conflict, anger, oppression, being unforgiving and being vengeful? Why do I enthrone these qualities in my heart? Why do I keep them in my mentality?"*

Are attitudes of harshness, conflict, anger, oppression, being unforgiving and being vengeful to be found anywhere in you? If so, you can easily replace these attributes with love, goodness, mercy, compassion, grace and forgiveness. When you make these finer qualities your focus, and enthrone them in your heart, all else will fade from view when you read the Bible.

The Infinite, our Heavenly Father, is a God of Love. The true God is All Good; and All Good is *all* that the true God is. Psalm 100:5 tells us: *"For the Lord is good: His mercy is everlasting: and His truth endures to all generations".* When the verse says that the Lord is good, it means more than just saying 'God is a good person'. It means that good is *all* that The Infinite is. Good is God; and God is Good.

The purpose of All Truth is to lead us to conscious oneness with Infinite Good. You may be wondering: *"If God is so good and so full of love, why is there so much negativity in the world? Why do bad things happen to good people; and why do good things happen to bad people?"* The answers to these questions will become crystal clear when we study Spiritual Laws at Level 2 of this Men's Bible Study.

The Wilderness Experience

We say a special word here to any man who for some reason has become spiritually weakened or has lost faith and trust in God. Perhaps you went through some difficult experiences, the reason for which you cannot fathom. Perhaps someone whom you looked up to as a religious leader did not live up to your expectations. Perhaps you have been through challenges which can only be described as hell on earth. Perhaps you feel as if God has abandoned you.

Please know that sometimes people go through a Wilderness Experience. Many people in the Divine Family have had to spend some time in *'the wilderness'*. We see this symbolized by the wilderness experiences of certain famous characters in the Bible as recorded in both the Old and New Testaments. Abraham, Jacob, Joseph on his way to Egypt, Daniel on his way to Babylon, Moses, David, Elijah, John the Baptist, Jesus, the list goes on. They all spent time in the wilderness, and it wasn't pleasant for any of them.

On the spiritual path, you will have 'mountain top experiences' and you will have 'wilderness experiences'. Mountain top experiences will show you who God is. By contrast, wilderness experiences will compel you to come to terms with who you are. Spending time in the spiritual wilderness is a spiritual rite of passage. It is sometimes called *"the dark night of the soul".* It is the prelude to great spiritual enlightenment. Your wilderness experience is your 'wake-up call' from the Divine Family. Nevertheless, at the same time, it's a challenge because the 'spiritual wilderness' is traversed in gloom and isolation. You feel cut off from God and from those around you. During this time of your life, God is silent. Your prayers go unanswered. Nothing goes right. You are sometimes attacked, mistreated, abused or betrayed and you can't figure out why. The more you try to do your best, the harder you are tested and tried. You feel heartbroken and lost. The closer you get to the end of the wilderness experience, the worse it gets. However, don't despair. It's all a part of your spiritual training. It won't last forever, even though it may feel endless.

Some men misunderstand the 'spiritual wilderness', and give up on God. However, it is for a divine purpose. When you come through the Wilderness Experience, you are on the path to fulfilling the divine purpose for which you were assigned to the Earth. Please understand that every person in the Divine Family has a particular role to play in the great drama of God's divine plan for the Earth. The 'spiritual contracts' regarding your earthly life were 'signed' before you came to Earth. You 'signed up' for your assignment. However, in your spiritual amnesia, you don't remember any of this, and so your Wilderness Experience seems pointless. (We will study this in depth at Level 2.)

However it is not pointless. If you have been through the Wilderness Experience and have come out victorious, you are *extremely valuable* in the Father's Kingdom. You are like gold which has passed through the furnace, and has emerged more valuable than before. When you take this time and the information in this book, and use them to upgrade your concept of God and of yourself, the 'spiritual wilderness' will build a strength within you which is second to none. There are certain lessons which you can learn only in the wilderness and in isolation. You will need these lessons later on. Only then will the reasons for your Wilderness Experience become clear.

Every son of God is called to give some type of service to humanity. Every son of God has been selected to draw sustenance out of his divine spirit in order to feed and bless others in some way. You are called to be 'bread' for some hungry souls. Therefore, the human aspect of every son of God has to be processed and refined to get to that point. Some bruising and crushing will happen, but it is only for a time and in measure. The Bible says: *"Grain must be crushed (ground, processed and refined) in order to make bread, but it is not crushed forever. The wheels of the cart and the horses will damage it, so it is not crushed for longer than is necessary. This insight comes from the Lord of the armies of heaven. His plan is wonderful and His wisdom is awesome"* (Isaiah 28:28-29).

So, if, for whatever reason, you have lost faith during the Wilderness Experience, please take courage and don't give up. Many before you in the Divine Family have gone through the same and worse and have survived and come out victorious. Many are going through it right now. You have not been singled out for any type of 'punishment', and you are not alone. Don't abort your divine mission and purpose.

You can use this time as a starting point for a different consciousness of God. You can re-evaluate and upgrade your concept of God, and ensure that you are a right-thinking truth-seeker in right relationship with your Heavenly Father. You can clear your mentality of any traces of mental bondage. You can give yourself the gift of Mental Freedom by knowing the truth that you are a beloved, free-born, spirit-son of God. You can let go of any feelings of fear, anger, hatred, resentment, disappointment, guilt, shame or self-condemnation, and assume your Divine Identity as a son of God. (We will go through this process at Level 2.) You can live each day with the conscious awareness of your Divine Self. If you are willing, the darkest of times can give way to the brightest of days; but only if you are willing. This is not to minimize whatever has happened to you in the wilderness. Rather, it is a confirmation that, as a beloved son of God, you are *greater* than whatever has happened to you.

The purpose of organized religion

Some men have had a positive experience with their involvement in organized religion. For other men, that experience has been very negative; so negative that it has caused them to lose faith in God. Whatever our experience may have been, it is necessary for all of us to recognize that religion is temporary. It had a beginning and it will end one day. Religion will last for a time, but *"Jesus Christ is the same yesterday, today and forever". (Hebrews 13:8)* As seekers of truth, our focus is 'eternal life' which is 'eternal conscious oneness with The Infinite'. Since religion is temporary, it cannot by itself give eternal life to us. Temporary things cannot produce eternal things. Eternal life is to be found in Christ.

This is why 1st John 5:11-12 says: *"...God has given to us **eternal life** [eternal, conscious oneness with God], **and that life** [that conscious oneness with God] **is in His Son** [His Manifestation]. **Any man who has the Son** [Any man who has the Manifestation of God] **has life** [has conscious oneness with God]; and any man who does not have the Son [Any man who does not have the Manifestation of God] does not have life"* [does not have conscious oneness with God]. Please read this passage of scripture a second time before moving on. Let it sink in.

The verses which we have just read tell us that Divine Sonship is the true and living Way to eternal life. Divine spirit-sonship is the way that we get to experience eternal, conscious oneness with God. This is why the Son of God said in *John 14:6: "I AM the way, the truth and the life"*, and why the Bible says *"any man who **has the Son** has life"*. When you know the truth of the Divine Sonship of Jesus Christ and the truth of your own divine sonship, you know that you are eternally one with God.

So then, what is the purpose of organized religion? It is a means of calling our attention to the divine side of life. When religion follows the teachings of truth and love, it creates a community of believers where we can worship and fellowship together, help and support each other, and minister to the needs of the wider society. However, religion is not the way to eternal life. Divine Sonship is the way, the truth and the life. Every time you see the expression 'eternal life' or 'everlasting life' mentioned in the Bible, be conscious that it actually means 'eternal, conscious oneness with Infinite God'.

The Bible gives a test which every son of God is required to pass, and here it is: *"Examine yourselves whether you are in the faith. Test yourselves: **Do you know that Jesus Christ is in you?** If not, you have failed the test." (2nd Corinthians 13:5)* When you know that Jesus Christ is in you and that you and Christ are one, you will "have the Son", and you will have "life" (i.e. oneness with God). Also, you will stop singing religious songs which say that Jesus Christ is "passing by" or "passing this way".

It is interesting to note that the believers in Christ, who are spoken of in the New Testament in the Bible, didn't call their beliefs 'Christianity' and they didn't call themselves 'Christians' at first. The word 'Christian' was a nickname assigned to them by non-believers which they later accepted. *(See Acts 11:25-26)* Rather, when they referred to the teachings of Jesus Christ and the values which He portrayed, they simply called these things **'The Way'** (meaning 'The Path'). *(See Acts 9:2, 18:25 & 22:4)*

Organized Christian religion is a signpost to point us to Jesus Christ who is the divine, outward portrayal of the inner Christ in every man; the perfect portrayal of Divine Sonship. However, if we set up camp around the signpost of organized Christian religion, and don't start actually progressing in the 'The Way', the way of Divine Sonship, the

Spiritual Path, we will never get to eternal life. We will never get to experience eternal oneness with God. The focus of the sons of God is not fixed on the external, temporary things. We are on this Earth for a limited time. Our focus is fixed on the internal, eternal things which will continue after earthly life is over. The center of our focus is the epitome of Divine Sonship: Jesus Christ, the same yesterday, today and forever.

It's good to do a bit of self-evaluation by asking yourself these questions: *"If tomorrow all churches were closed down, and there was no more organized Christian religion, and nobody available to preach to me, would I find that I am experiencing oneness with God in Divine spirit-sonship? Could I stand on my own and keep the faith because of the strength of my conscious awareness of my own Divine Identity? Could I make it without depending on following 'Church celebrities', or would I feel lost without them? Do I really have a relationship with the inner Christ?*

The spiritual path is your personal interaction and your personal journey with your God. So if your experience with religion and religious people has been negative, don't let it be a roadblock on your spiritual path.

The Truth about Jesus; the Truth about you

Many of us have been taught many things about Jesus Christ from early childhood. However, some of us have never paused to examine whether what we have been taught is the truth. For many people, when they hear the name Jesus Christ, an image comes to mind either of a baby in a manger, or a man wearing a robe and sandals or a man nailed to a cross. These are the *images* created by artists and portrayed in movies.

However, in order to be free to be like Christ, let's be willing to know who Jesus Christ truly is. Let's be willing to stop focusing on His temporary human body, and instead focus on His divine aspect which is unseen and eternal. The real Christ was not the physical body which could be seen and touched. That body was the 'house' in which the real Christ lived. The real Christ was the unseen, timeless, eternal Spirit who lived in that body. Jesus said in John 6:63: *"It is the spirit which gives life* (oneness with God); *the flesh profits nothing... "* (i.e. the physical body will never give you oneness with God). When Jesus Christ walked this Earth, He was more than just a man. He was Divine Spirit with a Divine Mind housed in a physical body. In order to perceive this truth about Jesus Christ, we cannot focus on His physical aspect.

Similarly, in order to know the truth about yourself, you cannot focus on your physical aspect, that physical body which you inhabit temporarily while on Earth. Instead, shift your focus from the physical Jesus to the divine Jesus, and shift your focus from the physical you to the divine you. Be willing to look at the thing which is not seen; *the inner, eternal you which has the divine connection.* That is where your eternal Truth is to be found. If you hold that image of a physical Jesus in your mind, you will be locked into focusing on the physical aspect. That physical image will block you from connecting with His divine aspect, and it will block you from connecting with your own divine aspect as well.

Jesus Christ was not 'only human'; and neither are you. The Bible tells us that we shouldn't think of Jesus as human anymore. 2nd Corinthians 5:16 says: *"So, from now on, we do not know anyone from a human point of view. And even though we used to think of Christ in that way, we do not know Him that way anymore."*

Our little i loves to focus on its individuality, so it can feel special and superior to other individuals. Therefore, it keeps creating criticism, prejudice and hostility so that it can feel 'better than' other individuals. However, when we come to the truth of our Divine Identity, we think of ourselves, not as human individuals, but rather as divine spirits in oneness with our Divine Spirit-Father. In that state of divine oneness, there is no room for criticism, prejudice or hostility.

Remember, the aim is to be like Christ. If you think of Him as Divine Spirit, as an expression of divinity, you will reflect that in your own life. You will see yourself and others in the same way, as divine spirits. You will give yourself greater access to your Divine I.

Letting go of the 'Old Man' image

And while we are on the subject of images, this is a good time to rethink any belief that God is an 'old man' or 'the Man upstairs'. It's time to re-evaluate any traditional image which portrays God as an old man with a long, white beard sitting on a throne up in the clouds. Is that image anywhere to be found in your mind whenever you think of God?

Jesus Christ taught us plainly that *"God is a Spirit: and those who worship Him must worship Him in* **spirit** (that's your divine spirit) *and in* **truth** (that's the divine truth of who you are)*" (John 4:24).* Anybody can praise God; but when we know the truth about God and the truth about our own divine spirit, we can be a true worshipper of God. Our little i can praise God, but it can't worship God. Only our divine spirit can connect with God in true worship.

God is a Spirit. Now, it's hard for us to hold the concept of 'Spirit' in our minds. So artists and movie makers have tried to portray God as an old man, in order to make it easier for us to have a concept of God. However, this image of God as an old man will create problems for any seeker of Truth. The Bible says that: *"No man has seen God at any time..."* *(John 1:18)* Now you may be wondering: "How can the Bible say that no man has seen God at any time? What about the people mentioned in the Bible who saw visions of God as having a human form and sitting on a throne?"

In any vision, what is seen is a representation of an idea. For example, in the Book of Genesis, chapter 41, when God wanted to show Pharaoh a vision of famine coming to Egypt, He represented the idea of 'famine' by showing Pharaoh seven bony, malnourished cows devouring seven fat cows. We understand clearly that the vision of seven bony, malnourished cows devouring seven fat cows was just a representation of the idea of seven years of famine wiping out seven previous years of abundance. We also understand clearly that this vision doesn't mean that there would actually be cannibal cows on a rampage in Egypt.

Similarly, when Isaiah the prophet said of his vision, *"...I saw the Lord sitting on a high and exalted throne and His robe filled the temple." (Isaiah 6:1)*, did Isaiah actually see God? No, he did not. "No man has seen God at any time".

Isaiah saw a representation of an idea. The seated figure on the throne represents a king. The exalted throne represents the idea of heavenly kingship in the spiritual dimension. The temple represents the idea that this is a spiritual king and not an earthly king. His robe filling the temple represents the idea that He controls the spiritual realm. It's just a physical representation of certain attributes of God so that Isaiah's human mind could understand.

Think about this. In order for Infinite God to actually sit on a throne, God would have to possess a limited, defined, physical form. The throne would have to be either as large as or larger than God. Also God would be smaller than whatever floor the throne was resting on and smaller than the temple that God was in. God would be confined to that throne and that temple, so there would be areas in space and in other dimensions where God would not be there.

God's 'throne' is not any type of chair or seat. God's 'throne', as mentioned in the Bible, is a symbol which represents the idea of the ultimate divine authority of Infinite God. The Bible is written in symbolic language. This is why, as seekers of Truth, we expand our minds to understand more and more and more of The Infinite. So if you are ever tempted to give a literal interpretation to Isaiah's vision or any other vision recorded in the Bible, you may find it helpful to say to yourself, "Cannibal Cows", as a gentle reminder that visions are just representations of ideas.

It is unwise to try to shrink God and assign a human form to God in order to make God fit within our human understanding. God is Infinite Spirit; too mind-blowing and too vast for us ever to fully comprehend in this life or in the life to come. Numbers 23:19 tells us plainly that *"God is not a man…"* We refer to God as 'He' and 'Him'; but not because God has a male human form, or any form at all. It is simply because our language is too limited to have a pronoun for 'Infinite Spirit', and it seems disrespectful to refer to God as 'It'. So, we say 'He' and 'Him'.

So when the Bible says that we are created in the image of God, that image is not a physical form. It is a spiritual image and a mental image. And when the Bible says that Jesus Christ is the express image of God (Hebrews 1:3), that image is not a physical form. It is a spiritual image and a mental image.

Here's a suggestion so you can let go of seeing God as an old man or as having any physical form: *Stop using the word 'person' to refer to God.* When you read the King James Version and some other versions of the Bible, you may see the word 'person' used in reference to God. (e.g. Hebrews 1:3) However, in the original Greek language, that word which is translated 'person' actually means 'essence'. So, if you have been using the word 'person' or 'persons' in referring to God, please release that from your mind and let it go. This suggestion goes against traditional teaching and traditional hymns, but here's why that word 'person' will shackle your mind to the 'old man image', and block you from remembering that God is Infinite Invisible Spirit. In human minds, the word 'person' brings up a human image: head, face, arms, hands, torso, legs and feet. This is how we have been trained to think over the years, and as far as our human minds are concerned, this is what a 'person' is. This idea, that God is a person, trains us to put a human form and human limitations on Infinite Invisible God. It is therefore a good practice to refer to God as "The Infinite". By doing so, we allow our minds to expand beyond human images and human limitations.

The higher meaning of Jesus Christ

Now that we have seen the importance of focusing on the eternal, unseen, divine things, let's go one level higher and get some more insight into the truth of who we really are and the truth of who Jesus Christ really is. This information may seem very strange at first because it is not traditionally taught, but please keep an open mind. Remember that the Bible is written at several different levels of meaning. When we move from the level of meaning with which we are familiar, and progress to a different level, it may seem strange at first. However, when we remain at that new level and let the information sink in, after a while we understand and benefit from the information. Are you ready? Here we go.

Understanding our Divine Identity is a crucial step in our development as sons of God. However, it is challenging for us to come to terms with our Divine Identity because it is hidden from our natural eyes. When we look at our reflection in a mirror, we cannot see our divine aspect. All we see is the human aspect of ourselves. Nevertheless, we are required to focus on this unseen, divine aspect since we desire to be like Christ. Remember our opening text: *"...we focus on the things that are not seen...the things that are not seen are eternal."*

The Infinite would not leave us to struggle in the darkness, ignorant of the divine aspect of ourselves. So in order to assist us, a representation of our own divine aspect is displayed in The Four Gospels (i.e. the books of Matthew, Mark, Luke and John in the New Testament) in such a manner that our human minds can see it.

Jesus Christ, as portrayed in The Four Gospels, is more than a historical figure, more than a man who lived over two thousand years ago, more than a man on whose teachings Christianity is based, more than a teacher, more than a healer, more than a prophet, more than a Savior and more than a figure on a cross. At a different level of meaning, Jesus Christ as portrayed in The Four Gospels is a pattern, a prototype, a template, a symbol and a visible representation of your own Divine Self. He is the outward, visible portrayal of your unseen, inner Divine Self. He is a representation of your own divine aspect, your higher self, your inner spirit, the real you, the eternal, everlasting you. This is why the Bible asks: *"Do you know that Jesus Christ is in you?"* (i.e. Are you aware that Jesus Christ is the outward portrayal of your own inner Divine Self?) *(2nd Corinthians 13:5)*

Remember what was said earlier about visions. In a vision, a person is given a representation of an idea. It is a way to make invisible things become visible and understandable. So our Divine Self is portrayed for us in a physical way in the Bible. It is portrayed in the person of Jesus Christ so that, by focusing on Him, we can focus on the part of us which is not seen, and that is our Divine Self. In Him, the invisible part of us becomes visible. When we read His words and study His life as depicted in The Four Gospels, we get insights into our Divine Self, into the divine aspect of who we are. This divine aspect is the part of us which has the 'God connection'.

Our Divine Self has to teach our human self how to conform to the Divine Mind. Our human self is called to serve, obey and follow our Divine Self. Remember, the Divine Self in us is the Master-Teacher; and all the faculties of our soul, mind, body, will, heart, and emotions are in fact the Disciples of the Divine Self. This is the higher, mystical meaning of Jesus Christ the great Master-Teacher and His Disciples. Many times when Jesus speaks in The Four Gospels, His words are actually a representation of what our Divine Self is teaching to our human self. When we study and follow these words, we can clearly understand what is being taught.

When you read The Four Gospels with this awareness of what Jesus Christ represents, your Divine Self comes to the forefront. Now you can see it. Now you can hear it. Now you can be instructed by it. Now you can be transformed by it. It's no more in some hidden place within. It has stepped out into the light of your conscious awareness.

Now we know it takes some mind expansion to see Jesus Christ in this way. This is why the Bible tells us that we shouldn't think of Him as a man. He is much more than that. This truth is beyond 'believing' and beyond 'knowing'. In order to get into this level of truth, you are required to do some 'watching'. Be willing to rise above traditional concepts and ideas. When you understand this truth: *Jesus Christ as portrayed in The Four Gospels is an outward representation of your inner Divine Self,* a whole new level of understanding opens up to you. You become aware of the higher significance of scriptures which you may have been reading for years.

Let's look at an example of this portrayal of the Divine Self in the person of Jesus Christ. Let's examine this well-known verse where Jesus says: *"**I AM** the way, the truth and the life; no **man** comes to the **Father** except by **Me**." (John 14:6)* What does this mean? At a basic level of meaning, these are words which Jesus spoke indicating that He is the way, the truth and the life, and that no one can access the Divine Father except by being like Him (i.e. being the son of the Father).

However, this verse is actually saying much more than that. As was said before "I AM" speaks of being divine; and 'man' speaks of being human. So, at a different level of meaning, these words are spoken by your Divine Self directly to your human self: *'I, your Divine Self, am the **way** to the divine aspect of life. I, your Divine Self, am the **truth** of who you are. I, your Divine Self, am the **life** of God in you, your 'oneness with God'. The human aspect (i.e. man) can only access the Divine Father by means of his Divine Self.'*

Let's read the verse again bearing in mind that it's your Divine spirit-Self speaking to you. When you keep that awareness as you read, you will hear the voice of the Divine Self clearly. *"I AM the way, the truth and the life; no man comes to the Father except by me."* Did you hear it?

Let's look at another example. Jesus Christ said in John 10:9: *"**I AM** the door; if any **man** enters in by **me**, he shall be saved, and shall go in* *and out and find pasture."* (Please read this verse a second time before moving on. Let it sink in). What does this verse mean? At a basic level of meaning, these are words which Jesus Christ spoke indicating that He is the access point to salvation of the soul, and when we like sheep follow Him the Good Shepherd, He will lead us to places where our souls can be nourished and fed.

However, at a different level of meaning, these words are spoken by your Divine spirit-Self directly to your human self saying: *"I, your Divine Self, am the access point (the door) which connects the natural realm to the divine realm. By accessing me, you will be saved (delivered) from the limitations of being human. By accessing me you get the benefits of both the natural realm and the divine realm. You can walk in both worlds and be nourished both naturally and spiritually [i.e. go in and out and find pasture]. You can access those 'green pastures' which Psalm 23 speaks of."* Do you see it? With this awareness that it is the Divine Self speaking to us, let's read the verse again: *"I AM the door; if any man enters in by me, he shall be saved, and shall go in and out and find pasture."* Did you hear it?

With this awareness, we can clearly hear the Divine Self calling to the human aspects of who we are; calling to our bodies, our minds, our hearts, our souls to be its disciples by saying: ***"Come unto me,*** (come to conscious awareness of your Divine spirit-Self) *all you who are laboring and are forced to bear heavy burdens and **I will give you rest.** Take **my yoke** (the doctrine of Divine Sonship) upon you and **learn from me,** for I am **gentle** and **humble** in heart and you shall find rest for your **souls.** For my yoke is easy and my burden is light."* (Matthew 11:28-30)

This is what is meant by the Bible being written at several different levels of meaning. One verse of scripture carries many messages; but the information is compressed into a few words, and so the Spirit of Truth has to 'open the scriptures' to us.

The true meaning of 'Take up your cross'

We have looked at three examples of the words of Jesus representing what our Divine spirit-Self is saying to our human self. Now that we have the understanding that at a different level of meaning Jesus Christ represents our Divine Self, let us look at some other well-known verses and see what they say. Let's read the following verses with the awareness that it is our Divine Self speaking to our human self.

In Mark 8:34-35, the Divine Self says: *"...if any **man** will be **my disciple**, let him **deny himself, take up his cross** and **follow me**. For anyone who will **save his life** shall lose it, but anyone who shall **lose his life** for my sake and the gospel's sake shall save it."* (Please read this passage of scripture a second time before moving on. Let it sink in.)

Many people have misinterpreted this verse, and have used it to justify suffering, hardship and even death in their lives. If they are faced with circumstances which are prolonged and difficult, they will sigh and say: "It's my cross to bear". Have you ever heard people say this? This notion of 'bearing your cross of suffering' is a favorite among Christian songwriters, and many people have accepted this interpretation of the verse without questioning it. But what is the verse really saying? What does this verse mean?

We see how this verse is usually interpreted. However, let us analyze it at a different level of meaning. Let's look at it from the point of view of the Divine Self speaking to the human self.

Your Divine Self is saying to your human self: *"If you (the human self) want to be like me and learn from me as **a disciple** of the Divine Self, you are required to **deny your (human) self, take up your cross**, and **follow where I, your Divine Self, will lead you**. Anyone who tries to **cling to his human life at the expense of his divine life**, will miss out on living the divine life. But anyone who will **merge his human life with the divine life**, and live the abundant life promised by the gospel, he will end up truly saving his human life."* With this understanding, please read the verses again and you will hear the voice of the Divine Self clearly.

Now let's dig deeper. What does the expression 'take up your cross' mean? That expression is a clue to the method by which you merge your human life with the divine life. This is what Jesus meant when He said: *"...I am come that they might have **life** (that they might experience conscious oneness with God) and have it more abundantly" (John 10:10).* Conscious oneness with God is true life; divine life.

As we have said before, Jesus Christ had a human aspect and a divine aspect. In His human aspect He is called "Son of man" but in His divine aspect He is called "Son of God". The same is true of you. You have a human aspect (son of man) and you have a divine aspect (son of God). After the resurrection of Jesus, His human aspect and His divine aspect were completely blended. We too want to get to a place spiritually where our divine aspect and our human aspect are blended. We want to live in the natural world in a human body, but yet be living under the auspices of our Divine Self. So, how did Jesus do it? How did He accomplish this merging of the two aspects of who He was? The answer is: *He took up His cross.*

The last act of Jesus in His human aspect was to take up His cross and go to a place called "Golgotha" which means "the place of a skull" (John 19:17). When He stretched out on that cross and died, He took His last breath in His human aspect. He left His human aspect on the cross. The Bible tells us that three days later when He was resurrected, His humanity and His divinity were completely blended. He lost His human life on that cross, but by doing so, He gained an access to His divine aspect which He did not have before. By taking up His cross, the full power of His Divine Self was fully manifested and His human aspect was totally subjugated. This process of taking up the cross, dying and rising again with a new life is a symbol of transformation.

How does this apply to us? As spirit-sons of God we follow the same process of transformation, but in a spiritual way. What did the verse say? It said: *"...deny yourself, take up your cross and follow Me."*

◎ DENY YOURSELF: First, be willing to 'deny yourself'. *Deny your human self.* Deny the notion that you are 'only human'. Deny that the real you is what you see when you look at your reflection in a mirror. Deny that you are just a son of man but not a son of God.

◎ TAKE UP YOUR CROSS: Next, make the commitment that you will no longer be led by your human thinking and your human nature. Your little i is called to be a disciple of the Divine Self. When Jesus Christ took up that cross, He was *committed* to giving His life. So 'taking up the cross' means a making a commitment that you will no longer cling to your human life at the expense of your divine life, but rather you are fully committed to let go of the ideas about life which you acquired in the world system, so that you will be free to experience the fullness and abundance of the divine life. The Divine Life is that abundant life which the Divine Self promises to give. When you 'take up your cross', you are committed to activate your Divine Self and to be in conscious oneness with God.

◎ FOLLOW ME: Then, be willing to follow your Divine Self as its disciple. Your Divine Self is leading you to the place where you release your attachment to your limited human aspect. You are both son of man and son of God, but these things are disconnected and in opposition. Your little i wants to take the lead, but it has to submit itself and follow the divine I to the place in the mind where it gives up control. When the human aspect gives up its control, it 'dies' symbolically. However, it is then 'resurrected'; fully blended with your Divine Self. There is no more conflict within the man. By 'losing its life', the little i saves its life. *It loses self-awareness and gains divine awareness.*

So 'take up that cross' in your mind and make a mental journey to "Golgotha", the "place of the skull", the place of understanding where you do your thinking, which is *your mind.* Form the clear commitment to give up thinking of yourself as 'only human'. And when you get into your mind, yield your limited human identity, so that the divinity in you, the Christ in you, can come to the fore. Give up completely the idea that you are 'only human'. Let go of human nature and follow divine nature. Let your limited human identity die *the death of the cross'.*

This is why the Apostle Paul said: *"I (the little i; the human self)* am **crucified with Christ**, *nevertheless I (the little i; the human self) still live. Yet I, (the little i; the human self; the son of man self) am not the one who is really living, but Christ (the big I; the Divine Self, the son of God self) lives in me. And the life which I now live in my human body, I live by the faith of the Son of God [the Manifestation of God], who loved me and gave Himself for me."* (Galatians 2:20) Do you see it?

We take that same journey in our minds to Golgotha, to the 'place of our skull', which is where we do our thinking. Our thinking changes to such an extent that we no longer see ourselves strictly from a human point of view. That human identity, which does not acknowledge or regard our divine aspect, is 'crucified' in our minds. We die to that old understanding of who we are.

Now, let's look at the last part of the verse: *'...anyone who will save his life shall lose it, but anyone who will lose his life for My sake and the gospel's sake shall save it'* What does this mean? It means that if we try to save our natural, human identity and not give it up to our higher self and our Divine Identity, we will lose the experience of the abundant life (abundant oneness with God) which our Divine Self is offering to us. However, when we lose our human perception of ourselves and become disciples of our Divine Self, we access 'the door' to our divine existence. We live in true self-knowledge and self-mastery. We live victoriously in this present world, no matter what the world system may throw at us.

So our Divine Self is saying to us: *"If you want to live from your divine aspect and not be confined to your human aspect, you are required to deny that your human identity is your only identity. Take up that cross in your mind and follow me, your Divine Self. Be obedient to me, your*

Divine Self, and be My disciple. Let your human identity die the death of the cross. Then rise to walk in full consciousness of your divine aspect."

When we are committed to 'lose our lives', committed to give our human aspect to the control of our divine aspect, only then will we be 'resurrected' as a 'blended being'. We will rise to *"walk in the newness of* **life***" (Romans 6:4).* Then we can live from the conscious awareness of our Divine Self.

The True Resurrection

In the episode of Adam and Eve recorded in the early chapters of the Book of Genesis, it is recorded that God warned Adam that if he ate the 'forbidden fruit' he would *"surely die"* (Genesis 2:16-17). When Adam and Eve later ate the 'forbidden fruit', they didn't die physically, but they were denied access to the fellowship, the conscious oneness with God, which they had previously enjoyed in the Garden of Eden (Genesis chapter 3). Being separated from God in consciousness, Adam and Eve 'surely died'.

Therefore, in the mystical teachings of the Bible, a person who is **'dead'** is a person who is not conscious that he is one with God. By contrast, in the mystical teachings of the Bible, to **'live'** or to **'be alive'** means 'to be conscious that you are one with God'. Therefore, *'Eternal Life'* is *eternal, conscious oneness with God.* This means that any man who is not fully conscious of his oneness with God is in fact 'dead' from a divine point of view, and needs to be 'resurrected'; to be brought back to life.

Now hear what the Divine Self says to the human self: *"I AM the resurrection and the life. He who believes in Me, though he were dead, yet he shall live. And any man who lives and believes in Me shall never die." (John 11:25-26).* What is the Divine Self saying to us? What does this mean?

The Divine Self is saying: *"I AM the resurrection and the life* [I am the only one who can bring a man back to his original state of conscious oneness with God]. *He who believes in Me,* [any man who believes in his Divine Self] *though he were dead* [although he was not conscious that he is one with God], *yet he shall live* [yet, because of his belief in his Divine Self, he shall become conscious that he is one with God]. *And any man who lives* [any man who knows that he is one with God] *and believes in Me* [and keeps believing in his Divine Self] *shall never die* [shall never stop being conscious that he is one with God]*" (John 11:25-26).*

Follow the pattern

Now, with this understanding of what it really means to *'deny yourself'*, to *'take up your cross'* and to *'lose your life',* let's circle back to a passage of scripture which we started to analyze in Lesson 1.

Philippians 2:5-8: "Let this **mind** [that's the Divine Mind] *be in you which was also in Christ Jesus who, being in the form of God, did not think it as robbery to be* **equal with God** [i.e. He did not deny His divine status, and did not see it as diminishing God in any way by thinking that He was divine]. *But He made Himself of no reputation* [He humbled Himself] *and assumed the appearance of a servant* [as the Son of God giving service], *and being* **in appearance as a human, He became obedient unto death, even the death of the cross..."** (Please read these verses a second time before moving on. Let them sink in.)

So here we see the pattern which Jesus Christ has left to us. Every son of God is required to have the same mind which was in Christ Jesus and to follow the same pattern. *Here is the pattern:* You are in the 'form of God' because you are created in the image of God. So you are a beloved, divine spirit-son of God. Nevertheless for the purpose of giving service in a physical world, you also have a human aspect and appearance. So you are 'son of man'. You humble yourself and live in this present world as a son of God giving service. Then you are required to continue to follow the pattern. The human aspect is required to be *"obedient unto death"* and die *"the death of the cross"*. Now that we have studied what it truly means to take up your cross and go to Golgotha, the meaning of this requirement is crystal clear.

As was mentioned in Lesson 1, some modern translations of the Bible have translated these verses to indicate that Jesus gave up His divinity and became a slave. But when you read His words in the Four Gospels, you will find that He always claimed God as His Father. This is one reason why the Pharisees hated Him. Even while serving others, Jesus always portrayed Himself as the divine Son of God giving service. He was never a slave or a bondservant.

Equal with God

Now here's a noteworthy point. The verse says: *"...**Christ** Jesus... did not think it as robbery to be **equal with God**."* You may be saying to yourself: *'When the man Jesus was on earth, He was in human form. How could God and any man in human form ever be equal?'* But notice that the verse doesn't say 'equal to God'; it says "equal with God".

It was the Christ (the divine) in the man Jesus which was in the form (the image) of God. It was the Christ (the divine) in the man Jesus which did not see it as diminishing God in any way by thinking that He (Christ) was equal with God. The human aspect can never be equal with God. Only the divine aspect can be equal with God.

This is why when a man once looked at the human aspect of Jesus and called Him *"Good Master"*, Jesus rebuked him and said: *"Why are you calling me 'good'?* (Why are you calling the human aspect 'good'?) *Only God* (i.e. only Divinity) *is truly good." (Mark 10:17-18)* Jesus Christ was not denying His Divine Identity. Rather, Jesus Christ recognized that the man speaking to Him had no inkling of the divinity within the human body of Jesus. The man could only perceive Jesus' human aspect, and it was just the human aspect which the man was calling 'good'. He could not perceive the Christ within Jesus. Therefore, Jesus rebuked him.

So **"Christ** Jesus (i.e. *the divine aspect of Jesus)...being in the form (in the image) of God did not think it as robbery to be* **equal with God."** What does this phrase "equal with God" really mean? The Bible gives the answer during an episode where Jesus had healed a man on the Sabbath day. According to the traditional beliefs of the Jews, no type of work should be done on the seventh day of the week (called 'the Sabbath day'). This was because the Jews interpreted the account of creation in the book of Genesis literally and not mystically. They believed that God literally stopped working on the seventh day of the literal week and literally rested. *(See Genesis 2:1-2)* Therefore the Jews were upset with Jesus because he had healed a man on the Sabbath day, and they accused Him of 'breaking the Sabbath'.

In response to their accusation, Jesus took the opportunity to set the record straight. He let them know that Infinite God has never stopped working. Jesus said to the Jews: "... *'My Father has always been working up until now, and I am also working.' Therefore the Jews looked even more for an opportunity to kill Him (i.e. Jesus), not only because He had broken the Sabbath, but* **because He also said that God was His Father, making Himself EQUAL WITH GOD."** *(John 5:17-18)*

Now this is a mind-blowing truth from the Bible. *Since God is your Father, you are a Divine Spirit-Being and therefore equal with God.* (Not equal **to** God, but equal **with** God.) In other words, if God is your Father you are in the divine category, in the Divine Family. You are Divine Spirit just as your Father is Divine Spirit. This is how Christ Jesus thought of Himself. He claimed His divine status. This is how the Mind of Christ thinks: *"God is my Spirit-Father and I am God's beloved divine spirit-son. I and my Father are* **one.** *As pure divine spirit, I am equal with God."* Let this Mind be in you which was also in Christ Jesus. Only the Divine Mind can think like this.

Now if a man's Natural Mind is locked within traditional thinking, it sounds presumptuous for him to say "I am equal with God"; for when he says "I", he is focusing on his human aspect and ignoring his Divine Self. He is thinking of his little i and not his divine I. He is locked into individuality and separateness. However, when Jesus said: *"I and my Father are **one**" (John 10:30)*, that was His divine aspect doing the talking. He was speaking from His divine I, and not from His human self. This is why the scribes and the Pharisees fiercely opposed Jesus. All they could see when they looked at Him was an ordinary man daring to claim divine status. They could not perceive the divinity within the human body. They could see Jesus but they couldn't perceive the Christ. Their beliefs blinded them to the Truth.

It takes a deep acceptance of Truth to *really* know that Infinite God is your Father. It takes a deep acceptance of Truth to *really* perceive the Christ in you. When you say, *"I am equal with God; I am in the divine category"*, that's not the human i speaking; that's the divine I. If you believe that you are just 'a human body plus a soul' but not 'divine spirit', you will be unable to perceive the real you, the divine you, the Christ within the body. You will block yourself from having the same mind which Christ Jesus had. Now is the time to start looking beyond the thing which is seen (your human aspect), and start focusing on the thing which is not seen (your Divine Self).

You may be wondering: Is God *really* my Divine Father? *Yes, He is.* Do you remember how Jesus taught us to pray? What are the first two words in the Lord's Prayer? *The opening words of that prayer are: 'Our Father'.* (Matthew 6:9) Since God is your Father you are equal with God. You are in the divine category, in the Divine Family. You are Divine Spirit just as your Father is Divine Spirit. You have the right to speak from your divine "I". That's the mind-blowing truth of Divine Sonship. Please take some time to meditate on this truth of who you are. The real you is a magnificent expression of Divinity. Come what may, never, ever deny your divine status. You are a beloved, divine, free-born, spirit-son of God, and you are in His family forever. (We will study this truth at Level 2.)

Like Christ Jesus, you are walking this earth in human appearance; and, like Christ Jesus, you are required to be obedient to 'the death of the cross' to merge your humanity with your divinity. You are required to give up thinking of yourself as 'just human'. Such thoughts are to be 'crucified'. That is how you die 'the death of the cross'.

As is the Head, so is the Body

And here's another thing. Jesus Christ is not just a pattern for the individual believer in Christ. He is a pattern for the entire fellowship of believers worldwide. The Bible tells us that Christ is the 'Head' and the entire fellowship of believers constitutes the 'Body of Christ'. *(Ephesians 1:22-23)*

Now we know that in any body, whatever DNA is in the head must be the same DNA which is in the body. Is it possible then that Christ our 'Head' is the divine Son of God operating in full divine authority and yet we, 'the Body of Christ', are vile, suffering beggars, sinners, wretches and worms, Gentile dogs, slaves and bondservants, all unworthy of the least of His mercies? *No, it is not possible.* The same spiritual DNA which is in the Head is also in the Body. If the Head is the Son of God, then the collective Body must be composed of sons of God. ***Since the Head is divine, then the Body must also be divine.*** It cannot be otherwise.

Jesus Christ is our Head because He is the One with the Divine Mind. When we collectively as the Body of Christ are connected to and governed by Christ our Head, we will automatically act according to the Mind which is in the Head.

Harmonizing Spirit and Soul

So, our goal is to merge our human aspect with our divine aspect, so that the life which we live is experienced and expressed as sons of God. When Jesus was resurrected, His human aspect and His divine aspect were merged. That is the real meaning of 'resurrection' and *'walking in newness of life'. (Romans 6:4)*

▣ YOUR SPIRIT: Your spirit is pure Divinity. It therefore gravitates to internal, heavenly, spiritual, eternal things.

▣ YOUR BODY: Your body is sacred. It is the temple in which Divinity lives. It thrives when it is treated with love, reverence and respect. However, your body is of the earth. It gravitates toward earthly, external, temporary things and needs divine guidance and discipline.

▣ YOUR SOUL: Your soul carries the components which make you feel like an individual, such as your human mind (memory), your human emotions, your life lessons and your mentality. Your *soul* can go either way. It can take the path of divinity or the path of the world system. Your soul is the link and the interface between your spirit and your body, between the divine and the human aspects of yourself.

This is why it is our souls which are 'saved'. Our souls are rescued from the path of carnality and led on the path of divinity. When our souls are led by the Holy Spirit of God, we become the sons of God in character. Our souls are purified of world system thinking. This is done by "obeying the truth through the Holy Spirit" which is the Great Spirit of Truth. *(1st Peter 1:22)* The truth which we obey is this: *I AM a divine spirit with the divine nature of God.* The soul is brought into obedience to that truth and becomes a disciple of that truth.

Why God is called 'Father'

When the Bible uses the term 'Father' in referring to God, it is not speaking of a male person or a male human form. The term 'Father' is a description of certain attributes of God. In the patriarchal society in which the events of the Bible took place, the father in the household was: the provider, the protector, the only one who could pronounce blessing upon the children of the family and the carrier and distributor of the genetic lineage or 'seed' of the family. So even though God is Infinite Spirit, the word 'Father' is used as one of God's descriptive titles because God is our Provider, our Protector, the only One who can pronounce The Blessing upon the children of God, and the Source and Distributor of the spiritual 'seed' of the Family of Divine Beings, of which we are a part.

We have the 'seed' of God in us, the 'seed of Divinity' which is the 'royal seed'. This is what makes us the sons of God. The sons of God are the true royal seed. We are divine royalty. We have the spiritual DNA of God. We are of the bloodline of the King of Kings. This is why, just after the Bible tells us that "right now we are the sons of God", a few verses later in *1st John 3:9* it says this: *" Anyone who is born of God does not commit sin for **his seed remains in him**; and **he cannot sin** because he is born of God."*

The Divine Self is the part of us which is 'born of God'. The Divine Self has never sinned, cannot sin, cannot miss the mark of the divine image. The seed of Divinity, which is in the Divine Self, remains untouched and unaffected by what the body does. The body and soul will conform to the divine image. We are preselected by God before the foundation of the world to bear this divine image, but the human aspect has to follow and obey the Divine Self. (We will study this at Level 2.)

When we call God 'Father', that's not our human aspect speaking. Only our Divine Self can call God 'Father'. God is *not* the father of our human aspect. When we call God 'Father', it is a confirmation that Divinity is the Source of our divine, spiritual aspect. Divinity is our origin. Divinity is the truth of who we are. This is why Hebrews 12:9 refers to God as "the Father of spirits".

Be willing to call out higher qualities in your soul, qualities which are in harmony with divinity. This is the work of the Holy Spirit. Be willing to allow your soul to be led by the Holy Spirit. The Holy Spirit allows the soul and the spirit to communicate. The Holy Spirit makes the soul receptive to truth. The Holy Spirit causes the soul to be purified and sanctified. When your soul and your Divine Self unite, and you become conscious of your oneness with God, you enter that state which Jesus called 'the kingdom of God'; which is the consciousness within you where Divinity reigns as king. The kingdom of God is not an external place; it is an internal state. In Luke 17:21 Jesus Christ says: "...the kingdom of God is within you".

The soul which sins shall die

Now, here's a verse of scripture which on the surface may seem puzzling but is really easy to understand. It says: "...The soul which sins shall die" (Ezekiel 18:4). What does this mean? How can a soul die? You will recall that, in the mystical language of the Bible, to 'die' means 'to be separated from God in consciousness' and to 'live' means 'to be one with God in consciousness'.

So let's look a little deeper into that episode in the Garden of Eden recorded in the book of Genesis which we started to study earlier. This episode is written in mystical language. We are told that "God breathed into his nostrils the breath of life, and man became a living soul" (Genesis 2:7). This 'breath of life' had nothing to do with inhaling and exhaling air. It was in fact the life of God, the divine spirit, being put into the man. This caused the soul of man (i.e. mind + emotions+ identity) to be in a state of oneness with the Divine Self.

The soul of Adam was fully connected to his divine spirit, and so from the viewpoint of eternity, Adam's soul was 'living'. Adam's 'living soul' was in communion and harmony with Divine Spirit. Later, God warned Adam about the 'forbidden fruit', and He said to this living soul: "...you must not eat from the tree of **knowledge of good and evil**, for in the day that you eat from it **you shall surely die**" (Genesis 2:17).

When Adam disobeyed, he did not die physically. However, his soul was disconnected from his divine spirit. He had lost contact with the 'God connection'. He was no longer able to fully express the image of

God. He 'sinned'. He 'missed the mark' of the divine image of God in which he had been created. His divine spirit was now caged within his human frame with no means of expressing itself through the physical body. He was barred from that place in which he used to commune and communicate with the Infinite Spirit. He had lost the conscious awareness that he was one with God as a divine spirit. Therefore, from the viewpoint of eternity, that living soul was now 'dead' by being separated from God in consciousness.

Jesus Christ came to save our soul and to set our spirit free; to restore the link between our soul and our divine aspect, that link which was broken in Adam. He came to rescue us from being separated from God and to bring us to a place where we are conscious of our oneness with God. He came to bring us back to the place where we can be in communion with Divine Spirit. He came to bring us back to the place where we can express the Divine image. He came to remind us of the truth which Adam had lost: **The Truth of Divine Sonship.** When we get to Level 3 in this Bible Study we will study the episode of the Garden of Eden in depth.

So *"the soul which sins shall die"* means *"the soul which misses the target of the Divine image shall no longer be conscious that it is one with God".* And who is God? God is Divine Spirit. And what is the target at which the soul is aiming? It is aiming at living as a son of God, thinking with the mind of Christ, having the conscious awareness of the divine aspect which is the 'God connection' and being one with God.

The soul which has missed the mark of the divine image shall, in consciousness, separate itself from the Divine Spirit who is God. The soul which does not blend with the Divine Self is not living as a son of God. That soul has mentally separated itself from the divine spirit and is 'body fixated'. It has restricted itself to just being 'a Natural Man with a Natural Mind' who is trying to imitate the character of Christ.

Living in Heaven

If we hope to enjoy 'heaven' after our physical body no longer exists, it is necessary to cultivate a heavenly state of mind in the here and now. Here's why: It is a Spiritual Law that God will deal with us according to the level of our State of Mind, the level of our mentality. This Spiritual Law applies while our physical body is alive, and still applies even after our physical body dies. Our mentality does not die when our physical body dies. Our mentality, our *'State of Mind'*, is a part of our soul, and so it continues to exist after our physical body dies. God will always deal with our soul according to its mentality, even after death.

Many Christians believe that 'heaven' is a place where people go after they die. However, spirits who are not attached to physical bodies do not live in places. *Rather, they exist in states.* Our physical body is the only attachment which our divine spirit has to this physical, earthly dimension. Our body keeps our divine spirit 'grounded' here on earth. Nevertheless, our divine spirit is always in a heavenly state.

So, our divine spirit is in a heavenly state and our physical body is in an earthly place, but our soul has the ability to alternate between that earthly place and that heavenly state. When we allow our soul to come under the influence of our divine spirit and both blend together, our soul also enters the heavenly state where the divine spirit is. This blending of soul and spirit will give us a heavenly state of mind. More and more, we will see everything in our life from the viewpoint of the heavenly state of mind. This blending happens when we renew our mind to the point where it is one with the mind of the Christ in us.

The more our mind is renewed, the more the divine aspect, the divine outlook on life, the divine character, the divine understanding and the divine state of mind create our comfort zone. More and more, we become sensitive to anything which is in opposition to divinity and will not allow it in our life. We enthrone in our heart and mind the beautiful qualities of the heavenly Father. We value His attributes and we allow them to have pre-eminence in our life. We enter deeper and deeper in the dimension of the heavenly King. We live in the truth of who we were created to be. We walk, more and more, in All Truth. We live with a heavenly state of mind. Our body is on Earth, but mentally and spiritually we are living in Heaven. There is no 'above and below', no division between Earth and Heaven; all is one.

One day, the physical body will die, and the blended soul and spirit will have no more attachment to this physical dimension. Ecclesiastes 12:7 tells us that *"...the dust* [i.e. the physical body] *shall return to the earth as it was, and the spirit shall return to God who gave it."* So, the body will go to the earth when it dies, but the spirit will return to God who gave it and will take with it the soul with which it is blended. They enter together into the fullness of the heavenly state, (that heavenly state of mind; that heavenly mentality) which they enjoyed even while attached to the physical body. That is Heaven.

Now you may be saying: *"I want to live with that heavenly state of mind. I want to live in the Kingdom of heaven. But there are so many challenges which I see in my mind and in my life. How do I completely overcome them?"* We will see just how to overcome them in our next Lesson. See you then. Please read the Supporting Scriptures, Affirmation and the Review which follow this Lesson.

Supporting Scriptures

Romans 8:29-31, 33- "Those persons whom He knew beforehand, **He also predestined them** [i.e. preselected them and chose their destiny] **to be conformed to the image of His Son***...And those whom He knew beforehand, those are the ones whom He called; and those whom He called, those are the ones whom He justified* [i.e. those are the ones whom He sees as being innocent of any wrongdoing]; *and those whom He justified, those are the ones on whom He bestows His glory...*

What shall we say in response to these things? Since God is on our side, can anyone be against us? Who can rightly accuse God's elected people of any wrongdoing when God sees us as being innocent of any wrongdoing?"

Ephesians 3:14-16 - "For this reason I bow my knees unto the Father of our Lord Jesus Christ, of whom the whole family in heaven and earth is named, that He would grant you, according to the riches of His glory, to be strengthened with might in your inner being [i.e. your divine aspect] *by His Spirit."*

Romans 8:14- "Those who are led by the Spirit of God, they are the sons of God."

Affirmation

I know the truth of just who I AM, the truth of God's design;
From one point of view, I am just a man; but within, I AM divine.
The Divine Self is the master self, the one with the God connection,
It is the way, the truth, the life, the door and the resurrection,
It is the Christ that lives in me, the Christ whom I will express,
So I won't be discouraged by anything I must face in the 'wilderness'.

God's purpose for me is much too great for anyone to hinder,
So I won't give up, won't accept defeat, won't retreat and won't surrender.
I yield to the work God is doing in me to process and refine,
I won't complain for I know, in the end, His image in me will shine.
If I don't yet see Christ's character in me, I know I'll see it later;
Yes, the troubles I've faced were truly great;
But as a son of God, I'm greater.

Review

Q. What is one of the main obstacles that I will overcome in order to know the truth of who I am as a divine being?
A. That obstacle is *'opinion'*. Release from your mind every opinion of yourself which is opposite to your being a son of God.

Q. Why is it important for me to renew my mind?
A. You are required to renew your mind so that true and permanent transformation to take place in your life.

Q. What will block God's ways and God's thoughts from becoming my ways and my thoughts?
A. If you, in your mind, create a gap between yourself and God and believe that God is 'up in the sky' and you are 'down here on earth', then you have separated yourself from Him in your mind. You are therefore separated from His ways and from His thoughts.

Q. What is true godliness and true righteousness?
A. Godliness means to be 'Godlike' or 'like God' in character. You can only be like God if you think like God, so Mind Renewal is important. To be truly righteous is to be *'right-thinking'*, which means 'to have the same mind in you which was also in Christ Jesus'.

Q. The Bible instructs me to look at things which are 'unseen'. How is it possible to see unseen things?
A. The Bible teaches that faith is the evidence of things which are not seen. By using your inner eye of faith, you can see unseen things which have not yet materialized in the physical world but are real nevertheless.

Q. What is the purpose of organized Christian religion?
A. Organized Christian religion is a means of calling your attention to the divine side of life. It is a signpost to point you to Jesus Christ who is the perfect expression of the Divine Self. If organized religion follows the teachings of truth and love, it provides a meeting place where believers fellowship with and support each other as they journey on their spiritual path. However, organized religion is temporary, and by itself it cannot give you eternal life. Eternal life is oneness with God.

Q. At a different level of meaning, what does Jesus Christ as portrayed in the four Gospels represent?

A. Jesus Christ is a representation of your own divine self. He is the outward portrayal of your inner divine consciousness. In many instances when you read The Four Gospels, the words of Jesus represent what your inner divine self is saying to your natural self or, in other words, what your divine spirit is saying to your soul.

Q. At a different level of meaning, what does it mean to deny myself and take up my cross?
A. It means that you deny your human self, deny that 'human' is all that you are, so that you can live your life from the conscious awareness of your divine self. You deny your human self when you completely give up the idea that you are 'only human', and when you understand the truth that you are divine spirit wearing a human disguise. Jesus took up His cross and allowed His human aspect to die, but then He rose again with His human self and His divine self fully merged and blended together. You follow His example and go to 'Golgotha', the place where you do your thinking, (i.e. your Mind). Then allow your limited, human identity to 'die' so you can experience life from the perspective of your divine aspect.

Q. According to Philippians 2:5-8, having the mind of Christ allows a man to say: 'I am equal with God'. We are instructed to have the mind of Christ, but how can I see myself as equal with God?
A. Notice that the verse does not say 'equal to God' but rather 'equal with God'. According to John 5:17-18, since God is your Father you are equal with God. This means that you are a divine spirit just as God is Divine Spirit, and you are part of the Family of Divine Beings. You are in the divine category.

Lesson 6: Your Facts are not your Truth

The eternal, everlasting You

Your Facts are not your Truth. It's a simple statement, but it is the key to self-knowledge. In reality, there is more than just one *'you'*. There is a temporary, earthly you (son of man) which is connected to Facts; and there is an eternal, everlasting you (son of God) which is connected to Truth.

Childhood experiences, geographical location, physical appearance, level of education, marital status, social position, skin color, ethnic background, religious background, income level, achievements, family history, experiences, relatives, ex-spouses, mistakes, failures, prison sentences, police records, weaknesses in character, a checkered past, things a man loves to remember and things he would rather forget, all of these things and more fall into the category of Facts. Facts are connected to the temporary, earthly man. When a man's body dies, all Facts, which now seem so all-important, will come to an end. People may have formed opinions about him based on Facts. He may have created his own definition of who he is based on Facts. Nevertheless, a man's Facts are not and can never be a man's Truth. When Facts are gone forever, the eternal Truth of who he is will still remain.

Your Truth, the Truth of who you are, is connected to the eternal, everlasting you. *And what is the Truth of the eternal, everlasting you?* You are a divine, free-born, spirit-son of God, created in the image of God, beloved of your heavenly Father, originated from God and returning to

God. You are divine spirit, linked to a soul, dwelling temporarily in a human body, on a mission to express the glory of God and to anchor the presence of God on Earth. You are 'the salt of the earth': a purifier of base energy and a producer of divine energy. You are 'the light of the world'. As was said before, 'light' represents 'awareness of divine truth'. You are the light of the world because you are created to be the living embodiment of divine awareness of Truth. *(Matthew 5:13-16)* You are created to be the outward expression of the inner Christ. You are to be 'the mind of Christ in expression'. You are a citizen of heaven. You are a powerful, masterful, majestic, victorious Divine Spirit-Being right now.

If you could see with your natural eyes the Truth of what you really are, you would gaze in awe at the beautiful, radiant, pure, Divine Being, made of pure Divine Love and Divine Light, which is the real you. The all-prevailing power of God, the wisdom of God, the love of God, the mercy of God, the goodness of God, the kindness of God, the true character of God, the peace of God, the patience of God, the joy of God, the intelligence of God, the beauty of God, the radiance of God, the light of God, the freedom of God, the ability of God, the perfection of God, the presence of God, the victory of God, the truth of God, the glory of God, ALL THAT GOD IS, is what you truly are. You are fully loaded, fully equipped.

So, your Facts are nothing to be compared with your Truth. The more you fully accept your Truth, the more you get dominion over the Facts of your life. No matter what happens to your body, the eternal, everlasting You will go on living. You begin to walk in authority when you identify more with the eternal, everlasting You than you do with the temporary, earthly You.

As a son of God, be bold enough to know the Truth of who you are, and be tenacious enough to hold on to that Truth and to live that Truth in the face of opposing Facts. Your little i is always preoccupied with the Facts of your life; but your divine I is always focused on the Truth of who you are.

Facts will lie to you

In the previous Lesson, we received the biblical instruction that we are to focus on the things which are not seen rather than the things which can be seen with our natural eyes. Why is this necessary?

It is necessary for this reason: *The invisible will always show us the Truth. The visible loves to show us only the Facts.* Many people are fearful because of the Facts of the past and the Facts of the present which confront them. They allow these Facts to convince them that they will never be their Ideal Self. They allow Facts to talk them out of living victoriously. They allow the Facts of their life to tell them: *"You're horrible! What you have done is unforgiveable!"* or *"You have made so many mistakes! You can't fix this! Your life can never be fixed!"*

However, here's another statement worth remembering: *Truth will never lie to you. Facts will lie to you if you let them; and Facts are very convincing liars.* Facts cannot hold you prisoner once you know the Truth. So then, have the Facts of your life been telling you negative things? Have you believed these lies and accepted them as your identity? You may say: "I am the way I am because I never got a break! Nobody ever gave me a chance!" Are you now willing to give yourself a chance by ignoring your Facts and focusing on your Truth?

Now, as strange as this may sound, it is possible for something to be a Fact and yet not be the Truth. Here's a practical example. If a man is being held in physical slavery, it is a *fact* that the man is a slave. However, 'slave' is <u>not</u> the *truth* of who he is. The truth is that he is born free just like every other person on Earth. His present circumstance of physical captivity is factual. It is visible and can clearly be seen with the natural eyes. Yet, this fact cannot alter the fundamental truth that he is born free; even though, at present, the truth that he is a 'free man' is not visible. So, his experience of physical enslavement, though factual and visible, is a lie. His physical freedom, though invisible and not presently experienced, is the truth.

However, if the man is not mindful, the facts of slavery will become so real to him that they will lie to him and convince him that 'slave' is the truth of who he is. Once he is convinced, he has become mentally conditioned to slavery. He has become mentally programed to accept enslavement as being the norm in his life. In order to be completely free from enslavement, the 'slave' must look away from the facts and accept the truth. Then and only then will he press for freedom, and at last be truly free both physically and mentally. If he believes in his lying facts, and clings to his identity as 'slave', he will have no real desire to be truly free. He will not see the experience of freedom as necessary, let alone possible. Even if the chains and shackles are removed from his body, his mind will still be enslaved to the lies of past facts.

The spiritual parallel is clear. It is a Fact that we all at some point in our lives sold ourselves out and became 'slaves to sin'. We 'missed the target' of our Ideal Self; and we accepted this as normal. Nevertheless, truthfully, we were born free as original sons of God. (We will study this in depth at Level 2). The Facts of our bondage to 'sin' were visible. The Truth that we were created in the image of God was not visible. However, if we are not mindful, the Facts of 'sin' will become so real to us that they will lie to us and convince us that 'sinner' is the Truth of who we are. Once we believe those lying Facts, we have become mentally conditioned to being 'slaves to sin', and will accept this as the norm. We will give up on our Ideal Self. We will not see freedom from 'sin' as being necessary, let alone possible.

As seekers of Truth, we look away from the Facts of 'sin' and accept the Truth of who we are in God. Then and only then will we press for complete freedom, and be free in Truth and in Fact. If we cling to the identity of being any type of a 'sinner', then even when the chains and shackles of 'sin' are removed from us, our minds will still be bound to the lies of past Facts. We will still be seeing ourselves as 'sinners' even though we are the sons of God. Do you see the parallel?

We understand therefore that it is possible to become so blinded by Facts that we cannot see Truth. Facts are major mental shackles from which we will free ourselves since we desire to be like Christ. Facts will torment and terrorize us if we let them. Facts can become tyrants in our life. When we free ourselves from the tyranny of lying Facts, then we will be free to live by the Truth of who we are.

Jesus Christ the Son of God is our pattern. He didn't say: 'I am the way, *the facts* and the life'. He said: "I am the way, *the truth* and the life." The facts of the life of Jesus were not exceptional. On the level of facts He was a simple man: born in Bethlehem in a manger and grew up in the village of Nazareth in an ordinary family. However, what was His Truth? He was the Son of God, the express image of the invisible God, living under divine authority, demonstrating divine power, fulfilling His divine mission, higher than all the kings of the earth. So, being a son of God is not about Facts; it's about Truth.

How to separate your Facts from your Truth

In order to live at the level of Truth, we train our minds to focus on the Truth regardless of what opposing Facts may be showing us. This is a personal choice which we make, and we persist in it until it becomes a way of life.

In the Parable of the Prodigal Son (recorded in the Bible in Luke 15:11-32), the younger son left his father's house, travelled to a far country, and gradually descended into a totally degenerate, wild and reckless lifestyle. He lost all his wealth and his reputation. He became a bondservant and found himself living with pigs. However, those were just the Facts of his life. The Truth was that, at all times, even while living opposite to his father's standards, and even while wearing rags in the pigpen and covered with stinking mud, the prodigal son was *always* a beloved son of his father. As soon as the prodigal son returned to the consciousness of the Truth that he was his father's beloved son, the Facts of his life had no more power to hold him captive. The circumstances of his life immediately began to improve. The prodigal son left the pigpen and returned home to his father's embrace and to all the privileges of his father's house. The prodigal son's Facts could not change the prodigal son's Truth. *Facts can change but truth never changes.*

Regardless of any mistakes, misdeeds or crimes which you have committed, you are a beloved, divine, free-born, spirit-son of the Divine Spirit-Father; a droplet within the infinite ocean of Divine Spirit, temporarily residing in a human body. You were in God before the foundation of the world *(Ephesians 1:3-4).* You are a citizen of heaven, you are spiritual by nature and you were designed to live on a higher frequency than 'normal'. These statements summarize the fundamental, irreversible Truth of who you are, no matter what the Facts of your life may be at present or may have been in the past.

No matter what you may have done, your Divine Father has never stopped loving you, and you have never stopped being His son. The Facts of your life may have *temporarily* blocked your fellowship with your Divine Father, but they could not break your eternal family relationship with Him. Why couldn't they? *Because your Facts are temporary, but your Truth is eternal.* The deeper your acceptance of this Truth, the more you will experience it in the Facts of your life. You are in the Divine Family forever. The eternal, everlasting you exists in the realm of Truth. The temporary, earthly you exists in the realm of Facts. The eternal, everlasting you did not originate on Earth. Truthfully, the Eternal, Everlasting You is much older than the Earth. We will study this in depth at Level 2.

It is a Fact that your soul was once separated from Divine Spirit because your mind was not conscious of your oneness with God. However, by faith in Jesus Christ and through the work of the Holy Spirit, your soul has been made aware of your oneness with the Divine. It is a Fact that because you were not living with the conscious awareness of your true identity as a Divine Being, you have made mistakes in life; (we've all made mistakes). It is a Fact that you have said and done things which, in hindsight, you can clearly see were not your best decisions. However, all these things in the past are just the Facts which pertain to the temporary, earthly you. In order to create better Facts, be willing to change your mind about yourself. You will not be free from the past until your mind is free from the past. Your past is nothing more than a collection of Facts stored in your memory; and scientists have proven, through exhaustive research, that memory cannot be trusted as being accurate. So feel free to let go of any bad memories from yesterday which try to define you today.

Your Ideal Self hasn't left you; it's still intact within you. Facts are temporary; Truth is permanent. So if at any time any Fact from the past tries to intimidate you, speak to it boldly and say: *"You may be a Fact but you are not my Truth. All debts are paid!"*

This is why the Apostle Paul said: *"...If any man is **in Christ** (i.e. in the Divine Self), he is a new creation. Old things (including the Facts of the past) have passed away. And look! All things have become new" (2nd Corinthians 5:17).* When you accept that you are a beloved, divine, free-born, spirit-son of God and that you and Christ are one, you begin to live from the Truth of your Divine Self as a new creation. It is not possible for a new creation to have a past.

Never let your Facts tell you who you are

So, your Facts relate to your human self, but your Truth relates to your Divine Self. The eternal Truth is that you are created in the image of God. You are a Divine Being. This is not subject to change, regardless of any Facts. If you have been trying to 'get past your past', you have been focusing on your Facts and ignoring your Truth. This is a symptom of mental bondage. You have been held in bondage by the Facts of the past. Those Facts have become like a slave-master keeping you in fear and doubt, preventing you from being free and from expressing your Ideal Self.

In our opening text, our WORD FOR TODAY, we read: *"...this is the one thing that I do: **forgetting those things which are of the past**, and reaching forward to those things which lie ahead, I **press on toward the goal** unto the prize of **the high calling of God in Christ Jesus**" (Philippians 3:13-14).*

This text tells us to forget the Facts of the past. We can only do so if we are focusing on the Truth. When we focus on Truth, Facts lose their significance. So we forget and mentally forsake the Facts of the past, and we focus on our goal which is to hit the mark of the divine image; to live as a son of God; to express our Ideal Self. This is *"the high calling of God in Christ Jesus."* This is the image we are called to express. The Facts of your life can hold you prisoner if you let them. They will mess with your mind. They will run guilt trips on you. They will try to tell you who you are, and who you can and cannot be. This is why it is so crucial for you to 'deny yourself', 'take up your cross' and follow Divine Sonship.

Your human self is the keeper and custodian of the Facts of your life. Be willing to deny and crucify that human definition of yourself so that your Divine Self can be manifested. Be willing to deny what your human self is showing you and to deny what your memories are telling you. Let the past be dead and buried, never to rise! Let go of those bad memories and all of those regrets. Let go of all the negative feelings which these memories hold. Today is a new day. Start believing in what your Divine Self is showing you and telling you. Rise to walk with the conscious awareness of your Divine Self.

The Divine Self says to the human self: *"...I am the resurrection and the life. He who believes in Me, though he were dead, yet he shall live. And anyone who lives and believes in Me shall never die. Do you believe this?" (John 11:25-26)*

What is your Divine Self teaching your human self here in relation to your past? It is saying that: *I, your Divine Self,* (i.e. the eternal, everlasting you) *am the resurrection and the life* (i.e. I am the part of you which will give you your life back after you have crucified your old definition of yourself. I am your oneness with Infinite God.) *He who believes in me, though he were dead, yet shall he live.* (i.e. As you believe in the Divine Self, then even though that limited, human definition of yourself, the 'old you' is dead, yet you shall live as a Divine Being in oneness with God.) *And anyone who lives and believes in Me shall never die."* (i.e. And when you live this way and keep believing in the power of your Divine Self, you shall never lose consciousness of your oneness with God for you shall have eternal life. You shall be eternally one with God.) Do you see it?

Your Divine Self is your authentic self. You were designed to live authentically. So there is no need to ask: "What would Jesus do?" Whatever Jesus would do is the same thing that your Divine Self would do. You are in Him and He is in you, but He is connecting with your Divine Self. That's where the mind of Christ is revealed. That's where the God-connection is. When you allow yourself to live authentically, you don't have to pretend. A man will only ask: *"What would Jesus do?"* if he sees Jesus as being different from himself, or as being separate from himself in some way, or if he believes that Jesus is one thing and he is something else. The man who needs to ask this question is not yet living authentically. He is trying to imitate Christ. He is not yet in Christ; and he does not yet know that Jesus Christ is in him.

▣ Here's a Technique to help you to raise your awareness of your Divine Self. Whenever you use the word "I", be conscious that it is your Divine Self speaking and not your human self. Practice speaking from this divine consciousness. Let the reality of who you are take hold of you whenever you say the word 'I'. Try out the Technique and say these words aloud with the conscious awareness that it is your Divine Self saying 'I':

I am a beloved spirit-son of God! I did not originate on Earth and I existed before there ever was an Earth! I proceeded and came forth from God! I am in the Divine Family forever! I am Divine Spirit! I am more than a conqueror! I and my Father are one! Did you hear it? Did you feel the difference? Did you sense the authority? That's not the human 'i' talking; *that's the voice of the Divine 'I'.*

Think on these things

As soon as we really know the truth that we are created in the image of God and that we walk this earth as beloved, divine, free-born, spirit-sons of God, a major mental shackle will be broken. We will be emancipated from being controlled by Facts, and we will begin to live the Truth.

Every mistake which we have ever made started out as a misguided thought. Maybe we rejected that silly, negative or unwholesome thought when it first came to us. However, after a while, we became intrigued by that thought; then we entertained it; then we took pleasure in it; then we became comfortable with it; then we became fascinated by it; and finally we conformed to it in our actions. Since we desire to transform, we are required to honestly identify the thoughts which led us into making those mistakes. Once we identify them, we kick those negative thoughts to the curb once and for all. We cut all ties with them. We disown them completely. We don't entertain those thoughts sometimes and then push them away at other times. Finally, we deliberately start thinking in the opposite direction until it becomes a habit. We will not be free until our mind is free. The only thing we ever need to work on is our thinking.

How can we train our minds to think good thoughts? The Bible gives us the answer. It says: "*...**the things that are true**, the things that are honest, the things that are right, the things that are pure, the things that are lovely, the things that are praiseworthy; if there is anything excellent and anything commendable, **think on these things**.*" *(Philippians 4:8)* These are the 'things' which will fill our state of mind. These are the positive 'things' which our faith will support when we expect to receive them. These are the things which will elevate us above world system thinking.

The first thing we are instructed to meditate upon is the Truth. We are to constantly think on *'things that are true'*. Therefore our minds ought not to be preoccupied with Facts of the past. Once we start out by focusing on the Truth of who the real God is, and on the truth of our Divine Identity, everything else will fall into place. All the high-frequency thoughts of love, compassion, joy, peace, power, freedom, forgiveness and oneness with Christ are to be found in the Divine Self. This is how our Divine Self thinks. As we allow our Divine Self to control our mind, our thoughts will automatically flow in the direction of these high-frequency thoughts. Everything around us will take on a different aspect when we start to think with the conscious awareness of our Divine Self, and when we keep our Divine Identity in the forefront of our mind. Our Divine Self always walks in victory.

Let your Divine Self emerge

We are told that a famous sculptor once said that when he looked at a rough block of marble, he could see encased within it a beautiful, polished, completed statue in all its marvelous detail. He said that, in order to create a masterpiece, all he needed to do was to chip away the unnecessary outer covering of marble to reveal the statue within.

The Divine Self is already within you. It is the real you. It is your authentic self, even if your past actions might have indicated otherwise. However your Divine Self is encased in the outer covering of inferior definitions and opinions of who you are. It is wrapped up in opposite Ideas and covered in opposing Facts.

Here's a suggestion: Since you have committed your life to Christ, please stop searching for the divine nature somewhere out there. Bring your mind to the place where you know that the divine nature of the Son of God is already in you. When you know this Truth, the outer covering of your human nature and all the opposing definitions and opinions will begin to fall away and the divine nature of Christ will emerge. You don't have to struggle for it. Just acknowledge it, live in conscious awareness of it and allow it to express itself. Like the sculptor revealing his hidden masterpiece, chip away at your strong identification with your human self, that temporary, earthly you. Chip away at everything which is opposite to the divine you. Allow your authentic self to emerge in all its beauty.

Made in the image of God

A man is not truly free unless his mind is free. The only way to free your mind is: *Know the Truth.* And what is the Truth? You are a beloved child of God created in the image of God and you are a divine spirit. You and your Father are one. We put a lot of emphasis on this truth because most of us have been taught the opposite for most of our lives.

Products which are manufactured today bear a stamp which states their place of origin. It may say: 'Made in the U.S.A.' or 'Made in the E.U.' You also bear a 'stamp' upon your spirit which says 'Made in the image of God'. As we have studied before, the word 'image' is not speaking of your physical appearance, for Jesus taught us that *'God is a Spirit' (John 4:24).* God has no human image or form, so we never think of God as 'a man'. So it's not your physical appearance which bears His image. The expression 'made in the image of God' is speaking of a similarity of character, substance and essence, not a similarity of shape or form.

It's a good practice to use the word 'Infinite' to refer to God. So, God is Infinite Unlimited Spirit, Infinite Divinity, Infinite Power, Infinite Wisdom, Infinite Truth, Infinite Life and Infinite Unconditional Love. It's good to feel the sense of expansion when you say these words. You can practice referring to God as 'The Infinite'. This will help you to free your mind from assigning a human image and human limitations to God.

It is vital that sons of God constantly affirm that they are created in the image of God. If you believe that you, (i.e. the authentic you), are anything less than divine, you have separated yourself from God in your mind. You have rejected the fundamental Truth of who you are. This is why you may hear people say they are trying to reach God, or trying to touch God, or trying to find God, or trying to connect with God. All of these expressions speak of being in a state of *separation from God.* These persons are seeing themselves as mere mortals, trying to connect to a God who is different from them and separated from them. They have created a gap in their consciousness between themselves and Divine Spirit. So they try to find God somewhere out there.

The truth about 'The Adoption of Sons'

It is only the divine spirit in you, the Divine Self, which can say and affirm that you are a son of God. This understanding can't come from your human self or your natural mind. Whenever you allow your authentic self, that divine spirit, to start affirming that you are a son of God, then the Holy Spirit, the Great Spirit of Truth, will come into agreement with your divine spirit and say the same thing.

This is why the Bible says in Romans 8:14-16: *"Those who are led by the Spirit of God, they are the sons of God. You did not receive the **spirit of slavery** which causes you to be **bound in fear**. Rather you have received **the Spirit of Adoption of Sons**, and this Spirit causes you to say to God: 'Father, our dear Father'. **The [Holy] Spirit testifies together with our spirit** [that's our divine spirit] **that we are the children of God**."* (Please read this passage of scripture a second time before moving on. Let it sink in.)

You will notice that this text speaks of *'the Adoption of Sons'*. Many Christians have misunderstood what this phrase means, and it has prevented them from living victoriously. They have interpreted this word 'adoption' in a modern sense, where a child, who from birth is not originally part of a family, is legally adopted into the family at some later date. This has brought many Christians to the conclusion that they are outsiders whom God in His mercy has adopted into His family. This idea causes them to feel unworthy to truly be the sons of God.

Truthfully, the expression which is translated 'adoption of sons', when looked at in the original Greek text, means something completely different to modern-day adoption. The Biblical expression "the adoption of sons" refers to *a father's formal acknowledgement of a son of the family by bestowing upon him the power and authority to represent the father and the family officially.* This is what the 'adoption' of a son really means in the New Testament.

We see this 'adoption' reflected in the Parable of the Prodigal Son. When the prodigal son returned home, his father bestowed upon the prodigal son not only beautiful clothing but also his signet ring. In ancient times, the family signet ring was used to impress the family seal on official documents, much as we would use a signature today. The ring, given to the prodigal son, was a symbol of power and authority to legally represent the father and the family in matters of business. *(See Luke 15:20-24)* The prodigal son was the father's son from birth; yet when he returned home, his father 'adopted' him.

We also see this 'adoption' occurring at the baptism of Jesus Christ, when the Holy Spirit descended upon Him, officially bestowing power on Him. At that very moment the Divine Voice spoke and declared: *"You are My beloved Son; in You I am well pleased" (Luke 3:22).* This declaration was the official bestowal of divine authority. So, we see a spiritual transaction taking place in the life of Jesus: *the official Adoption of the Son.* It was an official bestowal of power and authority upon the Son of God to represent the divine family, and it was an official acknowledgement that He was the Son of God.

So, the Bible says that we have *not* received the spirit of slavery which causes us to be bound in fear: fear of the past, fear of hell and damnation, fear of the future, fear of failure or fear of the shortcomings of our little i. We are not bondservants. We are not in servitude. We do not live in mental enslavement. Rather, we have received the Spirit of Adoption of Sons, for we have received power and authority to be fully functioning sons of God and representatives of the Divine Family. We are officially acknowledged by our Father as the sons of God. The text says that the Holy Spirit agrees with our divine spirit that we are the sons of God. It's a Spirit-to-spirit connection.

So if, for any reason, you were of the view that you are an outsider whom God has adopted into His family, you can now completely break that mental shackle. The truth is that you are, and have always been from eternity, a beloved, divine, free-born, spirit-son in the Divine Family. You are in the Divine Family *forever*. When we get to Level 2 of this Bible Study, we will go into the amazing details of this great and high Truth.

Now, your physical body is not divine in nature or in essence. It is of the earth and has no spiritual ambition. Nevertheless it is the means by which the divine spirit (which is the authentic you) has to express itself in this physical world. So your body has to be included in the 'adoption'. This is why the Apostle Paul wrote in *1st Thessalonians 5:23-24*: *"And may the God of peace make you completely and totally clean; and may **your whole spirit and soul and body** be preserved **blameless** unto the coming of our Lord Jesus Christ. **The One who has called you is faithful, and He will do it."*** He makes us blameless; not because we have never made mistakes, and not because our little i is perfect, but because we are completely forgiven. All debts are paid.

When spirit, soul and body harmonize in this manner, it causes *Romans 8:1* to be fulfilled in our life: *"Now there is no condemnation for those who are **in Christ Jesus** (in the Divine Self). They do not live according to the dictates of the body, but they are led according to the Spirit."* Does this mean that we will never again make a mistake? *No.* It simply means that the Facts of any mistake shall never again hold us prisoner. We will overcome them by keeping a conscious awareness of the divine Truth of who we are. The more we focus on our authentic self, the more power it wields in our life. Soon it becomes powerful enough that our body and soul become obedient to it. Circumstances become obedient to it. Other people become obedient to it.

We shall be like Him

You are a spirit-being of pure energy living temporarily in a human body. It is essential to keep your thoughts and your energy clean and pure. The more you focus on your authentic self and keep the Truth of who you are at the center of your mind, the more refined your energy will become. You will feel lighter in your moods, more free in your mind and you will find it easier to hear the Holy Spirit speaking within you.

Living as a son of God is living a life of spiritual development. This is why the Bible tells us in *1st John 3:2-3: "Beloved friends, right now we are the sons of God. **What we shall ultimately become is not evident now**. But we know that **when He shall appear, we shall be like Him, for we shall see Him as He is**. Every man who has this hope within him will purify himself to be just as pure as He is."* (Please read this passage of scripture a second time before moving on. Let it sink in.)

Many times, when these verses are read, it is believed that Jesus will return to the Earth at some future date, and when He appears on Earth, we shall be like Him. This belief creates a problem. A man can't wait to see Christ return to the Earth before getting to the place where he is like Christ. It will be too late then. May we tell you that when the verse says: *"...when He shall appear we shall be like Him, for we shall see Him as He is",* this is not talking about some future event? This is right here, right now.

What is the message in these verses? When we know the truth that we are the sons of God, and when we read the Bible with the conscious awareness of this truth, the mind of Christ will 'appear' before us in the Bible. When He 'appears' before us in the 'mirror' of the Word, and we look into the Mind of Christ, into that perfect law of mind which sets us free, we shall *be* like Him. We shall see Him clearly as the Son of God, and we will see ourselves clearly to *be* just as He is: *sons of God.* This is how we are like Him. The scripture goes on to say that since we hope to have this experience, we will put in the work and purify ourselves, i.e. purify your mind as the mind of Christ is pure.

So, being a son of God is not an exclusive experience. It is open to all people and for all people. It is *not* an opportunity for us to stick our noses in the air and feel that we are better than all of humanity. Rather, it is an opportunity to open our hearts and embrace all of humanity in unconditional love.

Now there may be some readers who even at this point in this Bible Study are still feeling a bit separate from God, and it may seem that it's still too big a leap to make in their thinking to accept their authentic self as being a son of God. However, it will become crystal clear when we study the well-known parable of the Prodigal Son. We will be studying this parable at a different level of meaning than is usually taught, so please be prepared to see this parable in a new light. This will be done in the next Lesson, which is the final Lesson at Level 1, in which everything we have studied in the past six Lessons will all fit together. See you then. Please read the Supporting Scriptures, Affirmation and the Review which follow this Lesson.

Supporting Scriptures

1st Corinthians 13:11-12: "When I was a child [i.e. a 'little child' spiritually]*, I spoke childishly, I understood childishly, I thought childishly: but when I became* [spiritually] *mature, I put away childish things. For at this time we see ourselves reflected in a mirror which is not clear; but then we shall see face to face. At this time my knowledge of who I am is* *incomplete, but then I shall know myself in the same way that I am known."*

Philippians 3:20-21: "For our citizenship is in heaven; and it is from heaven that we look for the Savior, the Lord Jesus Christ. He shall transfigure our lowly [physical] body, so that it may be fashioned to conform to His glorious body, according to His effective work by which He is able to make all things in us become as He is."

Affirmation

The mistakes of my past held me captive;
I've had issues to face from my youth,
But I'm free from the past; yes I'm free; free at last;
For my Facts are not my Truth.
From eternity I have been chosen, to reflect God's own image in me,
But the world system stripped my divine fellowship;
Yet I've kept my true identity.
My Facts may tell me: "You're a sinner!"
But Truth says: "You're God's divine son;
You're in God's family tree; no if, but or maybe;
It is real; it's a deal that is done."

Forgetting the things left behind me and reaching for good things ahead,
As God's free-born son, with the Father I'm one; and by His Holy Spirit I'm led.
People may have their opinions based on things from the past which I've done,
But now I clearly see God's perfection in me, and my true, ideal life has begun.

God's pure river of Love is now flowing, and it cleanses me body and soul,
And I now truly feel that my heart has been healed;
I am complete and whole.
I'm as pure as a new-born baby; I'm as clean as an angel bright,
For my record is clear and there's nothing to fear;
I am shining with God's own Light.

Review

Q. What is the difference between the Facts of my life and the Truth of my life?
A. The Facts of your life relate to the *temporary earthly you* and only relate to your earthly existence. By contrast, the Truth of who you are relates to the *everlasting, eternal you.* This truth relates to your living victoriously in this earthly life and to experiencing eternal life. The Truth is that you are a son of God and part of His family forever. Facts are temporary; Truth is permanent.

Q. The Bible says that I should focus on the unseen, invisible things. Why is this important?
A. The visible things can only show you the Facts but the invisible things will show you the Truth. Truth will never lie to you but Facts can be convincing liars. Facts can change, but Truth never changes.

Q. How do I free myself from being held in bondage by the Facts of my life?
A. Practice identifying more strongly with the *eternal, everlasting you* and relax your attachment to the *temporary, earthly you.* Whenever you refer to yourself as "I", do so with the conscious awareness that it is your Divine Self speaking through your mouth. The real "I" does not refer to your physical body. By practicing this awareness, you will train your mind to identify with your Divine Self. Also meditate on things which are true, honest, right, pure, lovely and praiseworthy. Create mental pictures of these things and hold them in your mind. (Philippians 4:8)

Q. Jesus taught us that "God is a Spirit". How do I train my mind to think of God as a Spirit and not as a human person?
A. Regularly use the expressions "The Infinite" or "Infinite God" to refer to God, and feel the expansion in your mind when you say these words.

Q. Why do some Christians feel a need to 'reach God', or to 'touch God', or to 'connect with God', or to 'find God'?

A. It is because somewhere in their minds they hold the belief that they are separate from God.

Q. The New Testament speaks of the "Adoption of Sons". What does this mean?
A. The term "Adoption of Sons" refers to a father's formal acknowledgement of a son of the family by bestowing upon Him the authority to represent the father and the family in an official capacity. We see this adoption reflected in the parable of the Prodigal Son when the father gave to the son his authority. We also see this adoption at the baptism of Jesus, where the Divine Voice spoke and said: "You are My beloved Son; in You I am well pleased" (Luke 3:22).

Lesson 7: Welcome home!

WORD FOR TODAY: "Surely goodness and mercy shall follow me all the days of my life; and I will dwell in the house of the Lord forever." (Psalm 23:6)

Heading home

We are about to begin Lesson 7, the final Lesson at Level 1 of this Bible Study. We have covered a lot of ground since we started our study. Therefore, in Lesson 7, we will be connecting together everything which we have studied in the previous Lessons. We will also be laying a foundation for some of the principles which we will be analyzing together at Level 2, which is the Intermediate Level of this Men's Bible Study.

So how are you feeling now in comparison to how you were feeling when you just started Lesson 1? Are the scriptures clearer to you? Have you given yourself permission to think differently? Are you feeling liberated in your mind? Have the facts of the past loosened their grip on you? Are you seeing yourself more clearly as a beloved, divine, free-born, spirit-son of your Divine Spirit-Father, and are you living more and more with the conscious awareness that this is your true identity? If you have answered 'Yes' to these questions, you have made great strides in your spiritual development. Now let's get started on our final Lesson at Level 1.

The Parable of the Prodigal Son

Jesus Christ taught many parables in order to illustrate spiritual Truth. One of the most significant parables He ever taught is the Parable of the Prodigal Son. If you are not familiar with this parable or if you need to refresh your memory, you may read this parable in Luke 15:11-32. We will be analyzing this parable in great detail and will be referring to it many times at Level 2 and Level 3 of this Bible Study, so please pay close attention to it. As we proceed, you will notice that the main principles which we have studied throughout this book will all come together in this parable. There are many facets to the Parable of the Prodigal Son. However, for the purpose of this Lesson, we will confine our study to just a few of them.

First, let's briefly summarize the facts of the parable and then we will investigate the Truth hidden within it:

A wealthy man lived in his house with his two adult sons. He also had many servants in his house. One day the younger son asked his father to give to him the portion of the wealth which he believed the father had set aside just for him. This wasn't his inheritance. It was just a means of livelihood. The younger son wanted to make his own living in the world, and he needed his father's help to get started. The older son didn't make any request for any wealth. A few days later, the younger son took all his wealth, left his father's house and travelled to a far country where he lived wild and reckless lifestyle. He made every mistake that could be made and he went as low as a man could go. He also wasted his riches in supporting this lifestyle. (This is why Bible scholars describe him as 'prodigal' which means 'wasteful').

When the prodigal son's fortune was gone, there was a great famine in the far country. He began to live in poverty and deprivation. So he became a bondservant to a citizen of the far country who was a pig farmer. The pig farmer promptly ordered the prodigal son to go into the field and tend the pigs. Even though he was working, the prodigal son was hungry, penniless and destitute. Neither the pig farmer nor anyone else gave anything to him.

Then one day, while dressed in rags, covered in muck and feeling the pangs of hunger, the prodigal son suddenly *'came to himself'*. He remembered the goodness of his father and the luxuries of his father's house. There and then he made the decision to return to his father. The prodigal son left the pigpen and journeyed home. His father saw him coming and ran to meet him, welcoming him joyfully. The son expressed to his father sincere regret for the mistakes he had made. The father commanded his servants to dress the prodigal son in the best robe and to put shoes on his feet. The father bestowed on the prodigal son his signet ring. By doing so, he elevated the prodigal son to the position of authority in the family, above the older son. The father completely disregarded all the negative things which the prodigal son had done in the past, and promptly and unreservedly accepted him as his beloved son. He threw the prodigal son a party to celebrate his return. Now, while the prodigal son had been away from home, the older son had remained in the father's house working and serving. When one of his father's servants told the older son the joyful news that the prodigal son had returned, and that the father had welcomed him back, the older son became very angry. Even though his father pleaded with the older son, he refused to go into the house to celebrate and welcome his brother home. These are the basic facts of the parable.

Over the years, this parable has generally been interpreted to illustrate that any church member who has left the Church, and has gone back to a life of complete servitude to sin, should return to the Church in penitence and regain his membership. This is the interpretation which many Christians believe. From our summary of the facts, we see that the parable does lend itself to that level of interpretation. However, there is much, much more to this parable. As it has often been said in previous Lessons, the Bible is written at several different levels of meaning. For the purpose of this Lesson, we will look at this parable with fresh eyes. We will investigate a higher level of meaning. We are now going to go one level higher than 'Believing'. We are going to study this parable from the level of *'Knowing'*. We will look beyond the traditional understanding. We will be going into some information which may seem strange to some readers at first. However, please keep an open mind.

The right State of Mind

As mentioned in an earlier Lesson, a parable is a means of using natural objects, persons and events to illustrate high spiritual truth. So let's begin to analyze this parable so that we may find the spiritual truth hidden within it.

*"...A certain man had two sons. And the younger of them said to his father, '**Father**, give me the portion of goods that is **due to me**'. And the father **divided between his sons a means of livelihood**." (Luke 15:11-12).* (Please read this passage of scripture a second time before moving on. Let it sink in.)

▣ THE MEANING OF THE FATHER AND THE TWO SONS: In this parable, the *father* represents the *Divine Father.* The *two sons* represent *two different States of Mind available to us.* Let us first examine the State of Mind of the younger son.

Traditionally, many persons have criticized the younger son because he desired and requested the portion of the father's wealth which was due to him by right of birth, so that he could have a means of livelihood. The younger son has generally been regarded as being greedy, selfish, disrespectful, impetuous and impatient. By contrast, the older son has traditionally been regarded as the better son, because he is seen as being hardworking, dutiful and humble. The older son is generally admired because he asked the father for nothing, but remained as a hard worker slaving away in the father's field while the younger son was in the far country. However, as the parable unfolds, we will see that the opposite is true. Despite all of his mistakes, it was the younger son who was truly the better son, because he was the son with the superior state of mind.

▣ THE STATE OF MIND OF THE YOUNGER SON: So, let's look at the state of mind of the younger son before he became a 'prodigal'. From the verses which we have just read, we see that the younger son started out in a good position. Contrary to popular opinion, the starting position of the younger son represents the state of mind which every son of God is required to have.

Now, the man of the house in this parable had both sons and servants in his house. He was *'Father'* to his sons but he was *'Master'* to his servants. Similarly, the Divine Father has both bondservants and sons in His house. He is 'Father' to His sons, but He is 'Master' to anyone who is living under the control of mental bondage. You will recall this principle from our study of Mental Captivity and Mental Freedom in Lesson 1.

◙ PRIVELEGES OF THE FATHER-SON RELATIONSHIP: The speech and attitude of the younger son indicate that he had clearly identified himself as a son of the father, and not as one of the servants. He addressed the man of the house as 'Father', and he was not in any way feeling *unworthy* of what was rightfully his by right of his status as the father's son. The younger son was consciously aware that he was in a father-son relationship with the man of the house, and he was also consciously aware that this gave him a certain status that the servants did not have. That status determined how the father treated the younger son, and that treatment caused the son to expect to have certain experiences which were far different from the experiences of the servants. The younger son was beloved of his father. The younger son knew that he had the right to enjoy the privileges of being the beloved son of a wealthy, generous and understanding father. He was elevated above the servants in the father's house, and rightfully so.

Similarly, every son of God is required to have a state of mind which causes him to know that he is a beloved son of his Divine Father. He becomes aware of the truth that he is in the Divine Family as a beloved son of the Father, and not as a bondservant. Sons of God are consciously aware of the privileges of being in a Father-son relationship with the Divine Father. They allow themselves to request and enjoy those privileges without being hindered by false humility or feelings of unworthiness.

◙ IDENTITY DETERMINES TREATMENT: From the bold request which the younger son made to his father, we can clearly see that the younger son was consciously aware that the father in the house was the source of every good thing which the son desired. He did not look to anyone or anything else as the source of his Good.

The son was also consciously aware of his identity in the household. He had taken the time to investigate his rights as a son of the father. This is how he knew that a means of livelihood was due to him, and why could ask for it. The younger son had firmly established in his mind his true identity. That identity as 'a son of the father' caused him to have certain expectations. He expected to be treated as a son and not as a servant. He expected to have privileges. He expected to have provision. The father generously bestowed on the son all that the son expected to receive. Faith is the substance of things expected. Those high expectations caused the younger son to have a positive experience in his father's house. His identity as a 'son of the father' determined his status. His status determined that the man of the house would treat him as a son and not as a servant. That treatment determined his experiences in that house.

The same is true spiritually. The Divine Father is the Source of every good 'thing' we could ever desire. Every son of God is required to focus on and to be consciously aware of God as the Source of All Good. The Divine Father in our 'house' has all the Good we could ever desire. Every son of God is also required to be consciously aware of his own identity as a beloved son of the Divine Father.

Our Divine Father deals with each man according to the level of his mentality. Anyone locked into mental bondage will be treated as a bondservant, because his inferior self-identity will determine his low status, which will determine the treatment he receives, which will cause him to have negative experiences. By contrast, anyone who knows the truth that he is a son of the Father will have 'son of the Divine Father' as his self-identity. That chosen identity will confirm his high spiritual status. His status will determine the treatment he receives which will cause him to have positive experiences.

The man who knows the truth that he is a beloved, divine, free-born spirit-son of God will take the time to search the scriptures and investigate what is due to him as a son of God. Like the younger son in the parable, he will not be afraid to ask the Divine Father for what is lawfully his by right of his divine identity, position and status.

▣ I AM WORTHY: The younger son was not like the Canaanite woman. He did not relegate himself to receiving "the crumbs which fall from his master's table". He was not like the Roman centurion. He did not think that he was in any way "unworthy". The younger son had a 'Zaccheus state of mind' when it came to his feelings of worthiness to receive. His attitude to his father was: *I have an opportunity to be blessed and I am going to receive my blessing. Father, since you say I am worthy to receive your blessing, then I am worthy.* The attitude of the younger son was not greed, and it was not arrogance. The attitude of the younger son demonstrated his recognition that he was in a father-son relationship, and it also demonstrated his conscious awareness of the Good to which he was entitled by virtue of that relationship.

Similarly, when a son of God puts a demand on the inexhaustible Good which is liberally made available to him by God, it is not greed nor is it arrogance. It is an acknowledgement of the wealth and the generosity of the Divine Father. It demonstrates his understanding of the privileges of being a son of the Father and his willingness to enjoy those privileges. It is recognition of the Father-son relationship which exists between him and the Infinite God, and a solid, conscious awareness of all he is entitled to by virtue of that relationship.

Just like Zaccheus, the younger son in this parable had his faults, but false humility was not one of them. We have seen the danger of false humility in the experiences of the Canaanite woman and the Roman centurion. Later in this Lesson, we will see that false humility was also the downfall of the older son in this parable.

◙ KNOW THAT ALL THINGS ARE YOURS: We see in this parable that the father had no objection to granting the younger son's request. He did not even hesitate in giving his son what he had requested. The father did not have to think about it. The son asked, the father released what he had already assigned to the son, and the son received. It was the father's good pleasure to shower his son with his goodness because they were in right relationship; the father-son relationship.

Similarly, your Divine Father has already bestowed on you all 'things' as a means of livelihood. 2nd Peter 1:2-4 says: *"Grace and peace be multiplied to you through the **knowledge** of God, and of Jesus our Lord, according as His divine power **has given** unto us **all things** that pertain to life and **godliness** by our **knowledge** of Him who has called us to **glory and power**: Whereby there are given to us exceeding great and precious promises that by these you might be partakers of the **divine nature**..."* (Please read this passage of scripture a second time before moving on. Let it sink in.) Do you see it? Whenever you put a demand on these 'things', they will be released to you when your state of mind is ready. *"It is your Father's good pleasure to give you the kingdom." (Luke 12:32)*

The younger son did not see himself as being in any way unworthy or undeserving of his father's goodness. He did not have the mental hang-ups that the Canaanite woman or the Roman centurion had. He did not plead or beg for what was his. Similarly, the sons of The Infinite don't beg.

The superior State of Mind

Now the question arises: *How did the younger son develop this superior state of mind?*

◙ KNOW THE FATHER: The younger son knew the truth that he was the father's son. He knew his position and status in the family.

However that was not all. *The younger son knew his father.* He knew his father's character, he knew his father's nature and he knew the extent of his father's generosity. He had spent quality time in his father's presence while growing up from infancy to adulthood. He had taken the time to really know his father; and he knew from experience that every request made to his father had been lavishly granted. This gave him supreme confidence in his relationship with his father.

Similarly, there is no substitute for having a personal relationship with your Divine Father. Ensure that your concept of God doesn't have any negative attributes. Ensure that your concept of God is only *Good.* This puts you in a confident state when you relate to God. Here's a question: If you have a kind, sincere and supportive friend, and you know beyond a shadow of a doubt that this friend loves you, wouldn't you be in a good mood when you are talking to him? So here's a simple but effective Technique in developing confidence in God: *Whenever you speak to your Divine Father, put a smile on your face and have a smile in your heart.* This simple act keeps you attuned to the infinite resources, goodness and generosity of The Infinite. You don't need any special words to talk to God. Speak sincerely from your heart. Sometimes you don't even talk. Just relax, sit in silence and be still.

If you are busy, you may find it helpful to make an appointment with God every day. Include it in your schedule and keep the appointment, preferably at the same time each day if possible. Be willing to let go of any negative impressions you may have developed about God, and understand once and for all that Infinite God is Infinite Good, and not a benevolent tyrant. (We will refine our concept of God when we get to Level 2.) This is why knowing the truth that you are a son of God must be paired with knowing your Divine Father for yourself. You will recall that these are two of the *'Keys of Understanding',* and we see them portrayed in this parable of the Prodigal Son.

▣ DESIRE TO LIVE IN YOUR FATHER'S IMAGE: The younger son grew up seeing his father as wealthy, successful and independent. He wanted to be just like his father. He wanted to be in his father's image. He was eager to allow the fine qualities which his father portrayed to also be evident in his own life as a son. This desire to be like his father is what prompted the younger son to request what was due to him. He wanted to get started in life and carry on his father's legacy of greatness. Similarly, every son of God craves the expression of the divine image in his personal life. Every son feels free to use the natural and spiritual resources bestowed on him by the Divine Father to assist him in expressing that image; that *'divine nature'*, by living powerfully, masterfully and victoriously right now.

▣ THE POWER OF FAITH + A HIGH MENTALITY: Now, in this parable, if the younger son knew the character of the father, it stands to reason that, over the years, the father also knew the character of the younger son. He knew that the younger son was inexperienced, and he knew that he would be likely to make mistakes. So we have to wonder: *With his knowledge of his younger son, why would the father grant the son's request so willingly?*

You will recall that in an earlier Lesson we learned that our Divine Father respects two things: *Faith and a High Mentality.* This parable reflects that principle. The younger son in the parable had both these things. He had faith in his father plus he had faith in himself. He had a high mentality. The father had to respect that, no matter what the shortcomings of the son were. So, no matter what our shortcomings may be, faith in God plus a high mentality will attract God's respect. We will see that the younger son would later lose these two things temporarily. However, once he regained them, they were his ticket out of servitude.

Pleasing the Father

Despite the mistakes that the younger son would make later in life, in the end he was elevated by the father above the older son. Authority and control of the household were turned over to the younger son. Why did the father do this?

The Bible teaches us that: *"It is your Father's **good pleasure** to give you the kingdom" (Luke 12:32).* The Bible teaches us that two things *please* God: *Faith and a High Mentality.* That is the deeper meaning of this well-known verse: *"But without faith it is impossible to **please** Him. For anyone who comes to God must **believe that God exists** [that's the faith requirement] and [must also believe] that **He rewards those who diligently seek Him** [that's the high mentality requirement]" (Hebrews 11:5).*

In this verse, we see faith and a high mentality working together. False Humility will suggest that we should not expect or seek or get a reward from God. False Humility will tell us that our only reward is 'up yonder' but not on this earth. False Humility will tell us that it is right to give financially to the Church, but that it is wrong to expect to receive from God anything in return. You will hear this sentiment expressed in a lot of hymns and gospel songs, this sentiment that Christians are to 'labor unrewarded'. However, sons of God do not sing the songs of bondservants; for the Bible says: *"The righteous* (i.e. those who think right) *will be rewarded here on earth..." (Proverbs 11:31)*

The younger son believed in his father, he believed in himself, he believed in his identity, and he believed in his reward. So he sought the presence of his father and put in his claim; and the father was pleased with his beloved son and released the goods to him. The younger son wasn't being rewarded for anything he had done. He was rewarded just because of his identity. The father was pleased with his son; not because of his son's deeds, but simply because the son was **his.** This is why before Jesus had ever performed a miracle or healed a sick person, the proclamation was made: *"You are **my** beloved Son; in you I am well **pleased".** Identity is everything.

Do you believe in suffering?

Many Christians today criticize the younger son for asking the father for what was his. However, we see that he was right in doing so. He was working with the ideal state of mind. Many people have convinced themselves of the 'unworthiness' of Christians, and that God requires all Christians to continually suffer and sacrifice and endure abusive conditions in order to qualify for God's goodness. Have you ever heard these ideas of unworthiness and suffering being expressed by Christian believers?

However, look at the parable of the Prodigal Son. There was no lifestyle of suffering and hardship in the father's house. Also, as we shall see later, the only thing which was sacrificed in the father's house was the fattened calf so that all of the household could feast and celebrate the prodigal's return home. When the Divine Father deals with His sons, He uses the principle of Exchange, not sacrifice. We surrender to Him something negative to which we have been accustomed or attached, and in exchange He gives us something of better quality. *(See Isaiah 61:3; Matthew 11:28-30; Psalm 40:1-8)*

Do you know what Jesus taught concerning this idea of suffering, this idea that all His followers will have to suffer and live in hardship for His sake? Do you know what He said about this idea that all His followers have to suffer in order to please Him? *Absolutely nothing!* These ideas are nowhere to be found in the teachings of Jesus Christ. It is good to go through the words of Jesus Christ as recorded in The Four Gospels. Read from a Bible where His words are printed in red ink, or listen to a recording of the books of Matthew, Mark, Luke and John.

Now at this point you might be wondering: "What about the verse of scripture that says: *'If we suffer, we will also reign with Him' (2nd Timothy 2:12)*? What about all those verses in the Epistles of the New Testament that speak of Christians suffering?" It is noteworthy that in many verses in the Epistles of the New Testament, the Greek word translated *'suffer'* actually means *'continue to the end'*. 2nd Timothy 2:12 is one such verse. It's also useful to bear in mind that the Epistles were letters written by persecuted people to persecuted people in a particular geographical location in the Roman Empire during a particular limited time in history. When we attempt to lift the statements made in the Epistles out of this context and generally apply them to modern life, we fall victim to warped interpretations of the Word.

Whatever temporary discomfort you endure as a child of God should be just that: *temporary.* That discomfort is not for God's benefit. It is for your benefit. The sole purpose for that temporary discomfort is to assist you to learn your lessons and change yourself. That's what happened when the younger son became a 'prodigal'. The discomfort he experienced in the far country and in the pigpen helped him to learn his lessons and change his thinking and himself. It brought him to his senses. Once that was done, the pigpen couldn't hold him any longer.

Once you learn the lesson which the temporary discomfort comes to teach you, and once you are diligent to make immediate adjustments in yourself and your thinking, the situation which caused you discomfort will leave your life. That's a 100% guarantee. However, if you do not learn the lesson and change yourself, you will be stuck in that situation. Even if you forcibly get yourself out of it, it will keep happening to you over and over again. So whenever you face tests and trials and challenges in life, remove your focus from the circumstances and say to the Holy Spirit: *"Please show me clearly **The Lesson** which I am supposed to learn from this challenge. Show me what I need to change in myself. Make it so plain that I can't miss it. Where I can't make the change myself, please help me to do it. Don't change the challenge. Change me!"*

Infinite God has no need to test you as a means of trying to find out what you will and will not do. The temporary tests of your faith will come so that you can know yourself. Whatever tests you fail, you will repeat. Somewhere down the line you will have to 're-sit that exam'. You will continue to be tested in that area until you learn and change yourself. If you fail to do so, the situation changes from 'testing' and becomes 'perpetual suffering'. So it's not about changing situations or fixing other people. It's about transforming yourself by the renewal of your mind. Your tests in life will show you your strengths and your weaknesses. *Every man is prone to fail at his weakest points and at his strongest points* (the strongest points being those areas in our character where we are certain we could never fail). So the test becomes our 'mirror', helping us to see ourselves clearly. Failing a test of faith is not to be used a reason for self-condemnation or an excuse for quitting. Rather it is to be used as motivation to go deeper into Mind Renewal.

Purification removes the dross from the gold

We all know that gold from the mine is very valuable. We also know that gold becomes more valuable after it has gone through the furnace which removes the dross from it, so that it can become pure gold. The refiner sits by the fire and heats the furnace to a certain degree. The temperature has to be just right. If there is too little heat, the gold would not be purified; if there is too much heat, the gold would be damaged. As the gold is heated in the furnace to the point of liquefying, the dross either rises to the surface of the liquefied gold or is burnt out and dissolved by the heat. The impurities on the surface are skimmed off. The heating process continues until the gold is pure. The refiner keeps watch over the gold during this process. He never walks away leaves it in the fire. *How will the refiner know when the gold is pure?* The gold is pure when the refiner can see his own face, his own image, reflected in the surface of the gold. Likewise, a son of God will be put through processes of purification, not suffering. These processes will require us to get rid of our impurities. During purification, impurities of thought and character will sometimes rise to the surface of our minds and our lives, and become clearly visible. This is so that we can identify them and 'skim them off'. Other impurities are deep in us but, if we are willing, they will dissolve in the intense heat of our process of transformation.

Many men get discouraged and frustrated with themselves when the impurities in them start showing up. However, discouragement at that point is self-defeating. If you see these impurities begin to surface, you can skim them off with the Mind Renewal Technique which we studied in Lesson 2, and keep skimming until your mind is pure. Once the dross is removed from the gold to the point where the refiner's own image is reflected in the gold, there is no need for gold to be put through the fire of purification any longer. So when we take the initiative and know ourselves, work on ourselves and voluntarily remove impurities from our mind to the point where we reflect the image of the Character of Christ, this will go a long way in shielding us from having to go through 'fiery trials'. Your State of Mind is all-important. God will always deal with you at the level of your mentality.

The younger son's mistake

So, the younger son started out with the right State of Mind. However, he then made a grave mistake which caused him to become known as a 'prodigal', meaning a 'waster'. He had requested and received a lavish means of livelihood from his father. This is what happened next.

*"And not many days after, the younger son gathered together **all that was his**, and journeyed into a **far country**, and there he **wasted his possessions** in wild and reckless living. And when he had **spent all**, there came a great famine in that land; and he began to be in want.*

*And he went and **joined himself to a citizen of that country**; and he [the citizen] sent him [the son] into the citizen's fields to **feed pigs**. And he began to have a craving to fill his belly with the husks which the pigs ate. And **nobody gave anything to him**." (Luke 15:13-16)* (Please read this passage of scripture a second time before moving on. Let it sink in.)

The prodigal's mistake was *not* that he asked for what was rightfully his. Rather, the prodigal's mistake was that he separated himself and his possessions from his father. It was after this separation that the quality of his life declined. He began to live opposite to his father's standards and became wild and reckless. Then for the first time in his life he experienced lack, suffering, hardship, deprivation, famine, toil and struggle for survival. In the father's house there was only peace and plenty; and he lacked nothing. However in the far country, separated from his father and with his mind now twisted, the younger son began to be in want. He had wasted everything, and was now a 'prodigal'.

In his haste to prove himself, the prodigal forgot that he had no possessions of his own. Truly, everything he had was the father's property; *The Father's Good*. He was merely entrusted with its stewardship as his father's son. Sons of God are always be mindful of this. All 'things' that we have, (whether spiritual 'things' or natural 'things'), belong to our Divine Father; and all 'things' which our Divine Father has belong to us for our stewardship and enjoyment. *"The earth is the Lord's and the fullness thereof"*. *(Psalm 24:1)* The earth and everything in it belong to God, but as His sons, *"He has given us all things richly to enjoy"* (1st Timothy 6:17). Our separation from our Divine Father is not a physical separation. However, if we are not consciously aware of our oneness with God, we become separated from our Divine Father in mind and in consciousness. We create a distance, a divide, a gap of separation between ourselves and God. Like the prodigal son, that is the single mistake we make which leads to all other mistakes. It is also why the sons of the Divine Father end up living as bondservants.

The prodigal State of Mind

After the prodigal son separated himself from his father, he complicated matters by making a bad decision. Jesus said that the prodigal son *"joined himself"* to a pig farmer who was a citizen of the far country. That expression "joined himself" literally means 'glued himself'. The prodigal bonded himself to the pig farmer. He forgot his true identity and became the pig farmer's bondservant.

▣ THE 'PRODIGAL' STATE OF MIND: The prodigal son in his wretched state also represents a State of Mind. The younger son became a 'prodigal son' because his State of Mind had changed from being 'a son who was one with his father' to being 'a son who was separated from his father'. On the long journey to the far country and during his period of adjustment to his new life there among strangers, he became 'lost'. *He lost the conscious awareness of his true identity.* In his father's house he was special, and had a higher status than the servants. In the system of the far country, he was seen by the citizens of that country as being inferior because he was a stranger. It was only a matter of time before the younger son fell victim to this inferior definition of himself. This is what caused him to sink into degradation. The younger son allowed the *opinions* which other people had about him to twist his definition of himself.

▣ SEPARATED FROM THE FATHER: The *'prodigal State of Mind'* is the State of Mind of any man who believes that he is separate from God. Such a man has separated himself from his Divine Father in consciousness. It is the State of Mind of a man who has lost the conscious awareness of his true identity as a beloved, divine spirit-son of the divine Spirit-Father. He has 'missed the mark' of Divinity. He is *'lost in sin'* because he has distanced himself from the divine within him. He does not know that he and the Divine Father are one. Any man with such a State of Mind is not living daily with the conscious awareness that he is a son of God. He is not living with his true identity at the forefront of his mind. He has forgotten that, as a divine son, he lacks nothing. He has succumbed to an inferior definition of who he is and has accepted it as the truth. He has fallen victim to the tyrant called "Opinion". He is a captive to world system thinking.

The prodigal son soon discovered that, in the far country, there was no 'father' to be found. When he bonded himself in service to the pig farmer, all he could find was a 'master '. The *'prodigal State of Mind'* is a mentality which believes in separation from the Divine Father. It's the State of Mind of anyone who believes that God is to be found up there somewhere far away in the sky. It is the State of Mind of anyone who is looking for a 'father figure' to put in God's place. It's the State of Mind of any man who does not remember that he is a son of God, and is thinking like a menial slave to his circumstances. Such a man has separated himself from Divinity and has joined himself to something inferior; to a low understanding of who he is.

Son of the Divine Father, you are the only one who can identify to whom or to what you may have 'joined yourself'. However, no matter who or what it may be and no matter how long you may have been in servitude to that person or thing, you can be free. And if you have accepted and justified negative conditions in your life because, for some reason, you believed that as a Christian you are required to suffer, then you have relegated yourself to suffering because of your chosen State of Mind. It's time to realize that if you have separated yourself mentally from the Divine Father: you still have a Divine Father who is waiting to welcome you; you still have a divine home; and you also have the God-given power to make your way home by being conscious that you are one with God. Facts can change; but the truth, that you are a son of God, never changes.

Rising above the pigs

Every pigpen is a mess. Any man who separates himself from his Divine Father in consciousness, any man who creates a gap between himself and Divinity, any man who believes that he is one thing and God is another, is going to end up in some kind of a mess.

The prodigal son suffered hunger while in that pigpen. Likewise, many men roam around in life seeking for satisfaction but to no avail. They have a hunger, a craving, a desire for something which will bring peace and fulfilment. That hunger can only be satisfied by being one with God who is The Source of All Good. It is futile to search externally for something that can only be found within you. This is why being consciously aware of your Divine Self is so crucial. Many men have wasted time, wasted years, wasted opportunities and wasted money in the 'far country' of self-isolation, far from their Divine Father. Many have lost their dignity, their self-respect and their self-esteem in the 'pigpen' of their past mistakes.

Son of the Divine Father, if these are the Facts of your life, please remember that your Facts are not your Truth. You are *not* born to be in servitude to anyone or anything. The 'far country' is not your home. There is a way out of any negative situation and here it is: *Come home to your Divine Source. Come home to your Father by being conscious of your Divine Identity as His divine son!*

I will arise

"And when he [the prodigal son] **came to himself, he said** [to **himself**], *'How many of my father's servants have enough food to eat and more than enough food, and I* [my father's son] *am here dying of hunger!*

I will arise and go to my father, *and will say to him, '****Father'...* " *(Luke 15:17-18).* (Please read these verses a second time before moving on. Let them sink in.) This was the turning point in the life of the prodigal son. Let's analyze what exactly happened.

◉ COME TO YOUR 'SELF': First, the prodigal *came to himself.* He became consciously aware of who he was. His amnesia regarding his true identity lifted from his mind. He remembered who he was. He remembered his true identity, position and status. He remembered the difference between servants and sons. He remembered his father and his father's house. Similarly, sons of God come to divine consciousness when we become fully aware of our Divine Self. When we stop thinking that we are 'only human', we come to our true self which is our Divine Self. Then our spiritual amnesia disappears and we remember who we truly are. (There is certain crucial information about ourselves which we need to remember; information concerning who we are and where we were before we came to the Earth, but we will investigate those things when we get to Level 2.)

◙ DESIRE MORE: Next, *the prodigal's desires and appetites changed*. He stopped craving pigs' food and started craving the father's food. Similarly, you know you have truly repented when your desires change. When the 'sinful' things which used to delight and fascinate you start to disgust you, and when you start craving the Truth, then you know you have truly repented; truly changed your thinking from 'sin' to 'godliness'.

When the prodigal son came to himself, he realized that his degraded, impoverished state was not normal. He got fed up with living at the level of less than enough and realized that as a son of the father he was supposed to be living at the level of more than enough. When we as the sons of God come to the awareness of our Divine Self, we begin to expect and desire more. Our Faith gets more to support. The boundaries of our State of Mind begin to expand beyond our present circumstances.

◙ RAISE YOUR STANDARDS: Next, *the prodigal lifted his mentality by raising his standards*. He said: *"I will arise..."* What used to satisfy him couldn't satisfy him anymore. He got fed up with his surroundings, fed up with the far country, fed up with deprivation and hunger and want. The mists had fully cleared from his mind. He realized that the pigpen was no place for a son of his father to be in. He became hungry for better things. Similarly, when the sons of God awake to their true identity, they become fed up with spiritual struggle and self-condemnation, and they become hungry for higher Truth. The understanding which comes from mental conditioning can't satisfy them anymore. They won't stop until they are one with the Father. They will search until they find Truth. They will rise to the level of their Ideal Self.

◙ CHANGE YOUR INNER CONVERSATIONS: The prodigal came to himself which brought about a change in his State of Mind. That new mentality was reflected in his inner conversations. So, he started to talk to himself about the quality of life and the privileges of those who lived in his father's house. He talked about who he was, what his true identity was, what his place of origin was. He talked about his loving and generous father. That is the power of Inner Conversations. They clear the mists from the mind and help us to see ourselves clearly. Once we can see ourselves clearly, we will know whether or not we are out of position. This is why there is an Affirmation which follows each Lesson in this book. These Affirmations boost your inner conversations. Please use them often, and feel free to create some of your own. The prodigal sent out his inner conversation as a 'messenger', and that 'messenger' paved the way for reconciliation between himself and his father.

◙ DECIDE TO LIVE AT A HIGHER FREQUENCY OF THOUGHT & EXPECTATION: Next, *the prodigal progressed from merely having a desire for more. He came to a decision.* He said *"I will arise and go to my father"*. He decided to live at a higher level. He decided to rise above other people's opinions of who he was: 'prodigal', 'degenerate', 'man with a past', 'black sheep of the family', 'rebellious', 'stupid', 'pig feeder' and 'bondservant'. Similarly, sons of God who have woken up out of spiritual amnesia will let go of every trace of a low mentality. They will rise higher. They will soar like eagles. They will rise above the level of the crowd, just as Zaccheus did. They will make positive decisions and follow through with them. These decisions lead to higher expectations.

◙ BEGIN YOUR JOURNEY OF TRANSFORMATION IN YOUR MIND: *In his mind, the prodigal son began to put distance between himself and everything negative in his life.* While his body was still in the pigpen, his mind had already arrived home. He renewed his Self-Definition. In his mind, he distanced himself from the pigs, from the pig farmer, from his past, from the far country and from his mistakes. In his mind, he had already taken the journey home. In his mind, he could smell the food at his father's table and see clearly its abundance. In his mind, he was standing in his father's presence, looking at his father through his own eyes and talking to him. What was the prodigal son doing? He was using the Mind Renewal Technique which we studied in Lesson 2.

Later in this Lesson, we will see that immediately after leaving the far country mentally, the prodigal left the far country physically. Journeys of transformation must first be made in the mind. Then they will play out in reality. This is the purpose of the Mind Renewal Technique which you have been using. Since you desire permanent transformation, feel free to identify the people and circumstances in your life from which you must distance yourself. Distance yourself from them without hesitation or regret. However, physically distancing yourself from unpleasant people and from negative circumstances is not enough. First, be sure to distance yourself mentally from these people and things. Permanent transformation takes place internally, in the mind. Then later it is expressed externally in circumstances. You will not be free until your mind is free.

⊡ LET GO OF THE PAST & STOP FEEDING THOSE 'PIGS': Once the prodigal son came to himself, he became independent of other people's reactions to his positive decisions. No doubt the pig farmer was upset when he found out that the prodigal son was gone. No doubt the pigs went hungry for a while because there was nobody feeding them. However, the prodigal son was not concerned about that. He was willing to forget the things which were behind him so he could progress to what was ahead. Is there anything in your life which is taking, and taking, and taking from you, and giving little or nothing back to you in return? Is it taking your good feelings about yourself and leaving you to survive on emotional 'husks'? Is it demanding to be 'fed'? Do you feel guilty if you don't give to it? If so, feel free to identify that thing as a *'pig'*, and feel free to stop feeding it. Just stop.

The prodigal son made the journey *in his mind* back to his father, back to his origin, back to his family, his home, his identity, his dignity, his comforts and the unconditional love which the father had for him. In his mind, he left the 'far country' of his mistakes and never looked back. Every son of God is also required to embark on this mental journey.

Breaking free

Now even after the prodigal son came to himself, the grip of mental bondage was strong and it showed up in his inner conversations. The same thing will happen to any son of the Divine Father who has come to himself and has decided to be consciously one with God. Habits of thought cannot be conquered; they can only be transformed, and this takes persistence. The prodigal's mental struggle showed up in his inner conversations as we see in these verses: *"And when he came to himself, he said* [to himself]...*'I will arise and go to my father, and will say to him,* **'Father, I have sinned** *against heaven, and before you, and* **I am not worthy anymore** *to be called your* **son***: make me as one of your* **hired servants'.***"* *(Luke 15:18-19)* (Please read these verses a second time before moving on. Let them sink in.)

▣ THE "I AM NOT WORTHY" MENTALITY: We see in the prodigal's inner conversations all the hallmarks of a mental captive: *'I have sinned and so I am not worthy'*, *'I am not good enough to be called a son of the father'* and *'I will settle for being a servant with a few benefits'*. On one hand, he was expressing his desire to return to his father, but on the other hand he was seeing himself as unworthy to be called a son. It's funny to hear the prodigal son say: *"**Father**, don't call me 'son'."* It's irrational and illogical, but that is how a mental captive thinks. We may even laugh at this statement and say it's ridiculous. However, it is the same thing that we do when we repeat the *'Our Father'* prayer while, at the same time, we are thinking of ourselves as sinners and feeling unworthy to be called a son of God. We are saying to God: "Father, don't call me 'son' ".

▣ THE DOUBLE-MINDED STATE OF MIND: The prodigal son had started out with an 'Isaac state of mind' where his only identity was 'son of the father'. However, during his sojourn in the far country, the prodigal had developed an 'Ishmael state of mind' where he was seeing the man of the house as both 'father' and 'master' at the same time. He was a son who was now thinking like a servant. This was why he was busy planning to return home and ask his father to treat him as a servant instead of a son. The prodigal son had become double-minded.

As we examine the life of the prodigal son, do you see the danger when you see yourself as a sinner and a bondservant instead of a son of God? Do you see the danger of uttering the dreaded words: 'I am not worthy'? Here was a beloved son mentally denying his true status and identity, and mentally asking the father to demote him to being just a hired servant. Has self-condemnation ever caused you to pray along these lines?

Always a son

Now here's one of the main lessons we learn from this parable. Even while the prodigal son was separated from his father, even while living wild and reckless, even while covered with stinking mud and coveting the pigs' food in the pigpen, the prodigal was *always* a son of the father. *The father never disowned the prodigal son, no matter how far he had fallen.*

So a son of God may be separated from God in consciousness. He may be in spiritual amnesia and, in that state of forgetfulness of his true identity, he may have made terrible mistakes. Nevertheless, the Divine Father does not disown him. No matter what, he is always a son of the Divine Father. Circumstances do not alter the truth of his identity. Facts may change but Truth never changes.

Traditional thinking has a very hard time accepting this concept, because traditional thinking is judgmental, and believes that all 'offenders' must be rejected, isolated, harshly treated and severely punished by God. There is no unconditional love, no compassion and no forgiveness extended. As we will see later in this parable, this is the thinking of the prodigal son's self-righteous older brother. The older brother became extremely angry when the father welcomed the prodigal son with open arms. This is why it is vital to think with the Mind of

Christ; so that we can think from the viewpoint of God's unconditional love instead of revenge.

Bible scholars tell us that, under Jewish tradition, if the father hadn't rushed to meet the prodigal son, the elders in the village would have executed him because of his misdeeds. However, instead of the death of the prodigal son, we see in the parable the death of the fattened calf which the father had prepared to welcome the prodigal son home. Symbolically, Jesus Christ is the 'fattened calf' who was killed to welcome us home. He took all our punishment. We are forgiven. All debts are paid.

◙ THE PHARISEES' VERSION OF THIS PARABLE: Bible scholars also tell us that the Pharisees (the religious leaders in Jesus' day) had their own version of this parable. In the Pharisees' version, the older brother heard that the prodigal was on his way home, and he went out and blocked the prodigal's path. He told the prodigal that, since he was such a disgrace to the family, he was unwelcome at home. He demanded that the prodigal live the rest of his life in exile in a distant village. In their version, the older brother made sure that the father never knew that the prodigal son had tried to come home. This is why every son of God is required to take the time to find and eliminate the *"Pharisee mentality"* which would like to control his mind. Always remember that the man who has 'missed the mark' has not given up his position as a son of the Father. His state of mental separation from God does not mean that he is 'unworthy', or that he is doomed to live the rest of his life in the exile of mental bondage. All he is required to do is to come to himself by seeing himself and his condition clearly, and without making excuses for himself. Then he comes home to his Father in consciousness. So when we look at the masses of people who are still serving world system thinking, let us not brand them as sinners. Rather let us see them as what they truly are: *Sons of The Infinite who are not yet conscious of their true Divine Identity and, as a result, are held in mental bondage as 'slaves to sin'.*

Keep on going until you arrive

◙ BODY FOLLOWS MIND: So what did the prodigal do after he travelled home in his mind and talked to his father in his mind? He went home physically and talked to his father in person. **Wherever the mind goes and stays, the body is bound to follow.** This is another key in the process of transformation and is worth remembering.

*"**And he arose, and came to his father**. But when he was still a very great distance away, the father saw him, and had compassion, and ran, and embraced him, and kissed him. And the son said to him, '**Father, I have sinned** against heaven and in your sight, and **I am no more worthy to be called your son.'***

*But the father said to his servants, **Bring forth the best** robe, **and put it on him**; and put a ring on his hand, and shoes on his feet. And bring the fattened calf; and kill it: and let us eat, and be merry. For this **my son was dead and is alive again; he was lost and is found'**."* (Luke 15:20-24) (Please read this passage of scripture a second time before moving on. Let it sink in.)

◙ POWER AND AUTHORITY IN THE DIVINE FAMILY IS FOR SONS, NOT BONDSERVANTS: When we see how the father treated the prodigal son, we understand the depth of our Divine Father's goodness, mercy and unconditional love. We notice that the father interrupted the prodigal son in the middle of his rehearsed speech. The father did not allow him to make the request that he be made a 'hired servant'. Why was this so? The father had a plan to bestow on the prodigal son that signet ring of power and authority. With that ring, the son would be authorized to represent the father and the family in matters of business. However, the father could not bestow authority on a son who was thinking like a servant. The prodigal son told the father: *"...I am **no more worthy** to be called your son..."* This indicates that before he left for the far country, the son *knew* that he was worthy. When he returned home, the father treated the prodigal son in a loving and doting manner in order to convince him that he was still worthy.

▣ FOCUS ON THE PRESENT, NOT THE PAST: Here's something worth remembering: ***Your actions are different from your identity.*** When the prodigal son expressed sincere regret for his past ***actions*** by admitting *"I have sinned"*, the father did not interrupt him. Sincere regret and remorse for wrong actions is a necessary part of the process of transformation. However, as soon as the prodigal son started to distance himself from his ***identity*** by saying *"I am no more worthy to be called your son"*, the father immediately interrupted his speech. The father would not allow the prodigal son to confuse his actions with his identity. Never allow any of your past actions to cause you to give up your Divine Identity. Never let a past mistake cause you to label yourself negatively. For example, a man who has stolen in the past should never label himself 'Thief'; a man who has a criminal record should never label himself 'Felon'; a man who has been in a gang should never label himself 'Gang Member'; a married man who has had an affair should never label himself 'Cheater'. It's a past action, but it's not your identity. Choose positive labels only; because your life will always match your labels.

Before the family power and authority could be bestowed, the father had to bring the prodigal son back to the state of mind which he had in the beginning. The prodigal's mind had to be renewed. So the father completely disregarded the son's mistakes. He did not ask for any details about the son's past. He wanted his son to be focused on the **now**, on the point of transformation in the son's life, and not on the past.

The limited wealth which the father gave to the younger son at the beginning of the parable was nothing to be compared to the vast supply of the father's wealth which he now had at his disposal as the father's official representative. He had started out with a means of livelihood, but now he would come into the fullness of his inheritance. The younger son's latter days would be even more prosperous than at the beginning. So be encouraged that if you have lost anything in the far country of your experiences, your Divine Father has much more and much better than that to give to you. Take no thought on what you may have lost. Your Father's supply of Good is infinite. Nobody can bankrupt God's goodness. He has more than enough goodness and mercy to accompany you all the days of your life.

◙ GET YOUR LIFE BACK: When the prodigal son ran to his father, the father started running to him, even when the son was a long way off. As soon as you remember and run to your Divine Father in consciousness, your Divine Father will run to you; even if you feel that you are far from the place mentally and spiritually where you want to be. Divinity is just waiting to meet you, waiting to run to you, waiting to bring out the best for you and in you. Just come home to God in your mind. See yourself as *being one with God* and *being at peace with God*. Know that you are a beloved, divine, spirit-son of the Divine Father. Think like a son and not a bondservant. Now that you have been studying these principles of freedom and have started on your journey home, please don't stop, don't turn back and don't feel nostalgia for any trace of mental bondage that you are leaving behind. Keep working on your State of Mind until it harmonizes with the Divine Mind.

When the prodigal son came home, he got his life back. The father said that this son was *"dead"* but is *"alive again"*. You will recall that in the mystical teachings of the Bible, to 'die' means to be separated from the Divine Father and to be 'alive' is to be one with the Divine Father. We see this meaning clearly portrayed in this parable. The son had closed the gap between himself and his father. They were one and at peace as in the beginning. We will always feel *"lost"* until we come to terms with our Divine Self, and accept our oneness with our Divine Father. Only then will our authentic Self be *"found"* in full awareness of our true identity.

Authority to be a son of God

Many men have a desire to express the Ideal Self which they

were created to express. However, they feel that they lack the power to be such a man. What solution does the Bible provide? We find the answer recorded in John 1:11-12: *"He* [i.e. Jesus] *came to His own people, but His own people did not receive Him. But as many people as did receive Him, to them He gave* **authority** *to become the sons of God* (in character).*"*

In many translations of the Bible, this verse says that Jesus gave them *'power'* to become the sons of God. However, the true meaning in the original Greek text is not *'power'* but *'authority'*. Our power comes from and is governed by the divine authority vested in us.

Authority is crucial. Do you remember what the Roman centurion said to Jesus in Matthew 8:9? He said: *"...I am a man* **under the authority of my superiors in the army**, *and* **I have soldiers whom I command**. *I say to this man, Go!' and he goes, and I say to another man, 'Come!' and he comes, and I say to my slave, 'Do this!', and he does it."* The centurion's lawful exercise of power was determined strictly by his level of authority; and so it is with us spiritually. When we live fully under the auspices of our Divine Self, we walk in divine authority. (We will study more on the subject of Power and Authority when we study Spiritual Laws at Level 2 of this Men's Bible Study).

▣ CHANGE YOUR 'GARMENT': The first step in being authorized to represent the Divine Family is to change our understanding of who we are. When the prodigal son returned home from the far country, he presented himself to his father ragged and barefoot. No doubt he was dressed in the filthy, old garment which he had worn in the pigpen. Under the practice of physical slavery, when slaves were freed, they were presented with 'freedom clothes' as a symbol of freedom. The father immediately commanded his servants to dress the prodigal in a new garment, the best robe. This was the first of three gifts which the father gave the prodigal son on his return home.

Now, the servants wouldn't put this fine robe on him while he was still wearing the filthy old garment. The prodigal would have to be willing to give up the old garment, become naked and then be dressed in the best robe which was the new garment. It was an Exchange. You will recall the Parable of the Garments which we studied in a previous Lesson. *'Garments'* represent *'spiritual understanding'* and *'nakedness'* represents *'spiritual ignorance'*.

The prodigal willingly gave up the old garment which he had worn as a bondservant and became naked. Then he was robed in the father's best new garment. Similarly, in returning to our Father in consciousness, we willingly give up the old understanding which we had under the world system, and allow our mind to become 'naked' by acknowledging that we are ignorant as to what the scriptures in the Bible truly mean. Then and only then will our Divine Father bestow on us the new garment, that higher quality of spiritual understanding. He will clothe us in our right mind. We will not receive the new without giving up the old. We step out of servitude and Mental Captivity, and we willingly accept and wear our 'freedom clothes'.

◙ ACCEPT YOUR POSITION OF AUTHORITY: The second gift that the father gave to the prodigal son was a ring. Bible scholars tell us that it was a signet ring used to impress the father's family seal onto documents, much as we would use a signature today. The gift of this ring was a symbol of the father's bestowal of his power and authority on the younger son. The prodigal son had 'unglued' himself from the pig farmer and was now one with his father in loving embrace.

With this ring, the prodigal became the father's official representative. He was not just representing himself anymore. He was authorized to represent the father and the family in all matters. Here we see the *'Adoption of the prodigal son'*. The prodigal son was the father's son from birth, but he now 'adopted' him by giving him power and authority to represent the father and the family. He was now at a higher level of authority in the family than the older son.

Traditionally, in ancient times, the older son was always

preferred above the younger, and the father's authority would be passed to his oldest son. However, the father in this parable was not following tradition. He was seeking for the right qualities and the right mentality which could handle power and authority in the family. This pattern, of a father going against tradition by preferring the younger son above the older, is seen in many stories throughout the Bible. We see it in the lives of Isaac, Jacob and Joseph just to name a few. This pattern has high spiritual significance which we will analyze when we get to Level 3 of this Bible Study.

Authority was passed to the younger son only after he willingly gave up his old, misguided understanding of himself as a bondservant and went back to his original identity as a *son of the father*. Freedom is our original state of mind which we temporarily lost. Now we can recover it by first changing our 'mental garments' to become conscious of our divine status as a son of God. When we fully return to our Divine Father in consciousness, we receive divine authority to be recognized as a son of God in the natural realm and the spiritual realm. We are authorized to represent God and the Divine Family. We are 'adopted' even though we have always been the sons of God.

▣ EXPRESS YOUR FATHER'S IMAGE: The third gift which the father gave the prodigal son was the gift of shoes. The father's servants actually put the shoes on the son's feet. Bible scholars tell us that under the system of ancient physical slavery, free people did not go barefoot. Being barefoot was a symbol of being enslaved. This gift of shoes represented the last break between the prodigal and his life in servitude. For us, it represents the requirement that we remove from our lives every symbol which identifies us as a bondservant instead of as a son of the Divine Father.

What was the overall purpose of these three gifts? Their purpose was to change the son's image. So we notice that once the prodigal son returned to his father and admitted his mistake, the father immediately started transforming his son's image. He came home wearing the image of bondage, but the father's gifts gave him the image of freedom. Everything about the prodigal which said 'bondservant' was removed from him at his father's command. The father was setting up the younger son to be successful as his representative. The father and the household then celebrated the son's return with a fabulous party. As soon as you return to God in consciousness, heaven will celebrate your return.

Our Divine Father has set us up for success in wearing the divine image, but only if we are first willing to mentally surrender the 'sinner' image. We cannot successfully wear the sinner image and the divine image at the same time. A choice is necessary. The prodigal could have rejected the father's gifts and continued wallowing in self-pity, thereby falling victim to False Humility. However, he chose wisely and accepted the image of 'son of the father'. The prodigal's mistakes could only temporarily break his fellowship with the father; but the family relationship never changed. The same is true for us. We have always been the sons of God.

The older son's State of Mind

So the prodigal son regained his original State of Mind of Mental Freedom. He allowed his mind to be renewed. He was back in his original fellowship with his father. There was great celebration in the father's family, but not everybody was happy. Every Eden has its serpent. There is another State of Mind that we have to watch out for. It is the State of Mind of the older son, the prodigal's older brother. As we shall see, it is a State of Mind controlled by self-righteousness, False Humility and the bondservant's mentality. Let's go back to the text:

*"Now his older son was **in the field**: and as he [the older son] came closer and approached the house, he heard music and dancing. And **he called one of the servants, and asked what these things meant.***

*And **the servant told him**, 'Your brother has returned; and your father has killed the fattened calf, because he has received him safe and* *sound'. And **the older son was angry, and would not go in:** therefore the father came out and pleaded with him.*

*And he said to his father, '**These many years I have served you,** and I have never at any time broken **your commandment**; and yet you have **never** given me even a young goat, that I might **celebrate with my friends.** But as soon as **this one, your son**, has returned, who has wasted his riches spending it on prostitutes, you have killed the fattened calf for him!'*

*And the father said to him: '**Son, you are always with me, and everything that I have is yours.** It is right for us to celebrate and be glad, for **this one, your brother** was dead and is alive again. He was lost, and is found'." (Luke 15:25-32)* (Please read this passage of scripture a second time before moving on. Let it sink in.)

▣ WHAT'S WRONG WITH THE OLDER SON: Throughout this Bible Study we have been sensitized to the difference between thinking like a son and thinking like a bondservant. With our awareness of this difference, we can clearly see what is wrong with the State of Mind represented by the older son. His State of Mind represents the mentality of a son of God who does not understand his true position in the Divine Family. It is the State of Mind of a son of God who is thinking and acting as a bondservant. He is a son who has a negative concept of his Divine Father. He is not consciously aware of his true identity. He is laboring under an inferior concept of who he is and he has a negative concept of the character of God.

▣ ARE YOU OUT OF POSITION? The older son in the parable was in the field toiling when he should have been in the house celebrating. He was not aware of the momentous event taking place in the family. He had his own agenda, his own clique of friends and he was doing his own thing. What was important to the father was not important to him. When he wanted information he did not ask his father, he asked a servant. This son was out of position. He was a son doing slave labor. He was so disconnected from his father that he looked to a servant for guidance. The prodigal son had been lost in the far country. The older son was just as lost, right there in his father's house. If we are not mindful, the same things will happen to us as sons of God. If there is a gap in our consciousness between us and God, we will have the older son's attitude.

◙ ARE OTHER CHILDREN OF GOD A 'THREAT' TO YOUR POSITION? Since the older son was thinking like a bondservant, he saw his younger brother as a threat to his position in the family. When speaking to his father, he didn't refer to the younger son as 'my brother'. He referred to him as 'your son'. When his younger brother was far from home, and possibly in dire straits or even dead, the older brother's desire was to *"celebrate"* and feast with his clique of friends. When his younger brother returned home safe and sound, the older brother was angry and resentful.

Do you see other children of God as a threat to your position in Church? Do you ever have a desire to *celebrate* the downfall of a child of God? If so, these are serious symptoms of the bondservant's mentality.

We have studied these symptoms of mental bondage. We saw that when a son of God is in mental servitude, every other son in the family looks like a threat to his position. He can't really see them as his brothers and sisters in Christ even though he may pay lip service to such a relationship. He is plagued by fear and insecurity. We see these same symptoms portrayed in the character of the older son.

◙ THE 'NOT GOOD ENOUGH' MENTALITY AND THE 'SUPER CHIRSTIAN' MENTALITY: We recall that the bondservant mentality usually shows up in one of two ways in Christians: (1) the 'not good enough' mentality; and (2) the 'super Christian' mentality.

We see that the prodigal son, in his wretched state, was suffering from the 'not good enough' mentality. However, the attitude of the older brother represents clearly what we learned about the 'super Christian' mentality: the fear and insecurity, the self-righteousness, the feeling of superiority, the boastfulness, the inflated ego, the craving for recognition, the desire for the limelight, the need for 'followers' (that's his clique of friends), his slander and character assassination of his brother whom he sees as a threat, and the self-serving lies. *(Can we really believe the older son never once disobeyed his father?)* Do you see the parallels?

▣ NO PUNISHMENT FROM THE FATHER: The older son expected the father to reject and punish the prodigal son. That's because the older son didn't really know the father. It's remarkable that the prodigal son received no punishment from the father; no harsh words, no severe treatment, no disapproval and no condemnation. The older brother dearly wished for all these things to be done to the prodigal, but he was disappointed. Those who choose to strongly believe in 'God's punishment' will be hard-pressed to explain the father's refusal to punish the prodigal. Knowing the true nature of your Divine Father makes all the difference.

The prodigal son had already punished himself after he had fallen victim to his low state of mind. He acknowledged that he had 'sinned against heaven' by living below the divine standard, and he had 'sinned' (missed the mark) of his father's plan for him. However, the 'punishment' which the prodigal son experienced in famine, want and servitude was a result of his own depravity of thought. And so it is with us.

Disobedience to our Divine Father always carries within it its own punishment. We will surely reap the harvest of whatever 'mind-seeds' we consistently sow in the soil of our minds. Our Father doesn't have to do anything to punish us. He has already put in place Spiritual Laws which are designed to carry out whatever divine discipline His sons need. If we go against Spiritual Law in our thinking, we go against our own divine self, and we go against our own best interests. If we think in accordance with Spiritual Law, we help ourselves. We will study this at Level 2.

Shackled by an inferior identity

You will recall that, in the Divine Family, the identity which a man assigns to himself will determine his character, status, expectations and experiences. In this parable we clearly see what identity the older brother had assigned to himself in the family. He told the father: *"...These many years I have served you, and I have never at any time broken your commandment."* This tells us that he had assigned to himself the identity of a bondservant. He had relegated himself to a life of servitude. He didn't say: "These many years I have loved you". He never once addressed his father as "Father". His chosen identity caused him to have the attitude of a disgruntled servant accusing his master and overlord of being unfair. The older brother was a man who had to be 'commanded'. You will recall from an earlier Lesson that sons don't need to be commanded in order to obey their Divine Father. His slightest instruction will be readily obeyed, for sons are in loving service to their Father, not in servitude.

You will also recall the statement: *"No two people believe in the same God."* The older son and the younger son in this parable were dealing with the same father, but they had very different concepts of the character of their father. The younger son's concept of his father was superior to the older son's concept of his father. The younger son saw the father as a generous, doting, forgiving father, but the older son saw his father as a benevolent tyrant. Both sons had the same father, but each son's relationship with the father was determined by that son's concept of the father. The father treated each son according to the concept of the father which each son had. *God deals with us according to our mentality.*

▣ THE PRICE OF LIVING IN SERVITUDE: The older son was in servitude in his mind. He gave service to his father and the family out of duty but not out of love. His angry words revealed that he had suffered and sacrificed for many years believing that this would qualify him for his father's favor. When he saw another son receiving the 'reward' and the treatment that he felt were rightfully due to him, he expressed all the bitterness, resentment and anger which he had kept bottled up inside him for many years. His mask of being 'the good son' fell from him. He showed his true colors. The same thing will happen to a son of God if he fails to remove the ideas of servitude from his mind.

◙ THE IMPORTANCE OF PLEASING THE FATHER: Christians who have the mentality of *'son of the Father'* understand that the love of the Divine Father is unconditional. It is not earned. Suffering and sacrifice are <u>not</u> the price we pay for God's acceptance. God is looking for sons who please Him, sons who believe in the Father's goodness and generosity. He is looking for sons who believe that He rewards His diligent seekers, not of His dutiful sufferers. He rewards those who diligently seek to please Him by having Faith and a High Mentality.

At the beginning of the parable, the younger son is in the house talking with his father while the older son is out toiling and working for his father's favor. The same thing happens when the prodigal comes home. The older son is never where he is supposed to be. He never learns how to please his father. The older son in the parable had subjected himself to servitude. The father's attitude to that was: "Well son, if you choose to live like a bondservant, go right ahead. You don't need to, but I'm not going to stop you. I'm going to deal with you at the level of your mentality." The younger son was therefore promoted over the older son.

Without Faith it is impossible to please God, but as we saw earlier, Faith works to support in totality whatever it finds in our State of Mind. Therefore, since we desire to please God, we will ensure that we have the right State of Mind. The Bible teaches us that: *"Letting your human nature control your mind is death* [is separation from God in consciousness and disconnection from our Divine Self], *but to be spiritually minded* [to be thinking from our divine aspect] *is life and peace* [is oneness with God and peace with God].....***Those who are under the control of their human nature cannot please God."*** *(Romans 8:6, 8)*

(Please read these verses a second time before moving on. Let them sink in.) When we please our Father, it will be His good pleasure to give us the Kingdom.

▣ THE DIVINE FATHER IS FAIR TO HIS CHILDREN: Christians believe that God is *good,* but sometimes Christians don't believe that God is *fair.* Do you sometimes feel this way? The older son had the same opinion, that his father was unfair. If we feel that we have been unfairly treated, let's check our State of Mind. God will always deal with us at the level of our mentality. The belief that the Divine Father is unfair is a symptom of the bondservant's mentality. At Level 2, our study of Spiritual Laws will help us to overcome this challenge.

The Character Traits of Mental Freedom

In previous Lessons, we studied many symptoms and character traits of a man living in *Mental Freedom.* We see these same symptoms and character traits in the younger son. Here are some of them:

- o Enjoying peace, protection and provision in accordance with his status as a son of the father;

- o Proper promotion in the family;

- o Confidence;

- o Being given authority to represent the family as a son of the father;

- o Power and freedom;

- o Portraying the image of a son of the father;

- o Love for the father, enjoying the love of the Father and complete assurance of his position in the family;

- o Seeing himself as worthy to receive the best that the father had;

- o Being in harmony with the father; being in a father-son relationship with his father, and not seeing his father as his master;

- o Knowing the truth of who he is in the family; knowing his rights as a son of the father, and being willing to claim those rights;

- o No fear, no insecurity, no rivalry, no 'backstabbing', no envy, no scheming, no manipulation and no promotion of his own agenda;

- o Respect for his father and knowing the true nature of his father;

- o Honesty; being able to face the facts of his life without being held prisoner by them;

- o Knowing the truth of his identity as a son in the family, and feeling free to fully express this identity;

- o Knowing the difference between being a son and being a bondservant;

- o A willingness to give service to father and the family which he loves;

- o A willingness to admit his mistakes without making excuses for himself; and

- o A willingness to renew his State of Mind.

The Character Traits of Mental Captivity

In Lesson 1, we studied many symptoms and character traits of a man living under *Mental Captivity*. We see many of these same symptoms and character traits in the prodigal's older brother such as:

- o Seeing his father as 'master' instead of 'father';

- Seeing himself as a 'bondservant' instead of as a 'son of the father'; and seeing his brother as a rival and a threat to his position;

- Bitterness, anger, resentment, self-pity, envy, gossip, rivalry, strife, false humility, living under pressure and stress;

- A belief in punishment and condemnation;

- A belief in the need to suffer and sacrifice to 'earn' the father's favor;

- Burdensome obligations;

- Feeling restricted from enjoying the privileges of sons;

- Lingering doubt as to his status in the family;

- Refusing to recognize the prodigal son as his brother; jockeying for an exalted position in the family; guarding and defending his position in the family;

- Disrespect to the father, and a belief that the father is unfair;

- A judgmental, self-righteous, 'holier than thou' attitude; obeying commandments to *'earn'* the father's favor;

- Trying to portray his brother as worse than himself and belittling his brother so he could feel good about himself; seeing himself as superior to his brother; imagining and digging up 'dirt' from his brother's past;

- Fear and insecurity;

- Lying to promote his own agenda; and

- A lack of forgiveness, a lack of love for his father, ingratitude, a lack of goodness of heart, maliciousness and causing disharmony in the family because it suited his own agenda.

Have you ever encountered any of these negative character traits in anyone in the Divine Family? More importantly, do you have any of these traits still in you? We can clearly see the end results of living under Mental Captivity and also of living in Mental Freedom. Let us feel free to distance ourselves from these negative mental traits and attitudes which the older son portrayed. Let us feel free to live as sons of God who are pleasing to the Divine Father.

The Price of False Humility

As mentioned in earlier Lessons, False Humility is an attitude adopted by a man who believes that by living under the bondservant's identity he is being humble. He believes that he is being humble when he speaks and thinks negatively about himself. The prodigal son tried to adopt a bondservant's identity when he returned to the father. He began to say, *"I am not worthy to be called your son..."* However, his father stopped him from making the request that he be made a hired servant. The father had a plan to promote him to a position of power and authority, so he could not allow the prodigal son to adopt the mentality of False Humility.

By contrast, the older son was a victim of the bondservant's mentality, even though he was a son. For many years, he seemed to be dutiful and humble. However it was False Humility. The older son truly did not believe in his father's goodness, and he did not believe that he was rewarded fairly by his father. In his mind, his father was a benevolent tyrant; (i.e. someone whom he should dutifully serve, fear and try to impress, and someone whose favor he should try to earn, but not someone whom he could truly love.) The older son didn't believe in his father, didn't believe in himself and didn't believe in his own worthiness to receive Good from his father. Therefore, the father could not be pleased with him.

Remember that the older son was assigned his portion of livelihood at the same time that the younger son received his portion. However, he refused to claim it as his own. He did not receive what his father had already given him. The father's storehouse was full to bursting with the goods he had assigned to the older son for his livelihood. He had been assigned his own herds of goats and cattle. However, the older son didn't have enough self-belief to claim and receive even a little goat from what was his. He was too busy covetously eyeing the calf that was being fattened for someone else.

False Humility caused the older son to be looking longingly at possessions which had already been assigned to him. As sons of the Divine Father, we lay False Humility aside and *"possess our possessions" (Obadiah verse 17)*. God has deposited into the storehouse of our minds all the natural 'things' and all the spiritual 'things' which He has already given to us. For many of us, that storehouse is full to bursting with Good which we have never claimed or received.

We know that it is our Father's good pleasure to give us the Kingdom; but where is this Kingdom to be found? Jesus told us plainly: *"...the kingdom of God is within you." (Luke 17:21)*. That's the Storehouse of the Mind. Then He gave us an instruction. *"Seek first the kingdom of God* (i.e. identify the storehouse in your mind) *and [seek] His righteousness* (i.e. be a right-thinking Christian and find out how to think right in order to open the storehouse) *and all these **things** shall be added unto you"* (i.e. you will receive the 'things' which you have already been given). *(Matthew 6:33)* Do you see it?

▣ EVERYTHING IS ALREADY YOURS: The father in the parable made a very telling statement of his generosity to his sons. This statement reflects the generosity of our Divine Father to us. The father said to the older son: *"Son, you are always with me, and **everything that I have is yours.**"* The younger son had asked for a portion of his father's goods, but it was the father's pleasure to give all his Good to his sons, not just a part.

Your Divine Father is delighted when you "purchase the orchard" and recognize that, as a representative of God your Father, all things are yours. May we also tell you that God has nothing more to give to you? 2nd Peter 1:3 says that: *"...He has given unto us all things* [all 'things'] *that pertain to life and godliness".* So He has already given us all natural 'things' and all spiritual 'things'. It's a done deal. It's up to us to cultivate the right state of mind so we can feel worthy to receive what our Father has given without any resistance on our part. And He hasn't given these 'things' to us grudgingly or with a heavy heart. Jesus said: *"... it is your Father's good pleasure to give you the Kingdom." (Luke 12:32)*

If we are not mindful, we will fall into the same trap in which the older son fell. We will be praying to God and begging for what has already been given. Then we will get angry and bitter because we feel our prayers are not being answered. That is the price we pay for False Humility; for assigning to ourselves an inferior identity and for being a victim of mental servitude. This is the price we pay when we forget that the sons of The Infinite don't beg. Visual Prayer will help us overcome this challenge, and we will study this topic more deeply at Level 2.

▣ THE BONDSERVANT'S MENTALITY IS CONTAGIOUS: *How did the older brother end up with a bondservant's mentality?* The older brother spent too much time in the company of servants and not enough time in the presence of his father. The bondservant's mentality rubbed off on him.

Mental Captivity is contagious. It will rub off on you. It is dangerous for you as a son of God to open your mind to people who are laboring under the bondservant's mentality. Rather, consciously and deliberately condition your mind to build immunity against such thoughts and attitudes. This is another reason why repeating the Affirmations in this book is useful. The Affirmations deepen and widen positive mental channels.

It is vital for us to spend quality time in the presence of our Divine Father in private. When we practice to quietly meditate on the nature, power, goodness and generosity of The Infinite, our minds will expand wide enough to receive what He has already given to us. Always meditate on Good: the infinite abundance of all the Good that is God.

This parable teaches us the importance of knowing who we are as the sons of God, knowing the true nature of our Divine Father and knowing our divine rights as the sons of God. However, there is much, much more to this amazing parable. When we get to Level 2, we will study this parable at an even higher level of understanding: *the level of 'Watching'.*

Dwelling in the House of the Lord

Our opening text, the WORD FOR TODAY, is a well-known verse from the 23rd Psalm. It tells us how to keep the goodness and mercy of God with us all the days of our lives. The psalmist David purposed in his heart: *"Surely goodness and mercy shall follow me all the days of my life, and **I will dwell** [live, remain, reside permanently] **in the house of the Lord forever."** (Psalm 23:6)* These words sound as if they have been lifted directly out of the inner conversations of the prodigal son, once he decided to return home. However, have we ever stopped to consider what exactly is "the house of the Lord" mentioned in this verse?

Many people have interpreted this verse to mean that the psalmist David would remain in a house of worship or a temple, and be a frequent attendee there. However, at a different level of meaning, this verse is saying far more than that. At a different level of meaning, the *'house of the Lord'* is not a building. *It is a state of conscious awareness within which you and your Divine Father dwell together in oneness.*

Your body is sometimes referred to in the New Testament as 'the temple of the Lord' because divinity is housed there *(2nd Corinthians 6:16).* That is the natural physical 'temple' which is your physical body. However, there is another 'temple', an inner, *unseen* temple, *a spiritual temple* which is not a building and is not your body. It is a place in your consciousness where there is oneness and communion between Infinite

Divine Spirit and your divine spirit. It is within this inner, unseen temple, within your own divine spirit, that you meet with God and commune with God. This is where you put in your claim for what has already been given to you. This is the state of consciousness in which you practice your Mind Renewal Technique and your Inner Conversations. This temple, this 'house of the Lord', is the place where diligent seekers find their God-connection.

With this understanding, we clearly see the higher meaning of what the psalmist David wrote in *Psalm 27:4- "One thing have I desired of the Lord, that will I **seek** after; **that I may dwell** [live, remain, abide permanently] in the house of the Lord all the days of my life, to behold the beauty of the Lord, and to inquire in His temple."*

We know that the psalmist David was not one of the priests of Israel; rather, he was the King of Israel. He did not live in any physical building which was known as 'the house of the Lord' or 'temple'. As a matter of fact, the temple in Jerusalem was built after King David had already died. So during his lifetime there was no physical temple within which King David could inquire of God. King David was a very spiritual man. He was speaking of this inner, unseen, spiritual temple, this place in our consciousness where we are one with God.

Jesus Christ spoke of this inner spiritual meeting place as well, but He didn't call it a temple. He called it a closet. He said: *"...enter into your closet and shut the door* [i.e. close your eyes and your mind to everything external and start looking through your eye of faith], *and pray to your Father in secret, and your Father who **sees in secret** shall reward you openly." (Matthew 6:6)* This is Visual Prayer not verbal prayer, as was mentioned in a previous Lesson. We will study this at Level 2.

This inner, unseen temple, this 'house of the Lord', this 'sanctuary of God', this 'secret closet' is also known as *'the secret place of the Most High'* and is spoken of in Psalm 91. Please read this beautiful

Psalm to see the rewards promised to those who will seek God diligently as they dwell in this secret place. When you enter this 'house of the Lord' and you 'shut the door' by shutting out of your mind all feelings of fear, insecurity and unworthiness, then you can commune in oneness with your Divine Father and behold the beauty of the Lord.

You may never have been in this inner temple, or maybe you have drifted away from this secret meeting place. You may feel separate from The Infinite. However, you can follow the example of the prodigal son and return to conscious oneness with your Divine Father by making it a habit to spend some time each day in quiet contemplation of how powerful and how loving The Infinite truly is. Know that God's only commandment is Love. If you are new to the teachings of the Bible, start by reading Psalm 91. When you have completed reading this Psalm, go back to its beginning and read it again. Keep reading it until you can *feel* it.

By consistently applying the principles which we have studied together in this book, you will live daily in the conscious awareness that you are a divine, free-born, spirit-son of the Divine Spirit-Father, and you are not His bondservant. Once you get to that state of consciousness, never leave it. Keep that consciousness with you as you faithfully practice the Mind Renewal Technique. Hold on firmly to the truth that you and your Father are one. When you do so, Goodness and Mercy shall remain with you all the days of your life.

Goodness and Mercy

What is goodness? Goodness is All That God Is. Psalm 100:5 tells us: *"...the Lord is **good**; His **mercy** is everlasting and His **truth** endures to all generations"*. His mercy for us is everlasting because His truth, the truth that He is our Divine Father, endures for all generations. So even when we 'miss the mark', when we admit that our wrongdoing is a result of our wrong thinking, and when we return in full consciousness to the

Father and dwell in that consciousness (dwelling in the house of the Lord), then our WORD FOR TODAY tells us that Goodness and Mercy will never leave us. They will stay with us all the days of our lives.

As was said in an earlier Lesson, when the Psalmist says, 'the Lord is good', it means more than saying, 'God is a good person'. It means that *God Is Good, and Good Is God.* Goodness is *All That God Is.* Everything that is Good is in God; and everything that is in God is only Good. Goodness is the only thing that can be found in God. This is the truth, regardless of what our mental conditioning says. It is easy to truly love a Good God, but hard to truly love a 'benevolent tyrant'.

With this understanding, we can clearly see the great significance of the well-known verse which says: *"We know that **all things** work together for **GOOD** to them that **love God**, to them who are the called according to His purpose." (Romans 8:28)* This verse states the overarching truth of our entire existence as a Divine Being, not just our existence on Earth. This verse is not referring to ordinary 'good'. This is at the level of Infinite Good, eternal Good. **Everything** *is working together for our eternal good as a Divine Spirit-Being.* When we fully accept this verse as truth, we will see more of the big picture of our existence. Then feelings such as bitterness, regret and worry will flee from us. The more we spend time in the inner temple beholding the beauty of the Lord, the more we will release any negative thoughts which we may have concerning the nature of God. We will let go of any thought that our Divine Father is a 'benevolent tyrant'. *God Is All Good; and Good Is All God.* Let's align our concept of God with the truth of God.

◙ GOD DOESN'T HAVE A SPLIT PERSONALITY: Here's something worth remembering: *Somebody told a lie on God when they told us that God is both good and evil.* The true God does not dwell in the realm of 'good and evil' or 'light and darkness'. Such things represent Duality which is a self-defeating state of mind. When you dwell in the realm of 'All Truth', you realize that *Duality is the doorway of evil.* This is why the Psalmist could say in Psalm 23:4: *"...I will fear no evil for You* (All Good) *are with me."* He was dwelling in the realm of All Good, not in the realm of 'good and evil'.

Infinite God does not have a split personality, and Infinite God does not dwell in the realm of Duality. There is no "light and darkness" or "good and evil" in God. God is only Good; All Good. Infinite God is Unconditional Love. God is Light, and in Him is no darkness at all. *(See 1st John 1:5 & 4:7-8)* The Israelites were instructed to understand that God is One; not dual. Jesus Christ said that this is the greatest commandment which was ever given. *(See Mark 12:28-31).* We will study how to be free from the deception of Duality when we get to Level 3 of this Bible Study.

The Paradox of the Parable

Now, one of the curious lessons we learn from the Parable of the Prodigal Son is that it is possible for a believer in Jesus Christ to be a faithful religious devotee and at the same time be a 'prodigal son'. This seems to be a paradox, but from our study we see that it is true. We may attend church services faithfully for years and yet not be truly 'dwelling in the house of the Lord'. We can be highly religious and still be separated from our Divine Father in consciousness.

The man Jesus Christ was a perfect example what it means to be one with the Divine Father. He was the perfect outward portrayal of the inner Christ. Since we desire to be like Christ, oneness with the Divine Father is our chosen State of Mind.

The Lessons in this book have been guiding us 'home', back to the 'house of our Father', back to a state of oneness with God. All the principles which we have studied in these Lessons have been guiding us to make the decision to know our Divine Father, to know the truth that we are sons of God and to sever all ties to the bondservant's mentality.

Having made this decision, speak from your divine 'I', and say these words with feeling. Be conscious that it is your Divine Self speaking these words: *"I am a Divine Spirit-Being. I did not originate on Earth. I proceeded and came forth from God. My origin is from eternity, and I am more ancient than the Earth. I am a beloved spirit-son of my beloved Spirit-Father. This has always been my identity. As divine spirit, I am one with God my Father, who is only Love. I am one with Peace. I am one with Unconditional Love. I am one with Truth. I am one with God. I am conscious that I am one with God. I and my Father are one. Even while living temporarily in this human body here on Earth, I am still in the divine category. Therefore, I am 100% worthy to receive and enjoy all of my Father's Good. I let go of all resistance to God's goodness. I now claim and accept and receive All Good, and I expect to experience All Good. Thank you, Father. I am walking in my true identity. I am who my Divine Father says I am. I am divine royalty; that is my truth. Even while living in this human body, I am worthy; because of my Divine Identity. My human actions and my Divine Identity are not the same things. And no matter what my human aspect has done or what has been done to my human aspect here on Earth, and regardless of anyone's opinion of my human identity and appearance, I, Divine Spirit, have always been and shall always be a beloved spirit-son of God my Spirit-Father. That will never change. Facts may change but Truth never changes. I am in the Divine Family forever!"*

Can you feel these words resonate in your spirit? Can you feel the connection with your divine "I"? Now that you truly feel it, we say to you: 'Welcome Home, beloved son of God!' We have analyzed the parable of the Prodigal Son from the level of Knowing: knowing your Divine Father, knowing that you are His son and knowing your status and privileges in the Divine Family. We have just scratched the surface of the meaning of this amazing parable. When we get to Level 2 in this Bible Study, we will be analyzing this parable at the level of *Watching*. We will be removing our focus from earthly things, and we will be looking into the realm which existed before the world existed. We will be looking into the realm of the eternal everlasting you which existed before your human existence. When we do, we will more fully understand who we are and why we are here on Earth. We will also be delving deeper into the many hidden secrets to an empowered life. So be sure to be back and study with us at Level 2.

Work on you

You have gone through these 7 Lessons and you may have greatly expanded your conscious awareness of the different levels of meaning found in the scriptures. You have been drawn to this information because you are ready for it. Others may not be ready yet. Don't criticize, judge or condemn anyone. Just let your light shine. So, thank you for allowing this book *Feeling Free To Be Like Christ (Level 1)* to serve you, and for helping to spread the word to many other men about this book. You don't need anybody's validation of the information in this book, and you don't need anybody's validation of the positive change in you. If this book has helped you, *you* know it has helped you, and that's enough. All that is required is that every day you live consciously in an atmosphere of peace.

Now as we close, you may still have some questions such as:

What does the Parable of the Prodigal Son mean when we study it at the level of 'Watching'? • Who am I? And why am I here on Earth? • Doesn't the Bible say that our Father is in heaven? It even says so in the 'Our Father' Prayer. Since I am to come home to the Divine Father, how can I do this while I'm still living on Earth? • Who were we and where were we before we were born here on Earth? • Why do bad things happen to good people, and why do good things happen to bad people? And how can I keep the bad things from happening to me?

These are just a few of the topics which we will be studying together at Level 2. Level 1 has just barely scratched the surface of the information available to you. Much, much more awaits you at Level 2. See you then. Please read the Supporting Scriptures, Affirmation and the

Review which follow this Lesson.

Supporting Scriptures

Psalm 92:12-14: "The righteous [i.e. the right-thinking man] shall flourish like the palm tree: he shall grow like a cedar in Lebanon. Those who are planted in the house of the Lord shall flourish in the courts of our God. They shall still bring forth fruit in old age. They shall be fat and flourishing."

Psalm 91:1: "The man who dwells in the secret place of the Most High shall abide under the protective shadow of the Almighty."

Psalm 103:2-4, 10, 12-13 "My soul, bless the Lord! And do not forget all His benefits. He forgives all your wrongdoing. He heals all your diseases. He ransoms you from destruction. He crowns you with loving kindness and tender mercies. He has not dealt with us in the way that our sins deserve, neither has he rewarded us according to our wrongdoing. As far as the east is from the west, so far has He removed our wrongdoing from us. Just like a father is merciful to his children, so the Lord is merciful to those who respect Him."

1st John 4:4; 14: "You are from God, little children; and you have been victorious: because greater is He who is in you than the one who is in the world... We love God, because He first loved us."

Here's the final Affirmation at Level 1:

Always A Son

Wandering alone in the desert;
No friend to cheer or console;
No escape from the shame on my family name;
No rest to be found for my soul;

Nowhere to run from my failure;
Nowhere to hide from my sin;
Adrift and forsaken; the path that I'd taken had left me no peace within.
I paid a high price for low living;
I thought I could do things my way;
But in my naïve haste, all I had went to waste;
The wolves had escaped with the prey.
Famine and Loss came and robbed me;
Pigs were my pillows at night;
Hunger was my meat; from the swine I would eat;
There was no hope left in sight.

Then I remembered that God is my Father, and that I am forever His son,
And that long before birth and my life here on Earth, I and my Father were one.
I remembered His love wrapped around me;
Oh, the peace in His tender embrace!
His care and protection, His love and affection,
His mercy, compassion and grace;
I remembered my place at His table, and the abundance which freely was mine,
Before my mind had run wild, this truth I'd known as a child:
'I'm a son in the Family Divine.'
I remembered that He's always faithful, and that He is forever the same,
And though I'd gone astray, He wouldn't turn me away,
For *Infinite Love* is His name.
I remembered He said He'd forgive me, for all wrongs, present, future and past;
So I lifted my eyes, and said, "I will arise! I won't quit till I'm home at last!"

My Father was waiting and watching; and He saw me so far, far away,
He could not wait to greet me; so He ran out to meet me;
And He welcomed me home to stay!
I told Him that I was not worthy, to be called his own son anymore,
But He silenced that thought when the best robe was brought
and replaced the old rags that I wore,
I said, "Father, I've sinned against heaven. In your sight, I can't stand as a man."
But my Father Divine, said, "Son, you are mine.
To promote you was *always* My plan.
On your own, you've tried *so* hard to make it; but you had many lessons to learn.
I've always chosen you; but you had to choose Me too;

So I've been waiting on you to return.
I give you My power and dominion; My ring on your finger you'll wear;
You will represent Me with My authority. You're My son; never worry or fear.
Your feet are now bare and so weary; but lean on Me, and you will stand.
You'll walk with new shoes on, for you have been chosen
My blessings divine to command.
For too long we've been separated; but now you are home safe and sound.
Let's all feast and rejoice, for the son of My choice
who once was lost has now been found!"

My Father didn't ask any questions as to why I had lived as a slave;
Didn't punish or chide, didn't hate or deride;
Instead, He just loved and forgave.
My true love I give to My Father, whose heart is so pure and so kind;
And I'm truly free, for I clearly see ALL GOD IS in my heart and my mind.
Nevermore will I stray from my Father; nevermore like a wanderer I'll roam,
For my ears have now heard the sweetest of words, when my Father said:
"Son, welcome home!"

Review

Q. In the parable of the Prodigal Son, what do the two sons represent?
A. The two sons represent two different states of mind. The younger son, before he separated himself from his father, represents the ideal state of mind of a son of God. The older son represents the state of mind of a man who is in mental bondage and servitude.

Q. Was it wrong for the younger son to ask his father for the good that had been prepared and set aside for him?
A. No. It was his right to request and receive all that the father had prepared and stored up for him. And it is also your right as a beloved son of God to request and receive all that the Father has prepared and stored up for you.

Q. How does a son of God separate himself from his Divine Father?

A. A man cannot be separated from the love of God, just as the prodigal son even in his wretched state was always loved by his father. However, a man can create a gap, a distance, a separation in his own mind between himself and his Divine Father by failing to recognize that he is a divine being and that he is part of the Divine Family forever.

Q. What was the sign that the prodigal son 'came to himself'?
A. His inner conversations changed. He remembered his true identity as a son of the father, and his condition of suffering and separation from his father became so intolerable to him that he immediately left it never to return.

Q. At a different level of meaning, what is 'the house of the Lord'?
A. The house of the Lord is an inner temple, an inner sanctuary in which the Divine Spirit communicates with our spirit. When we meditate upon Divine Truth which is the law of the Lord, the prefect Law which sets us free, we are given admittance to this inner temple. This is explained in *Psalm 1.* When we dwell at this level of conscious awareness of truth, and mentally align ourselves with it, we step out of the realm of 'good and evil' and dwell in the realm of Good.

Congratulations!

You have completed your study of *"Feeling Free To Be Like Christ (Level 1)"* which is the Introductory Level of this Men's Bible Study. Be sure to read the next book in this series, *"Feeling Free To Be Like Christ (Level 2)"*, which is the Intermediate Level.

Let's hear from you! You can give your feedback about this book by clicking on the Stars on Amazon.com. It's quick and easy. On your Amazon.com home page, click on *'Orders'*, then click on the *'Write a product review'* button, then click on the number of Stars. One Star is the lowest rating; Five Stars is the highest rating. After clicking on the Stars, you have the option to also share your thoughts about this book by writing your comments if you wish.

To receive Jackie Goldsmith's free 30-day Devotional titled **"Walk in the Light"** in your email inbox, send your request to:
voiceoflightforchrist@gmail.com

About the Author

Jackie Goldsmith is a Minister of the Gospel, a bold truth-teller and a conference speaker who has given years of service in Christian ministry. Jackie extracts from the Bible insights which are simple but profound and life-changing, and explains them in a practical, user-friendly manner.

voiceoflightforchrist@gmail.com

Made in the USA
Columbia, SC
07 July 2025

60478387R00217